Career Paths for Programmers

Career Paths for Programmers: Skills in Senior Software Roles

By

Jack Downey

CAMBRIDGE
SCHOLARS
PUBLISHING

Career Paths for Programmers: Skills in Senior Software Roles, by Jack Downey

This book first published 2009

Cambridge Scholars Publishing

12 Back Chapman Street, Newcastle upon Tyne, NE6 2XX, UK

British Library Cataloguing in Publication Data
A catalogue record for this book is available from the British Library

This research has been supported by the Science Foundation Ireland Investigator Programme, B4-STEP (Building a Bidirectional Bridge Between Software ThEory & Practice).

ISBN (10): 1-4438-0242-5, ISBN (13): 978-1-4438-0242-0

TABLE OF CONTENTS

LIST OF TABLES

LIST OF FIGURES

List of Appendices

LIST OF ACRONYMS

3GPP	Third Generation Partnership Project
AI	Artificial Intelligence
API	Application Programming Interface
B.A.	Bachelor of Arts
B.Comm.	Bachelor of Commerce
B.E.	Bachelor of Engineering
B.Eng.	Bachelor of Engineering
B.Ind.Eng.	Bachelor of Industrial Engineering
B.Sc.	Bachelor of Science
BSC	British Computer Society
B.Tech.	Bachelor of Technology
CASE	Computer Aided Software Engineering
CATP	Customer Acceptance Test Plan
CCITT	Commité Consultatif International de la Télèfonique et de la Télègraphique
CD	Compact Disc
CM	Configuration Management
CMM	Capability Maturity Model
CNRC	Cellular Network Resolution Centre
COTS	Commercial Off The Shelf
CSR	Customer Support Request
CTO	Chief Technical Officer
CV	Curriculum Vitae
DSS	Decision Support Systems
EC	European Community
ETSI	European Telecommunications Standards Institute
EU	European Union
EVA	Earned Value Analysis
FDI	Foreign Direct Investment
FERB	Front End Review Board
FRDB	Feature Request Database
GAA	Gaelic Athletic Association
GPRS	General Packet Radio Service
GSS	Group Support Systems
HR	Human Resources

HRM	Human Resource Management
H/W	Hardware
ICT	Information and Communications Technology
IEEE	Institute of Electrical and Electronic Engineers
IITD	Irish Institute of Training and Development
IMI	Irish Management Institute
IP	Internet Protocol
IS	Information Systems
IT	Information Technology or Institute of Technology
ITU	International Telecommunications Union
J2EE	Java 2 platform, Enterprise Edition
JDBC	Java Data Base Connectivity
JFC	Java Foundation Classes
JMS	Java Messaging System
JNDI	Java Naming and Directory Interface
KSA	Knowledge and Skills/Abilities
LDAP	Lightweight Directory Access Protocol
MAP	Mobile Application Part
M.Eng.	Master of Engineering
M.Eng.Sc.	Master of Engineering Science
MIS	Management Information Systems
MMS	Multi-media Message Service
M.Phil.	Master of Philosophy
MS	Microsoft®
M.Sc.	Master of Science
NPV	Net Present Value
O&M	Operations and Maintenance
OEM	Original Equipment Manufacturer
OO	Object Orientation or Object Oriented
PC	Personal Computer
PERL	Practical Extraction and Reporting Language
PERT	Project Evaluation and Review Technique
PMBOK	Project Management Body Of Knowledge
PMI	Project Management Institute
QA	Quality Assurance
R&D	Research and Development
RADIUS	Remote Authentication Dial In User Service
RF	Radio Frequency
RFID	Radio Frequency Identification
RFI	Request For Information
RFP	Request For Proposal

RFQ	Request For Quotation
SCM	Software Configuration Management
SDL	Specification and Description Language
SEI	Software Engineering Institute
SFIA	Skills Framework for an Information Age
SIP	Session Initiation Protocol
SMS	Short Message Service
SOC	Standard Occupational Classification
SWEBOK	Software Engineering Body Of Knowledge
S/W	Software
TCL	Tool Command Language
UML	Unified Modelling Language
UMPS	Universal Mobile Telephony Service
VB	Visual Basic
XML	eXtensible Markup Language

FOREWORD

EILEEN M. TRAUTH, PENNSYLVANIA STATE UNIVERSITY

In these difficult economic times it is more important than ever to strengthen the connection between academic preparation and workplace skills. This is particularly the case in the globally competitive field of software development where the stakes have never been higher. The ability to educate and retain a software development workforce is no longer just an issue for educational institutions and the software industry. For countries such as Ireland, whose economies depend heavily on a robust information economy, it is a matter of national importance. In this well written and highly accessible book, Jack Downey makes a unique contribution to the software development literature. He does this by addressing a clear gap in the IT skills and knowledge literature. Whereas I and others have been writing for some time about the skills and knowledge needed in the information systems profession, little systematic research has been carried out in the software development field. In response to this need his book details the research that was conducted in order to better understand the connection between the various software development roles and the skills needed to successfully carry them out.

There are several important audiences for this work. Clearly, members of the software industry would benefit from reading this book. In particular, managers who have responsibility for staffing projects or recruiting new personnel would want to read it. The artefact-centric framework that he developed can be of use not only in the recruitment process. It can also facilitate an overall understanding of the various roles carried out by members of a software development group in the course of enacting a project. In doing so, this framework provides a useful mechanism for determining the skills that are needed to develop software. It also serves to highlight the skills that every team member needs – to communicate, collaborate and to support the decision-making process. Contrary to many stereotypes about the nature of work in the information technology professions, this study reinforces the need for software developers –

particularly those in management roles – to posses both the 'back end' technical skills and the 'front end' interpersonal skills needed for customer interaction, requirements analysis and domain understanding.

But in one of the most distinctive characteristics of this book, Jack Downey has reached out to an audience that is atypical of software development writing: national policy makers. While some may find this unusual, those of us who have studied the connection between the development of an information economy and the economic development of a country know precisely why he addresses this audience. And there is no better country in which to do this than Ireland. As I explained in my 2000 book, *The Culture of an Information Economy: Influences and Impacts in the Republic of Ireland,* the case of Ireland was one of the first to document the connection between the growth of an IT sector and the increase in economic prosperity. While my book traced the policies and processes put in place over a thirty year period to bring about Ireland's Celtic Tiger, Downey's book addresses the issue of sustainability in the current economic climate. Whereas Ireland had little competition in the 1970s when it first began to attract multinational IT firms, that is not the case at present. In this highly competitive and global information economy of the twenty-first century, Ireland must constantly strive to stay ahead of the trend that moves software development work to lower wage countries.

For these reasons Downey's critical assessment of the skills needed by the software development profession is not just a matter for academics to consider. It should be taken to heart by policy makers as well. His interviews with senior software developers reveal a dilemma for educators and policy makers in Ireland. The informants indicated that little or no business skills are required, and -- because they work mainly on mature products – neither are high-end research skills. But if Ireland's software sector is to be sustainable, it needs to provide more value, Downey argues. Irish software facilities need to engage with *research* as well as development. By identifying the lack of roles for people with business/entrepreneurial and research skills, this study introduces a factor that may have escaped notice by policy makers: how to gain the skills needed for the next generation of software development when such environments are few and far between. Thus the implications of Downey's critical assessment of the roles and skills of software developers are significant beyond industry and academe. Perhaps the best reason to read this book is for this connection. One of the factors that accounts for Ireland's success in creating an information economy was the way the university curricula adapted to the skills and knowledge required of those who sought employment in the multinational IT sector. Jack Downey's findings argue that continued cooperation among the multiple stakeholders – academe, industry and policy makers – is as important now as it ever was.

CHAPTER ONE

INTRODUCTION

Commercial software development is significantly more complex than programming as a hobby (Weinberg 1971). When writing a program for personal use, the amateur programmer understands the requirements and will not have to explain to third parties how the program works. Similarly, if the program contains faults, the author decides if they are worth correcting or not. In contrast, commercial software development is dominated by the need for communication. For instance, during his studies of TRW, Barry Boehm observed that roughly two-thirds of the time spent in a development project leads to documentation, while only the remaining third produces code (Boehm 1981; Boehm, Penedo, Stuckle, Williams and Pyster 1984). Similarly, during his days in IBM Fred Brooks (1972) noted that only about one-sixth of the development activity is coding. He also discovered that half of the development time is taken up in various levels of testing. A factor that Brooks does not consider in his breakdown is maintenance, which Boehm (1981) estimates takes up around half the development lifecycle but, according to Hatton (1998), makes up four-fifths. So, comparatively speaking, the low-level design, coding and unit testing activities – what McConnell (1993) calls software construction - is a small fraction of a commercial software development project.

This suggests that the other activities, such as software testing (Roper 1994; Myers 2004) and maintenance (Swanson 1976) or evolution (Lehman 1998) should command more attention than they do. Even so, bearing in mind Dijkstra's point that: "Testing shows the presence, not the absence of bugs" (Dijkstra 1969, p.66), a comprehensive testing strategy will not address the fundamental goal of computing science: "How not to make a mess of it" (Dijkstra 2001, p.92).

Because software is inherently complex (Brooks 1986), often needs to satisfy disparate customers (Birk, Heller, John, Schmid, Masser and Muller 2003) and is regularly expected to meet 'hard' deadlines (Miranda 2002), not making a mess of it - i.e. developing software on time and without error - is easier said than done. Moreover, because computers are becoming more pervasive, flawed software can have tremendous consequences (Colwell 2002). Also, many projects never get to completion (DeMarco and Lister 1999) and some should never even have been started because they were either technically or commercially infeasible (Boehm and Huang 2003).

Why is software development so error-prone and time-consuming? Boehm (1981) makes the point that the cost in terms of time and effort of repairing an error increases by a factor of ten from one phase of development to the next. This suggests that attention to the earliest phase, requirements, would pay dividends. However, as noted in Norris and Rigby (1992), "the time and effort devoted to [requirements definition] is usually minimal" (p.47). This leads to the situation where, "in any development effort, the requirements make explicit some – but only some – of the desired properties of the final system" (Bass, Clements and Kazman 2003, p.6). Turski (1986) describes the essential difficulty of software as having to work with one formal system – the hardware – and one informal one – the application domain. "Strictly speaking, a description of non-formal domain properties cannot be proven" (p.1078), therefore software developers can never guarantee that their solutions totally address the given problems.

However, the software industry seems to prefer devoting its time to managing the software development process than improving its requirements elicitation process. For instance, despite the fact that each project is unique (Turner and Muller 2003) efforts are being made to standardise the software development process, an example being the Capability Maturity Model (Carnegie Mellon Software Engineering Institute 2008). Alternatively, it is argued that reducing the process (and documentation) overhead will lead to shorter development cycles and quicker responses to changing requirements. Thus, various 'agile' management techniques have emerged, such as Extreme Programming (Beck 2000) and SCRUM (Schwaber 1997). Although regarded as a new step in project management, Larman and Basili (2003) argue that these are simply forms of 'iterative and incremental' developments that trace their roots back to the 1970's. While these are very popular with developers, they appear to be most effective on small projects (Boehm and Turner 2003) or non safety-critical ones that have volatile requirements and which are developed by small, skilful co-located teams (Williams and Cockburn 2003).

No matter what management approach is used, the development of commercial software products requires the skills of a multi-disciplinary team. Between them, the team members must determine what the customer wants, decide on the most cost-effective way to do it, plan the steps needed and produce the end product - a deliverable comprising tested software, user manuals and training materials. For larger systems, the software must be installed on site and the end-users trained in its operation and maintenance.

Therefore, in addition to the detailed technical skills needed to develop computer programs, members of the team must have customer-facing skills, business skills, management skills and general communications skills that allow the team members interact effectively.

With the emergence of China and the Andhra Pradesh region of India as software development forces, as well as the accession of Eastern European states to the European Union (EU), Ireland's software industry is under threat from lower-wage economies. The Irish government is concerned about this and has commissioned one of its advisory bodies (Forfás) to investigate the problem. Their report recommends that the various industrial sectors, including information and communications technology, add more value to whatever they do by developing new skills (Forfas 2003).

Although the Irish government must ensure that the workforce has sufficient skills to attract investment and, by doing so, create employment, the skills needed to develop software are of concern to many parties: Universities want to make certain that their graduates are equipped to obtain employment in industry. Practitioners need to have the necessary skills to pursue careers in the software industry. Professional bodies strive to transform software practitioners into true professionals having the characteristics identified by Ford and Gibbs (1996); one of these characteristics being the continuous development of professional skills. Finally, industry requires a wide range of skills in order to develop its products; it would like to acquire these skills as economically as possible.

Extensive skills research has been carried out in the information systems (IS) arena, although such research has not been done in the software engineering discourse. While it is useful to learn from the IS research, it must be noted at the outset that there is considerable confusion over the definition of IS (Kaarst-Brown and Guzman 2005) and the work done in the IS area may not have direct relevance for commercial software development.

Therefore, while the literature cannot list the skills needed to develop commercial software, IS skills research may provide useful guidance, as shown in the following examples:

For educational institutions, charged with developing relevant curricula in the changing world of information systems, efforts have to be made to bridge the gap between what skills the institutions are equipping their graduates with and what industry needs from its staff (Trauth, Farwell and Lee 1993). A problem for the institutions is that recruitment adverts emphasise the required technologies, but final selection is based on the person's communications or 'soft' skills (Litecky, Arnett and Prabhakar 2004).

Trauth et al (1993) consulted IS practitioners in industry to determine what skills employers are looking for. Respondents recommended that university programmes should place greater emphasis on 'real world' experience, communication skills, analytical ability and problem solving. They went on to note that companies need high quality people with general intellectual depth, solid inter-personal skills and some functional business knowledge. In a later report from this study, these researchers identified the importance of business functional knowledge and inter-personal and management skills (Lee, Trauth and Farwell 1995):

Another study motivated by IS curriculum design was carried out by Bailey and Stefaniak (1999). They divide their skills findings into three headings: 'soft', business and technical. The authors place particular emphasis on listening skills, whose importance is emphasised in the literature. For instance, Nichols and Stevens (1957) note that "business is tied together by its systems of communication. This communication, businessmen are discovering, depends more on the spoken word than it does on the written word; and the effectiveness of the spoken word hinges not so much on how people talk as on how they listen" (p.85). The general impression from Bailey and Stefaniak's (1999) work is that technical skills are easier to teach than non-technical ones. Indeed some IT companies would prefer to hire people with minimal technical skills so long as they can demonstrate solid soft and business skills.

In Singapore, Shi and Bennett (1998) draw on earlier work and use four knowledge (general IS, organisational overview, organisational unit and IS product) and two skills (organisational and technical) categories in their IS skills survey:

One IS study, (Misic 1996), focuses on the skills needed by systems analysts. Misic reaches the conclusion that strong technical skills are not necessarily the most useful ones for analysts to have. He predicts that tomorrow's analysts may come from business disciplines rather than from the programming pool, citing how some end-users are proving very adept at designing and developing their own PC-based systems.

In the Irish context, Forfas (2003) recommends that courses teaching industry knowledge, technology entrepreneurship, team working, team leading, project management and understanding the customer perspective be added to software-related curricula.

To summarise, the key skills required in the IS arena are: technical, business, interpersonal and the application of technology to business problems - which leads me to ask: are similar skills needed by commercial software practitioners?

Judging by the wide range of activities involved in commercial software development, it is expected that an eclectic range of skills is also required in this field. Because software is developed by multi-disciplinary teams, then the necessary skills are likely to be distributed among the team members. This conjecture is supported by Weinberg (1971) who observes that not everyone on the team needs to have all the skills. If this is the case, how are the skills allocated across the different roles seen in software development teams?

When the literature considers roles, it tends to focus on a single role at a time and, generally, its concern is with what makes a good exponent of that role. So, for instance, while Misic (1996) determines the skills employed by systems analysts, other studies look for the characteristics of a good systems analyst (Vitalari and Dickson 1983; Schenk, Vitalari and Davis 1998; Wynekoop and Walz 2000), a good project manager (Cheng and Dainty 2005) or a good software engineer (Turley and Beiman 1995).

While this is significant research - highlighted by DeMarco and Lister's (1999) assertion that the best software people outperform the worst by a factor of ten – the literature does not seem to consider other roles in the software development team. Customer-facing roles, such as product management and customer support, are not studied; neither are the training and documentation functions.

So, what are the skills needed to carry out the various roles in software development? This is an important question to ask as it affects all the stakeholders listed in Figure 1. The educators need to know what skills their graduates will need. The government will want to draw attention to the high-value skills that the country boasts in order to attract investment. Practitioners are interested in positioning themselves to best advantage. Professional bodies will want to develop their members' careers so that they tailor their skills to the areas in most demand. Finally, industry will only continue to trade in a country if it offers the skills a company needs. Considering the increasing competition for foreign direct investment, this question is of particular importance in an Irish context.

Figure 1: Skills Stakeholders

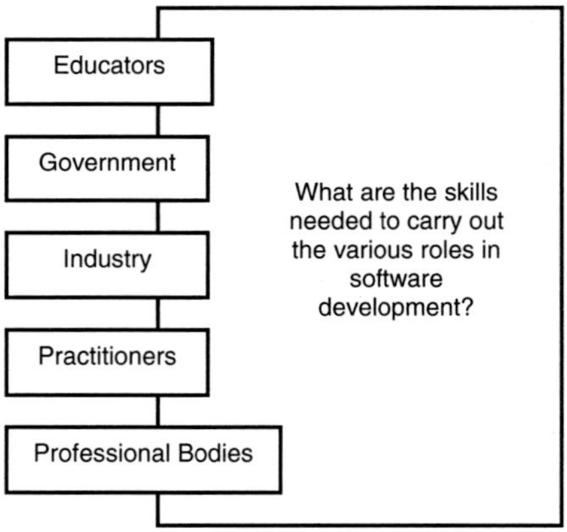

Research has been done on the skills required in the software development sector, but the tendency has been to group all the roles under one heading. For instance, the British Office for National Statistics places team leaders, systems architects, software developers and testers under the same heading – standard occupational classification code 2132 (Office for National Statistics 2000b). Similarly, Irish studies (that make use of the British codes) offer recommendations for the Information and Communications

Technology (ICT) sector as a whole (Forfas 2003; Enterprise Strategy Group 2004).

Professional bodies have also avoided role distinctions. The Irish Computer Society (2008) is promoting the use of the Skills Framework for an Information Age (SFIA Foundation 2008). This framework provides a list of skills and asks practitioners to assess themselves on each one. They can then plan their development by improving existing skills or by gaining new ones. However, what constitutes an ideal skills profile for a particular role is not discussed.

In summary, there are noticeable gaps in the literature. Firstly, skills surveys have not been carried out in the commercial software development industry. The skills surveys carried out by IS researchers have revealed the need for technical, business, interpersonal and the application of technology to business skills. Because the IS environment mainly concerns the development of software solutions for in-house use, the skills identified for this sector may not be appropriate in the commercial software industry. Secondly, there are no satisfactory role definitions for software development practitioners.

Being able to identify the skills needed for particular roles will allow stakeholders to target their efforts effectively. By gaining insights into what the key roles in the software development process are, academic courses can be targeted to produce graduates capable of these roles. For instance, how do testers and customer support people currently prepare for their positions? Indeed, for any given role in a software development project, how do people advance into senior grades – what sort of career progression can a new graduate look forward to?

The remainder of this book will describe a research project, based in Ireland, that set out to answer the question: what are the skills needed to carry out the various roles in software development? The insights gained through this research will contribute to the software engineering literature by addressing skills needs and role definitions in the software development industry. It is hoped that the research will also be of benefit to Irish policy makers.

CHAPTER TWO

REFINING THE QUESTION

2.1 Introduction

What exactly does the research question mean? It seeks to equate skills with various roles. But what roles need to be considered and what precisely is a skill? The next sections will explore these ideas.

2.2 Selecting Roles

A first step is to decide what software development roles to concentrate on. The roles chosen for study should reflect the software development lifecycle, so that the people involved in bringing a product from initial requirements elicitation through to final product installation and maintenance are considered.

Capers Jones (2003) notes that, the bigger the organisation, the more distinct and specialised the roles. In his survey, he identifies a total of thirty roles in software development. However, many of these roles seem like specific tasks within a larger role, suggesting that a smaller organisation would merge some of these responsibilities. Table 1 shows a possible merging, one where the roles reflect the entire development lifecycle.

Table 1: Combining Roles

Role	**Activities**
Architect	Cost analysis Cost estimation Function point analysis Human factors Performance analysis Reliability Reusability Security } Non-functional requirements Software engineering Systems analysis Education & training (preparing material for customers)
Programmer	Configuration control Networks Integration Librarians Data administration Database design Data quality
Project manager	Metrics and measures Project planning Quality assurance Standards
Technical writer	
Tester	
Customer support	
Product manager	Assists in cost analysis and estimation Assists with systems analysis (domain knowledge) Globalisation

These roles can also be seen in the Standard Occupational Classification (Office for National Statistics 2000b):

Table 2: Work Areas

Role	SOC Code	Sample Job Titles
Architect	2132	Architect, systems (computing)
	2131	Architect, software
	2132	Designer, software
	2132	Engineer, design, software
	2123	Engineer, staff, telecommunications
	2132	Programmer, analyst
Programmer	2132	Developer, software
	2132	Developer, systems
	2132	Engineer, development, software
	2132	Engineer, software
	2132	Engineer, software, senior
	2132	Engineer (professional, software)
	2132	Programmer, computer
	2132	Programmer, systems
Project manager	1136	Manager, development, software
	1136	Manager, development, systems
	1136	Manager, project, development, software
	1136	Manager, software
	1137	Manager, development (*research and development*)
	2132	Leader, project, software
	2132	Leader, project (software design)
	2132	Leader, team, software (computing)
Technical writer	3412	Author, technical
	3412	Writer, technical
	3412	Writer, technical, senior
Tester	2132	Tester, software, computer
Customer support	2131	Consultant, support, software
	2131	Consultant, support, technical
	2131	Engineer, support, software
Product manager	1137	Manager, product (*research and development*)

As noted in chapter 1, most of the research into roles concentrates on a single role at a time and the characteristics needed to be effective in that role. As DeMarco and Lister (1999) point out, the best developers outperform the worst by 10:1; they outperform the median by 2.5:1. These studies find that skill is only one factor in determining performance.

For instance, Turley and Bieman (1995) attempted to determine what differentiates good and bad software engineers. Their findings show that experience is an important factor and "that personal attributes and interpersonal skills are most closely linked with performance differences. Skills associated with task or situation did not generally emerge as differential." (p.37) High performing engineers tend to have an appreciation of the 'big picture'. The researchers' work results in a list of thirty-eight competencies, which are classified as task accomplishment, personal attributes, situational and interpersonal skills.

Research in the information systems (IS) area also suggests that non-technical skills and personal attributes relate to performance. For instance, the systems analyst is a key player in IS developments. Several studies have been carried out to determine what characteristics and skills are needed to succeed in this role. In their early study, Vitalari and Dixon (1983) identify two problems with this task:

1. There are no well accepted job performance criteria
2. There is no understanding of how different skills relate to job performance

They interviewed a total of eighteen systems analysts, nine of whom had been identified by their managers as effective and the remaining nine as poor. The hypothesis they sought to test was: that effective analysts will have different problem solving behaviours to less effective ones. To a large extent their argument is substantiated and they conclude that highly-rated analysts demonstrate the following types of behaviour:

- Analogical reasoning – trying to fit the problem into a previously experienced scenario.
- Planning and goal setting.
- Hypotheses management.
- Application of heuristics (rules of thumb).
- Good inter-personal relationship with the customer

Vitalari returned to this area in an effort to understand how problem-solving approaches differed between novice and expert systems analysts (Schenk et al. 1998). This research results in five potential reasons for error-proneness in novice analysts:

1. Less domain knowledge utilisation.
2. Superficial concern with user involvement.
3. Use of general versus specific triggers.
4. Less hypothesis testing and rejection.
5. Less goal generation.

A later study by Wynekoop and Walz (2000) uses Delphi analysis to identify twelve traits of high-performing systems analysts:

Table 3: Traits Associated with High-performing Systems Analysts

Knowledge or Skill	**Personality Trait**
Can abstract business problems and translate into computer systems.	Is analytical and logical.
Is a creative problem solver.	Prefers challenging work.
Has good interpersonal and communications skills.	Is organised.
Has a high level of technical knowledge.	Is both dependable and reliable.
Has leadership skills.	Is team oriented.
Has a high level of business knowledge.	Is self-motivated.

Those traits containing a knowledge or skill component can be taught. However, Hackman and Oldham (1980), warn us that management training has not been wholly satisfactory and it is unlikely that someone can be taught to be creative.

Systems analysts are not the only people to be assessed in this way. Although Cheng and Dainty's (2005) study concentrates on building construction project managers, when they categorise projects as being: "inherently unique, tend to be awarded at short notice, are reliant on a transient workforce and exist within a complex multidisciplinary team-oriented environment" (p.26), it can be seen that their findings should be relevant to software development project managers also. Like Vitalari and Dixon, these researchers compared good and average project managers and found that the high performers used their initiative to gather information, focused their efforts on their clients' needs, worked well in teams and showed leadership. They also proved to be flexible and had self-control as well as an "achievement orientation". Finally, they displayed analytical and conceptual thinking.

In summary, technical skills are absolutely necessary but alone are insufficient to make an effective practitioner, be that a commercial software developer or an IS professional.

2.3 Defining Skill

It is interesting to observe how important interpersonal skills and domain knowledge are in the studies recalled by the previous chapter. This suggests that knowledge is something that this project should also be concerned with. Indeed, the term: "knowledge, skills and abilities", or KSAs, is often used in the literature (Bailey and Stefaniak 1999; Curtis, Hefley and Miller 2001; Forfas 2003; Ryan and Tippins 2004). But what do these terms actually mean?

- **Knowledge.** According to Cook and Seely-Brown (1999), there are four different types of knowledge: individual, group, tacit and explicit. They describe knowledge as something that is possessed and has to be applied to be of any use. In essence, knowledge is a psychological state resulting from education.
- **Skill.** Reifer (2005) distinguishes skills from knowledge and abilities as follows: "For the most part, skills are developed on the job while knowledge and abilities are fostered in the classroom" (p.8). Skill is needed to apply knowledge to the problem domain. Skills are acquired by means of training and honed by practice.
- **Skill set.** The skills possessed by an individual.
- **Ability.** Fleishman (1975) discusses four types of ability: physical, sensory-perceptual, psychomotor and cognitive. This suggests that an ability is a natural talent or aptitude. It would be expected that software practitioners possess keen cognitive abilities.

However, the terms skill and ability seem to be used interchangeably in the literature, in dictionary definitions and in everyday speech. For instance, Misic (1996) describes the ability to employ system development techniques, when he should have referred to the skill of employing them. Therefore, although this project is concerned with knowledge and skills, the way the terms are used in daily life will be acknowledged by adapting the term KSA to mean: knowledge and skills/abilities.

As far as the research question is concerned, it now must be expanded to: what knowledge and skills/abilities are needed to carry out the various roles in software development - where the roles are those selected in section 2.2.

2.4 Scope of the Study

Miles and Huberman (1994) caution researchers to determine if the proposed sample population is feasible "in terms of time, money, access to people, and your own work style" (p.34). These factors automatically limit the scope of the project as there is only so much that can be done by a single researcher in a limited time span. Specifically, the following factors have been considered:

1. **Practitioner Scope.** The Forfás recommendations - that Irish software practitioners must increase the value they add to the development process – provides a useful constraint: Senior practitioners, in order to justify their higher salaries, already have to add more value than entry-level recruits. The skills they employ should be those that will be needed if Ireland is to succeed in competing with low-wage economies by providing more value-added services.

   The focus on senior people restricts the study to practitioners at or approaching what Dalton, Thompson and Price (1977) term 'Stage III' of their careers. That is, they have reached a level where they begin to achieve through guiding and mentoring others, as distinct from achieving by themselves. These employees are in their thirties and forties, having a minimum of five years software development experience.

2. **Geographical Scope.** Would the Republic of Ireland be an appropriate country to study? Ireland's software industry has benefited significantly from foreign direct investment (FDI); in 2003 Ireland ranked fourth in the world in terms of overall investment inflow (Lhermitte 2004). However, low-wage economies in Asia and in Eastern Europe are proving increasingly attractive to companies

striving to lower their cost base. Being unable to compete in terms of unit labour costs, Irish government advisory agencies, such as Forfás and the Economic and Social Research Institute (ESRI), are recommending that Irish industry develops skills along the entire value chain. They argue that Ireland must provide skills in business, sales and marketing, high-end research and basic communication (Forfas 2003; Enterprise Strategy Group 2004). Given this threat to Ireland's competitiveness, research into the knowledge and skills/abilities needed by Irish software practitioners would be of immense interest to policy makers.

It might also be interesting to study software practitioners in other countries, such as those in Eastern Europe and Asia, in order to compare them with their Irish counterparts.

Some preliminary investigation showed that this would not be a successful avenue to explore. Joe Walsh, the head of Logica-CMG's operation in the Czech Republic warns that Czechs are suspicious of outsiders and is confident that they would not cooperate with an Irish researcher, invited into the company by an Irish manager. Or, as Walsham (2002) puts it: "structure in the minds of actors in cross-cultural interaction affects the way they think and behave, and the way in which they perceive others from a different culture, which may result in disagreement and conflict" (p.368).

Brendan Keane, a University of Limerick student, spent time in India as part of his M.Sc. project (Keane 2005). He found it extremely difficult to arrange interviews with Indian software personnel. He explains that 'face' is a central concept in the east and software professionals have to make sure they are always busy in order to be perceived as important.

Given these cultural differences, an appropriate restriction would be to limit the study to Ireland.

3. **Industry Scope.** Because software has been applied in so many different problem domains, this study is limited to a single industry, representing a single facet of the ICT sector, specifically software development. This approach serves to reduce the project to a manageable size, as well as removing certain cultural variables (Schein 1999). Hofstede (1984) offers an analogy that helps put

culture in context: "culture is to human collectivity what personality is to the individual" (p.21). Therefore, by restricting this study to one industry, aspects of the problem domain's culture can be ignored.

4. **Company Scope.** How many companies need to be studied? Would a single software development team be adequate or do several companies need to be considered to create a reasonable picture of Irish software development personnel?

   According to the Industrial Development Authority's (IDA) web-site: "Over 800 software companies, both Irish and foreign owned, employ approximately 32,000 people, generating 10% of Ireland's exports and have total annual revenues of €12 billion" (IDA Ireland 2008). In 1997, half of the total employment in the software sector was made up of Irish indigenous firms (O'Malley and O'Gorman 1997, p.46); the other half comprised subsidiaries of foreign, trans-national corporations. By 2003, employment slightly favoured the multinational sector with these companies employing 56% of the software workers (Martinez-Solano, Giblin and Walshe 2005, p.8). This could be due to the fact that even "the most successful [indigenous] ventures, though, never grew up to be large organizations. Most Irish-owned software companies rise and fade in less than a decade" (Sterne 2004, p.7). To understand the entire sector then, project teams from both types of company must be included.

Restricting the scope of this study along practitioner, geographical, industry and company lines leads to a further refinement of the research question: what knowledge and skills/abilities are needed to carry out the various senior roles in a single industry within Irish software development? What that industry will be is dealt with in the next section.

2.5 Choosing an Industry

Given that my background is in telecommunications software development, I regard this as a good sector to concentrate on. However, an objective assessment of this industry should be made.

The telecommunications sector has advanced considerably since the first 'stored program control' telephone exchanges were announced. Traditionally, telecommunications service providers were concerned with transporting voice traffic from one telephone to another. For the most part, these providers were government departments.

Once the technology existed to transmit and route digitally encoded voice traffic, the potential for using the telephone network to transmit data was realised, with facsimile transmission being among the first data services.

However, the equipment providers were more concerned with real-time call processing activities than with the provision of novel billing and call routing services. A new release of telephone exchange software could take from eighteen months to two years to deliver because of its extensive testing interval. When the telephone service industry became deregulated, this situation was unacceptable to newly licensed operators.

The International Telecommunications Union (ITU), or CCITT (Commité Consultatif International de la Télèfonique et de la Télègraphique) as it was then known, created its Q.12xx series of recommendations to address this situation. Titled 'intelligent networks', this initiative called for billing and number translation to be moved from the telephone exchange (the service switching point) and migrated to a computer platform, called the service control point. The CCITT defined the communication protocol used to interface between the two devices.

This development allowed small software houses to enter the telecommunications market in order to create differentiating applications for the service providers. The demand for these applications grew in Europe when the pan-European digital cellular network was set up for mobile telephony. Newly licensed service providers depended on tailored billing packages and unique services to distinguish themselves from the competition.

In this context, the nature of the software changed from embedded real-time code to high-level languages. The service control point needed a high speed database to store subscriber configurations and secure Internet applications that allow the subscribers customise their own accounts. Thus, while software developers in this sector are still concerned with real-time call processing, they may also find themselves designing web applications and tuning database products. As such, this sector is considered to be an excellent exemplar of a software development industry.

It should also be noted that the telecommunications discourse is uniformly technical. By exploring the KSAs required to develop telecommunications software, this project has the potential to make a genuine contribution to our understanding in this area.

2.6 The Elicitation Framework

Knowledge of concepts can be obtained from classroom education (Misic and Russo 2000). However, skills need to be developed via training (Weinberg 1971). Training takes time; the new skills need to be developed with practice. As DeMarco (2001) explains it, training involves carrying out new tasks in a slower manner than an expert would.

The software practitioner needs to develop a skill set that has practical application. This is achieved using a combination of theoretical learning, vocational training and practical experience. This combination is similar to 'experiential learning' and can be illustrated as follows (Kolb 1984):

Figure 2: Experiential Learning

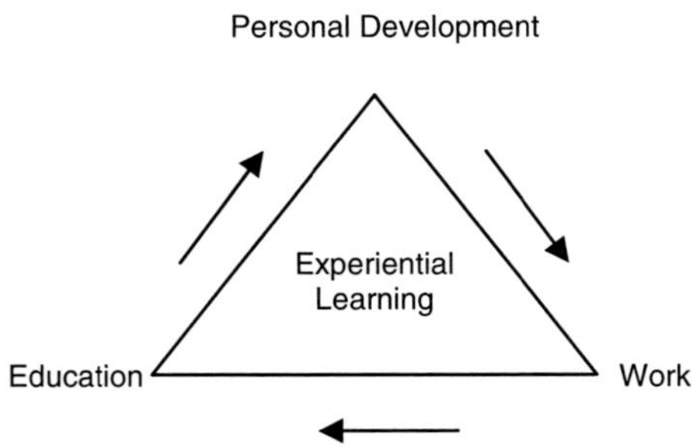

The learning process can be modelled as a feedback loop where experience leads to reflection that in turn leads to abstract concepts that can be tested out in new situations. Figure 3 shows such a model:

Figure 3: Kurt Lewin's Experiential Learning Model

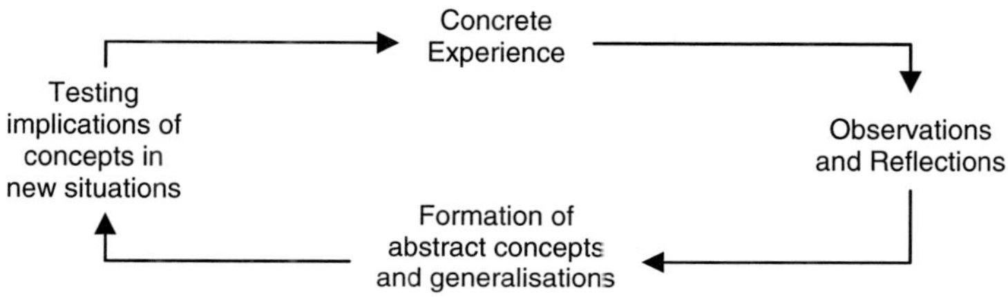

In summary, every person has innate talents (aptitudes) or abilities. Each can use their abilities to acquire a store of knowledge and develop the skills necessary to perform certain tasks through a combination of education, training and experience. This relationship is shown graphically in Figure 4:

Figure 4: Factors Leading to Skills

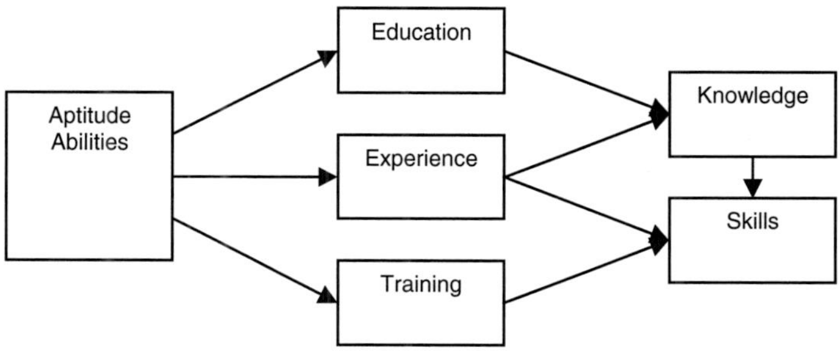

The active pursuit of education and training is a form of behaviour and Lewin has defined behaviour as a function of personality and the environment: "In principle it is everywhere accepted that behaviour (B) is a function of the person (P) and the environment (E), B = f(P,E), and that P and E in this formula are interdependent variables" (Lewin 1952, p.25).

Albert Bandura has expanded on this idea and relates all three factors bi-directionally. He argues that the person, their behaviours and their environment all determine one another. These relationships he terms "triadic reciprocal determinism" with the term reciprocal meaning "the mutual action between causal factors" – see Figure 5. This model of behaviour is called "social cognitive theory" (Bandura 1986).

Figure 5: Triadic Reciprocal Determinism

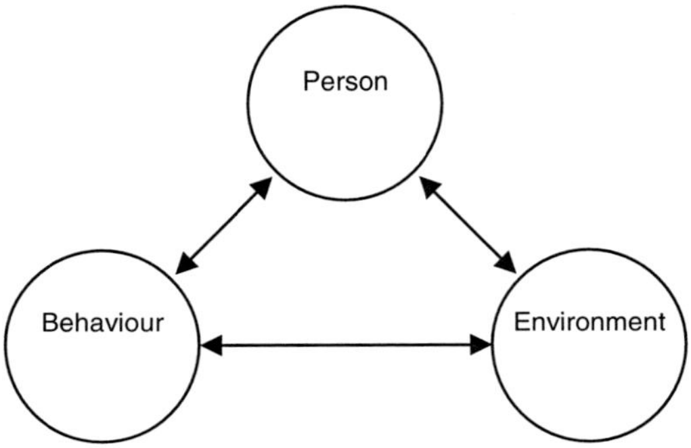

In this study, social cognitive theory is the basis for the theoretical framework informing the research instrument. The framework was developed by considering each of Bandura's three factors - personality, behaviour and environment – and identifying relevant attributes of each as shown in Figure 6.

Obviously, the research instrument will have to probe the software practitioner's skill set, which is a personal attribute. This skill set has been developed as a result of learning behaviours, which must be explored to determine how the skills were obtained. Another behaviour that is of interest is the practitioner's application to work which reveals how motivated s/he is. Motivation is determined by the work environment (Herzberg, Mausner and Snyderman 1959), which can be considered under the headings of the work itself and the context in which this takes place – generally in some sort of business organisation. In turn, these environmental attributes will influence the practitioner's personal attitude. Attitude is manifested by behaviour (Lemon 1973) and thus the pattern of influences is revealed: The work the practitioner does, coupled with organisational context, will foster that person's attitude. This will be seen in the types of learning behaviours and work habits, which in turn contribute to skill set development and application to the work itself.

Figure 6: Social Cognitive Framework

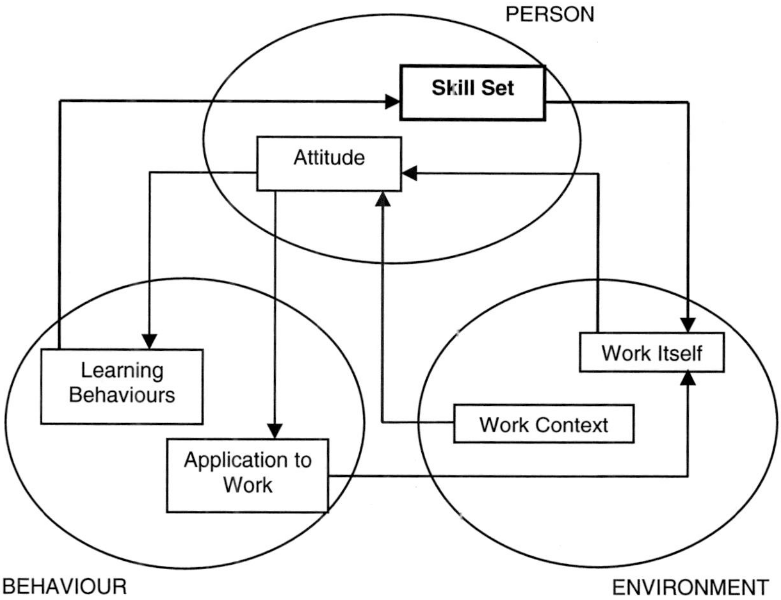

The specific factors given in Figure 6 will be elaborated in the next chapter.

2.7 Summary

In this chapter, the research question is analysed in order both to clarify understanding of the terms used and to define the scope of the project. Thus, the software development roles to be studied have been identified and the notion of skill has been elaborated to include knowledge and ability.

There have been some restrictions made to make the project feasible for a single researcher. To summarise, the scope of the project can be defined as:

a. Location: Republic of Ireland.
b. Industry: Telecommunication software

c. Companies: Multinational subsidiaries and Irish indigenous
d. People: Those with five or more years experience
e. Roles: Product manager
Project manager
Systems architect
Programmer
Tester
Technical writer
Customer support

The analysis carried out in this chapter has produced a more precisely defined research question: This project seeks to determine what knowledge and skills/abilities are needed to carry out the various senior roles in the Irish telecommunications software development industry.

A theoretical framework based on social cognitive theory has also been presented that will be used in the next chapter as a basis for the research design.

CHAPTER THREE

RESEARCH DESIGN

3.1 Introduction

In order to determine what knowledge and skills/abilities are needed to carry out the various senior roles in the Irish telecommunications software industry, an appropriate research instrument is needed. This chapter will explore the options available in terms of the research question and the theoretical framework.

3.2 Selecting a Research Method

The research method to use is dictated by the research question. Suppose the question was: do practitioners in the Irish telecommunications software industry require the same skills as those identified in the computer personnel research literature as pertaining to the information systems (IS) field? Then a 'confirmatory' study would be appropriate, using "mathematical & statistical techniques to identify facts and causal relationships" (Fitzgerald and Howcroft 1998, p.10). Such a study would either support or reject the hypothesis that these two types of practitioner need the same knowledge and skills/abilities.

However, because the goal is to determine the knowledge and skills/abilities that practitioners in an area other than IS require, an 'exploratory' study is needed. As Lethbridge, Sim and Singer (2005) note: "Many of the field studies in software engineering tend to be exploratory in nature, because we are still gathering basic knowledge about the human factors surrounding software development and maintenance" (p.314). Ultimately, what this study needs to do is to create a theory that satisfactorily answers the question. Thus, the goal is to build a new theory rather than to test an existing one.

More formally, an 'inductive' as opposed to a 'deductive' methodological position is appropriate. Inductive research is a posteriori – based on experience, while deductive studies are a priori – prior to experience. Inductive methods, such as grounded theory (Strauss and Corbin 1998) or case study research (Eisenhardt 1989; Yin 1994), seek to gather information and build theories from this – i.e. they argue from the particular to the general. Deductive approaches, such as surveys and laboratory experiments, are designed to confirm or disprove pre-defined theories – i.e. they test the general rule by applying it to particular instances.

Having decided on an exploratory study, what techniques are available firstly to gather information and secondly to analyse that information? If the research question suggests an exploratory, inductive methodology, then the theoretical framework (Bandura 1986; Downey 2005) and the scope of the project will influence the technique to use.

Lethbridge et al (2005) divide the possible techniques into 'inquisitive' and 'observational' ones. Observing practitioners across the seven roles identified earlier would be extremely demanding on a single researcher. It also might be difficult to get permission to make such observations. Therefore, inquisitive techniques provide most potential. These include focus groups, interviews and questionnaires.

Confidentiality is an important ethical consideration in this project and a potentially interesting focus group - people carrying out similar roles across the subject companies – might not be possible as practitioners would have to discuss work processes in the presence of their competitors. Another potential danger is the reluctance of companies to allow their people to describe aspects of their work in such a public forum. Even without the ethical considerations, focus groups can be dominated by individuals and the facilitator has less control than over a one-on-one interview (Maguire 2004).

Questionnaires have proven popular in the IS skills surveys. However, these questionnaires either drew on the literature or the researchers' own interviews and focus groups for their hypotheses. For instance, Trauth et al (1993) took a four phase approach and used brainstorming, telephone interviews, focus groups and questionnaires to identify the expectation gap between academia and industry. Both Shi and Bennett (1998) and Noll and Wilkins (2002) devised questionnaires based on previous skills surveys found in the literature. A series of focus groups, followed by a questionnaire survey was used by Lee et al (1995). Sawyer et al (1998) drew extensively from the literature and used interviews, focus groups and questionnaires to elicit their information.

Because of the exploratory nature of the research question, a questionnaire would not be adequate at this point to determine the knowledge and skills/abilities needed by senior practitioners. If the questionnaire was based on IS research, then how can we determine if the telecommunications practitioners need other skills, ones unknown in the IS world?

Lethbridge et al (2005) offer some caveats relating to questionnaires. Because "there is no interviewer, ambiguous and poorly-worded questions are problematic" (p.322). Also, a good response rate is difficult to achieve, 5% being typical in software engineering surveys.

With focus groups, the issue is one of control; with questionnaires, it is the need for a hypothesis to test. For this study, we need to build up a picture of the personality and behaviours of practitioners who work in the Irish telecommunications environment. Because the Irish practitioners work in either multinational subsidiaries or indigenous companies, a series of case studies across examples of these organisations is required. According to Yin (1994), what is needed here is a multiple-case embedded case study. In an embedded study, several people in either one (single-case) or many (multiple-case) organisations may be studied. Thus the people are termed 'units of analysis'. Yin also states that "interviews are an essential source of case study evidence because most case studies are about human affairs" (p.85). He also hints at how we can include some of the benefits of questionnaire-based research by creating a 'focused' or structured interview. This is an important refinement because there are several factors to consider before arranging interviews:

1. Access to practitioners is difficult to obtain, so the primary goal of each interview must be to gather all necessary information – it is unlikely that a second attempt will be allowed.
2. On the other hand, interviews can not be allowed to digress into irrelevant areas. Goldkuhl and Cronholm (2003) point out that if "you are too open minded in the data collection phase, you will probably end up with a large and diverging amount of data" (p.3). Or, as Coffey and Atkinson (1996) observe, open mindedness should not be the same as empty mindedness.

3. There is a very real chance that some of the interviewees will be reticent or inarticulate people. A reasonably comprehensive checklist is needed simply to keep the conversation going.
4. The goal of this study is to identify knowledge and skills/abilities for particular roles. Thus these interviews will be compared with one another and a common structure facilitates this process.

While it is useful to place a structure on the interview, the informant must be allowed to describe the role without too much intervention from the interviewer. By drawing on the social cognitive framework, an overall interview structure comprising three questions can be developed. In the following sections, each question will be considered in turn and the literature will be examined in order to provide a checklist for each question. The interview checklists are given in Appendix A.

3.3 The Environment ("What do you do?")

Job titles provide little insight into what a person actually does. A person called a "programmer" in one company may carry out similar duties to a "software engineer" in another. To understand the person's work environment, we need to learn about the work itself and the work context.

To determine the work itself, a general question: "what do you do?" is posed. To keep the conversation moving and to ensure that the person's answer can be compared to that of another interviewee, a checklist of functional areas is associated with this question. This draws on various IEEE standards and recommendations, specifically those for purchasing (IEEE Computer Society 1998), documentation (IEEE Computer Society 2001), project management (IEEE Computer Society 2003) and the Software Engineering Body of Knowledge (IEEE Computer Society 2004).

The work context can be considered in terms of two factors: the organisation the interviewee works in and the profession to which s/he belongs. This information is elicited in more subtle ways than the work itself. The formality of the development process (obtained from the descriptions of the work itself) will indicate the level of process-maturity in the company. Later parts of the interview, those probing for inter-personal skills and the person's experience, will also offer insights into the corporate culture and the way it has influenced the interviewee's career path.

3.4 The Person ("What skills do you need?")

The goal of the interview is to identify the skill set needed to perform a given role. The interviewer seeks out this information explicitly by asking: "what skills do you need in your role?" To prompt the interviewee, another checklist provides a list of skills. These skills are classified under technical, business and inter-personal skills. These lists are broadly similar to those used in comparable surveys made in the information systems field (Trauth et al. 1993; Lee et al. 1995; Sawyer et al. 1998; Shi and Bennett 1998; Noll and Wilkins 2002). They also map well to the acting, valuing, thinking and deciding skills described in (Kolb 1984).

The second personal attribute we need to consider is the person's attitude. This is not probed directly. Instead the person's behaviours – their learning behaviours and their application to the work – are examined. For instance, a positive learning behaviour could be shown by a person who has taken the initiative to pursue a degree course at night. Their application to the work itself tends to come across in the degree of enthusiasm with which they describe their work.

3.5 The Behaviours ("How did you acquire these skills?")

The question: "how did you acquire these skills?" uses a checklist that seeks to determine the person's initial motivation to enter the software world and the way the necessary qualifications and experience were built up. The checklist behind this question looks at their academic history as far back as their school days. It also explores outside interests, such as team sports and membership of clubs and societies. It is possible that such outside interests have helped them develop useful inter-personal skills.

The interviewee's learning behaviour is further examined by looking at mentoring experiences; how promotions arose; what journals are subscribed to; what views of professional training courses are held and whether or not the person attends night classes.

3.6 Summary

This chapter explains the decision to gather data using an interview instrument. Being based on Bandara's (1986) social cognitive theory, the instrument must determine as much as possible about the work environment, the interviewees' personalities and their relevant behaviours.

The interview instrument corresponds to this breakdown by asking three main questions: The first seeks to understand the work environment by determining what the interviewee does. As was seen in chapter 1, software development is a multi-disciplinary activity including significantly more than simply writing computer programs. To understand what a person's role is in the development process, it is important to determine what that person does in the context of a project.

Another environmental factor to consider is that all the people interviewed in this study work in organisations. Within these organisations the status of the practitioners needs to be considered. How do software developers consider themselves in relation to other professions? Indeed, should software developers regard themselves as professionals in the first instance?

The second concern of the theory relates to personal factors, including the person's skill set. Software development is a labour-intensive activity, so an appreciation of human personality is needed to understand practitioners in this field. Also, as noted above, the people we are interested in work in organisations, so their career path possibilities must be considered in the context of organisations. Being human, their performance and their progression in the organisation will be shaped by their attitudes towards both the work and the company. However, as we have seen in earlier chapters, even the most positive attitudes will not lead to success unless the person can draw on a relevant skill set.

For the third question, we need to learn something of the interviewee's behaviour. According to Lewin (1952), behaviour is a function of environment and personality. Thus personal attitude and organisational imperative should shape how practitioners acquire the necessary skills. They should also influence how well or how badly they apply themselves to their work.

This wider understanding adds a measure of confidence to the interview instrument, suggesting that it will be sufficient to elicit enough information to facilitate meaningful analysis. To validate the instrument, a pilot study was carried out. This study is described in the next chapter.

Hart (1998) uses a table to list the issues and options available when designing a research project. This list of issues is used here to summarise the design of this study.

1. *What is the purpose of the study?*
   This project seeks to determine the knowledge and skills/abilities that are needed to carry out the various senior roles in the Irish telecommunications software development industry.

2. *What is the scope of the study?*
   a. Location: Republic of Ireland.
   b. Industry: Telecommunication software
   c. Companies: Multinational subsidiaries and Irish indigenous
   d. People: Those with five or more years experience
   e. Roles: Product manager
      Project manager
      Systems architect
      Programmer
      Tester
      Technical writer
      Customer support

3. *What is the focus of the study?*
   The focus is on the skill sets of individual, senior practitioners who work as part of development teams.

4. *What are the units of analysis?*
   a. For information gathering: Individual software developers.
   b. For analysis: Project artefacts.

5. *What is the sampling strategy?*
   Companies and individuals were chosen in a purposeful fashion, acting as exemplars.

6. *What types of data will be collected?*
   Qualitative.

7. *How are the data managed?*
   a. Interview recordings stored digitally on a computer.

  b. Interview reports maintained using the QSR Nvivo® analysis tool

8. *What analytical approach is used?*
   Inductive: conclusions are drawn from the gathered evidence.

9. *How is validity addressed in the study?*
   a. The skills used were both implicitly (by asking about the interviewee's contribution to the project) and explicitly (by asking which of the skills listed on a checklist are used) canvassed.
   b. The interviews were summarised and sent to the interviewees for approval – i.e. they were member checked.
   c. The overall findings of the study were discussed with experts in the industry (a management consultant and a senior manager).

10. *When did the study occur (interview dates)?*
    a. Pilot study: 13 January 2004 – 4 February 2004.
    b. Main study: Company 1: 29 June 2004 – 31 August 2004
    Company 2: 2 July 2004 – 3 December 2004
    Company 3: 25 September 2004 – 1 February 2005
    Company 4: 11 August 2005 - 4 October 2005
    c. Expert opinions: 8 December 2005 and 29 December 2005

11. *How is the study justified?*
    a. By providing independent verification of the Forfás recommendations; the rationale behind these is not published.
    b. By providing a means of addressing the role ambiguity problem encountered in the literature, for instance (Belbin 2000; Shaw 2000).

12. *How are ethical issues handled?*
    a. Every effort is made to ensure both company and individual confidentiality. No work will be published where the company or an individual informant could be recognised.
    b. No company, product or individual names are used in the analysis stages.
    c. Interviews with practitioners were arranged with the approval of the companies and, where necessary, non-disclosure agreements were signed.

13. *How are logistics handled?*
    d. Companies were approached through personal acquaintances.
    e. The companies selected are within a 100km radius of the university.

CHAPTER FOUR

THE PILOT STUDY

Introduction

Lethbridge, Sim and Singer (2005) strongly recommend that interview- or questionnaire-based studies be piloted before approaching the principal informants. In this case, the semi-structured interview checklist needed to be evaluated and revised. Also, the information gathered as part of the pilot would be used to limit the scope of the main study and to highlight topics that could be examined in more depth. To gain experience using the interview instrument, a number of software practitioners were interviewed. The aim was to explore a wide variety of roles and industries. Candidates were approached if they satisfied the following criteria:

- They develop software. The interpretation of 'develop' is as wide as possible, from customising a third-party product using scripting languages to developing new applications from scratch.
- They have at least five years software experience.

In total, seven practitioners were interviewed. Their job titles are listed in Table 4 and the industries they work in are detailed in Table 5.

Table 4: Job Titles

Number	Job Title
2	Systems Architect
1	Software Engineer
1	Software Test Engineer
1	Business Development Manager (start-up company)
1	Projects Manager
1	Editorial Software Consultant

Table 5: Industry

Number	Industry
3	Telecommunications systems vendor
1	National daily newspaper
1	GPS tracking and rf identification (RFID) systems integrator
1	Process tracking systems developer
1	Warehouse identification and communication systems

As well as recording the interviews, extensive notes were taken during the conversations and the act of note taking seemed to put the interviewees at ease. While the interview was structured, all questions were open-ended and the person was allowed to describe their work in as much detail as they wished.

The benefit of the structure was shown when it came to writing up the interview. Rather than make a verbatim transcript, the notes were written up as soon as possible after the interview. Then the recording was replayed and the text added to, corrected and clarified as appropriate. The finished product was e-mailed to the interviewees for their approval, as a form of 'member checking' (Miles and Huberman 1994).

The following sections describe the findings. They broke down into two main headings:

1. How the interviewees began their careers.
2. How the software development environment appears from their perspectives.

4.2 From Motivation to Work

Figure 7. The Origins of a Software Practitioner

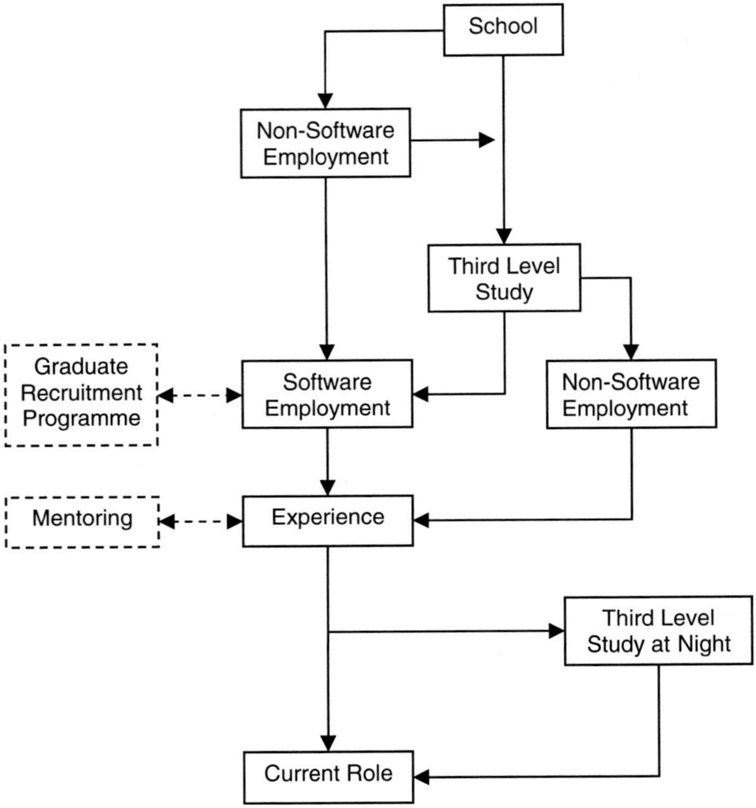

Figure 7 illustrates the various paths that the pilot study participants took to reach their current status. For most of the interviewees, an aptitude for mathematical subjects in school triggered an interest either in computers per se or electronics in general. For the others, they had no clear idea what they wanted to do after school or failed to obtain places in their preferred courses.

Not all of the practitioners went directly from school to a third-level institution. One did a secretarial course while another served an apprenticeship to be a compositor (printer/graphic designer).

For those who did pursue third level education directly after school, feelings are mixed. Opposing views were expressed about the relative merits of a university degree versus the more practical courses available in Institutes of Technology (ITs).

> "Students who came from the I.T.s were better prepared for the workforce; they had spent a lot more time doing, I think, project work or work that was more related to industry. I think that a lot of, say, the academics, the professors that are in the third level institutes are not tuned in to what's happening in industry."

Ironically, a person who had studied in two ITs condemns these courses for being too theoretical:

> "It was all artificial intelligence and physical electronic systems which is absolutely of no benefit."

Those who studied electronics, however, all cite their courses as providing solid problem analysis skills.

> "You have to do that much more in hardware because if you're designing a circuit you know and you have something that gets so far and doesn't come out the other end. To fix that you kind of have to be methodical in terms of how you – you know you have to say: 'Okay is it getting through the first bit and getting through …' – you know and being methodical as to where it's going through. So as part of learning how to design in hardware you have to learn how to debug hardware and analyse your hardware."

One interviewee sums up the value of third level education by noting that it gives you the skills:

> "To know what book to look up and be able to understand it when you read it."

Entering the work-force saw most of the practitioners receiving mentoring, either as part of formal graduate recruitment programmes or by being assigned mentors on a more informal basis.

> "Your supervisor would do a lot of work with you and different people kind of showed you – there was a lot of close interaction. I found that was great actually. It was a good place to learn that kind of stuff and learn how projects were run because you tended to be involved in a project group even if you only do a little bit of it. … You got to see how a project worked and how it ran through the process."

Those who experienced mentoring highly recommend the practice; one commentator noting that mentoring is less available the more experienced you become. It is interesting to note that the interviewees whose roles are the least demanding have never received any form of mentoring.

Some of the interviewees have subsequently pursued further studies through the Open University. All are very satisfied with their courses and each cites the ability to pick modules that are immediately relevant to work or provide a basis for their future careers. One interviewee completed the Irish Management Institute's supervisory management two-year course and the Irish Institute of Training and Development's one-year course, both at night.

These interviewees note how useful it is to have practical experience before undertaking coursework. The block release structure of the apprenticeship is also strongly recommended, lending weight to the software apprenticeship proposed by Surendran et al (2002).

This observation informs the interviewees' views of short professional courses. Most are of the opinion that, before attending a course, you "have to know what you need to learn". To get value from the course depends on "whether you should be on the course in the first place." As well as being prepared, the knowledge picked up in training needs to be applied immediately.

Practical experience and learning by trial and error is cited by all interviewees as where most of their skills are obtained. One notes that:

> "With all these engineers coming out of college, computer programmers coming out of college, you're in competition with them. You're probably on twice their salary and you're going to have to keep pushing yourself to keep ahead. … Fortunately or unfortunately trial and error is there with us. You might lessen but you will not get rid of it in a competitive environment."

The bulk of the interviewees in this study have been with the same company for many (in one case, twenty-four) years and have built up strong domain knowledge.

4.3 Roles and Interactions

The seven people interviewed for this pilot study describe their work in detail and explain the skills they employ in their roles. Technical skills are not regarded as the most important, lending weight to the findings of the skills surveys described in chapter 1.

For a senior person, the role evolves into one involving interaction with functions outside the development arena. Figure 8 shows the major interfaces to the development group. The remainder of this section will explore these interactions in the context of the interviewees' experiences.

Figure 8. Software Development In Context

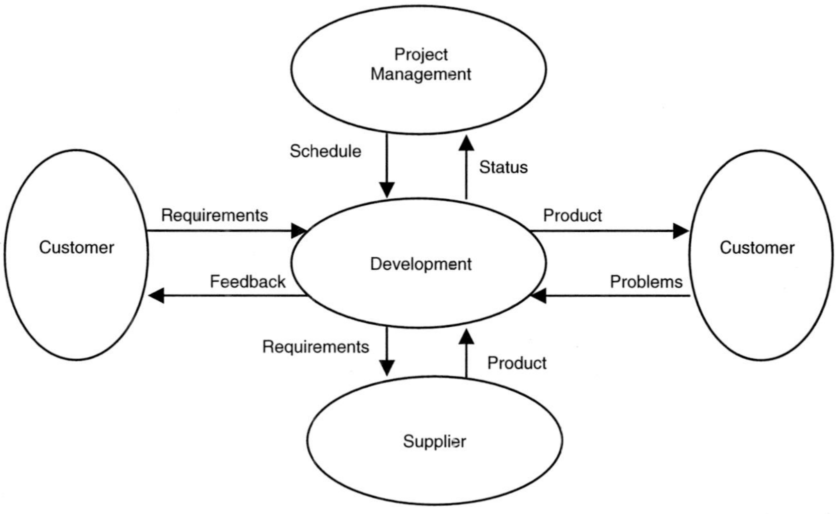

For someone involved in the development of software, the following interactions will, eventually, take place:

1. Interaction with technology. This is the area where a newcomer to the commercial software development world spends most time working. The focus of this work is the design, coding and testing of software products.

2. Interaction with customers. It can be seen from Figure 8 that customers figure twice in the software development context. At

the front end, organisations and individuals must be converted into customers by the sales operation. Only one of the interviewees is directly involved in sales. However, due to the customisable nature of software products, many of the interviewees have to elicit and clarify customer requirements. At the back end, once the software is ready, the product must be installed on the customer's site and documentation and training provided. A mechanism must be put in place to allow customers report problems and get adequate support.

3. Interaction with suppliers. These interactions range from the straightforward acquisition of computers, through the purchase of large software systems, to the outsourcing of entire software sub-system components. This role sees the interviewees in the guise of customers themselves and they are faced with providing adequate requirements and testing the resulting deliverables.

4. Interaction with project management. Having mastered the technical aspects of the software development process, many developers get involved in the project management role. Indeed some may be required to continue their mainstream development work while also managing the overall effort.

4.3.1 Interacting With Technology

Figure 9. Technology Interaction

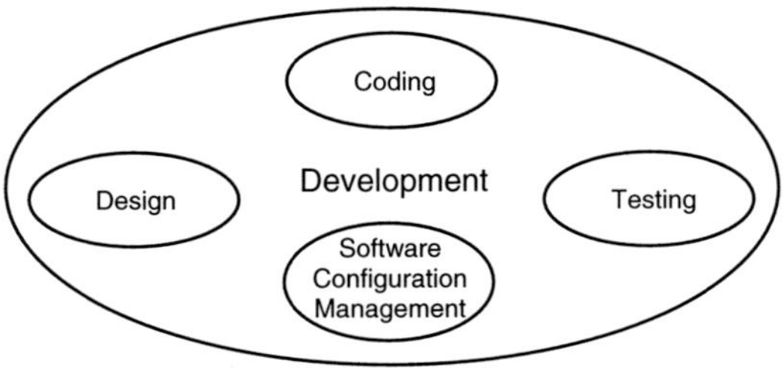

According to the Software Engineering Body of Knowledge, mainstream software development is covered by the following knowledge areas: software design, software construction, software testing and software configuration management (IEEE Computer Society 2004). It was expected that most of the interviewees would have extensive experience in these areas and would follow either a corporate or personal process in carrying out these tasks. Of the people who actually work in these areas, only one follows a recognised process.

Of most concern is the lack of formal design methodologies. There were vague references to object oriented design and flow charts, with one noting that the use of Visual Basic promoted object oriented thinking.

> "I usually start at the front end in terms of what they're going to see – the interface to the customer - and work back to how that then is going to be stored in a system and look at it from that point of view."

While those with an electrical engineering background are happy that they know how to design, there was no mention of any particular methodology such as those by Jourdan (1975) or Jackson (1983) for structured design, or object oriented techniques such as the Unified Software Development Process (Jacobson, Booch and Rumbaugh 1999). At least the architect who has the most mature development environment does emphasise the importance of well-defined interfaces in a design.

Finally, the person without any formal training in software development observed that his training in graphic design proves helpful in the design of Visual Basic programs. He feels that design is a transferable skill. This is in agreement with the studio based design training described by Kuhn (1998).

Coding shows the emergence of Visual Basic as the language of choice for commercial products with significant end-user interaction. The telecommunications sector mainly uses C and C++ with a strong element of PERL scripting.

While coding standards apply in two of the companies, formal code inspections are used in only one:

> "We would inspect under an inspection process which was developed under CMM, the Capability Maturity Model. We inspected the code under that four person review process."

They also employ program templates to enforce coding standards. Because the product is mature, these templates provide a reasonably good fit.

The projects manager makes an important observation about how code is very rarely developed from a clean sheet. Her observation suggests a different meaning to code reuse:

> "To actually start a project completely from scratch – like blank screen – can often be rare enough. You usually end up chopping a bit out of something else or even if you are starting, you'll say: 'I know I did something like that before' and you'll look up your old project and take out that chunk of code that does that bit that you want to do so you do a lot of re-using of code."

The Visual Basic applications seem very easy to test – suggesting limited functionality. Again, only one interviewee mentions a formal testing regime where unit tests are based on the designs as per the 'V' development model.

> "That came from a key process area of CMM. One of the main goals in unit testing is to have each individual branch tested. Now that's a pretty large requirement in itself. We didn't always achieve full unit testing because sometimes you write more code to test your own code than the actual code itself so we would do it within reason and test all the major branches."

None of the interviewees showed any appreciation of the theory of testing (Roper 1994; Myers 2004), with testing being done on an ad-hoc basis. This is true even for the software test engineer - experience dictating what symptoms to look for if a system is not working.

> "I suppose it's something you built up over the years really. There's nothing you can sit down and read and say that should kind of do this. I suppose you could read through old test cases or something. It's about identifying what a system does and what it should do and how to know if it doesn't."

The two companies that had adopted coding standards also feature software configuration management. In one case, the emphasis is on change control. This is motivated by having to synchronise between two remote development sites. A person was hired for this role and the code is placed under strict control. In the other, build control is the main concern. The company likes to get beta versions to customer sites as quickly as possible. These versions contain small functional increments and the developers hope to get feedback as soon as possible. This feedback may influence the contents of the next increment.

4.3.2 Interacting With the Customer

Figure 10. Front End Customer Interaction

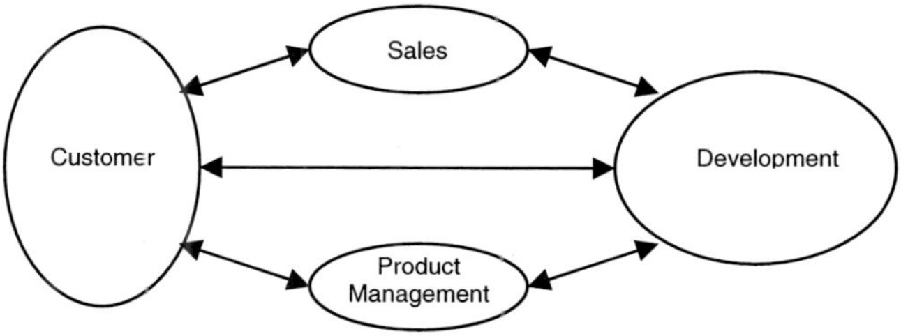

The interviewee with direct sales responsibility provided most detail in this area. Before any product is fully developed, extensive market research is carried out to determine what products will sell. Some of this research involves talking to existing customers where they learn how the existing product can be developed. If feedback from the marketplace is positive, a prototype system is developed and presented to possible customers. Unless someone makes a firm order, no further development work will take place.

> "A lot of it is down to whether you can see an application that can make money for a company as opposed to coming up with a product and then trying to sell it."

The costing of the product is also worth noting. The price is not determined by the estimated development cost; it is based on a reasonable return on investment for the customer. The sales presentations illustrate how the adoption of the product can either increase revenue, reduce costs or, ideally, both.

For the others who deal with customers at the front end, their role is to clarify and manage requirements. In one case, a sales support role is involved where technical input is fed into tender responses.

If the person does not interface directly with the customer, s/he deals with sales personnel or product managers. The goal of these interactions is to clarify requirements. These can come from existing or new customers. Many of these requirements are similar and the interviewees try to develop the products as generically as possible; customer specific features are often enabled using configuration files. Requirements are prioritised by product management. All of the interviewees are very concerned with identifying common solutions or sensible groups that would make useful software releases. However, only one company uses formal requirements tracking throughout the project.

> "… the requirements were held in this package called Doors and they were managed through that and we would have had one requirements liaison person in our office in Cork who would work with the requirements group over in Holland in the updating of the various requirements from the customers into this package itself … we had full traceability."

The person who carries out the sales role emphasises the need to get into the customers' mindsets and understand their businesses, as recommended by Graham (2003). However, those who interface with product management groups actually never meet the customers face to face. While unclear requirements are well known in the software industry, this study uncovered the situation where requirements are described in terms of a solution.

Because of the problems with mapping designations (domain terms such as "touch down") to definitions (exact requirements such as "wheels turning"), Michael Jackson (1998a) proposes the whole area of description as a discipline in its own right. However, in this study, only the newspaper analyst notes some problems with terminology. Nobody else acknowledges any difficulties in coming up with a common vocabulary when dealing with customers or suppliers.

The significant observation about front end customer interaction is that none of the interviewees have training in sales or formal requirements engineering. Even the person involved in sales admitted that he needs training in presentation skills.

Figure 11. Back End Customer Interaction

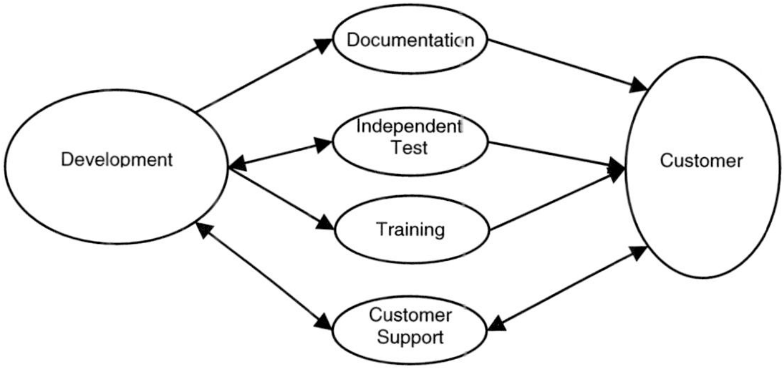

All of the interviewees have to deal with some aspect of the delivery to the customer. A commercial piece of software is more than working code. Because software is intrinsically complicated (Brooks 1986), user manuals have to be produced and training given. Also, a support arrangement must be put in place to correct defects. For larger systems, like telecommunications products, the support group provides useful feedback to development. This contributes a deeper understanding of how the product is actually being used.

Several of the interviewees understand the importance of testing although none use any formal methodology. For instance, one product that had a large user interface component was given over to other employees to play with.

> "Doing usability test on it, you know, try and break it; check that it does what it's supposed to do first of all and then, if I don't do what I'm supposed to do, what happens? Does it kind of cope with me putting in the wrong thing or leaving something empty? … Then it would go to somebody else in the company as well, to get a few people to look at it and get different attitudes on it."

Formal independent testing is seen in the telecommunications companies, where system testing requires expensive equipment to simulate a real telephone network. These laboratory systems can be configured to emulate whatever customer installations are required.

Few of the interviewees express any interest (or aptitude) for technical writing. Indeed one company takes the novel approach of hiring contract writers and training them in how to use the product. Once they can use it themselves, the writers are well placed to write the user manuals from a user perspective. Besides relieving developers of what appears to be an onerous task, it also ensures that the resulting documentation is not technically biased.

Another interviewee finds working with technical writers distasteful as he has to write out what needs to go into the documents and then has his work reformatted by the documentation group.

> "They don't understand the technical side of it so you had to write the descriptions of what's actually going on. It's painful when you go away and go to the trouble of writing down what actually the product does from the customer point of view and then, you know, the technical team come along and say: 'That's wrong' or: 'That's written the wrong way'. You know you write more like a developer than a technical writer. The fact is that they don't have the raw material; you have to supply them with the raw material."

For one company, on-site installation is the project phase requiring most planning, as overruns in installations are liable to penalty clauses and directly affect the bottom line. This product requires the installation of hardware devices and the software is installed on "ruggedised" PCs, so installation is a non-trivial activity. Another has an easier time with a software package that is up and running within a few hours. As a final example, a company faces the problem of providing a customised version of a third party product. Every time the supplier upgrades their software, all the customisations have to be tested to ensure that they still work after the upgrade.

Training is another aspect of product delivery. In some companies, informal training is given to customers as part of the installation process; in one case, the sales representatives provide training in the generic product, with the interviewee explaining the workings of new customisations.

The newspaper consultant's main role is the provision of training to over 250 in-house end users. Because so many of the editorial staff members are not familiar with computers, they are inclined to panic when dealing with them. Similarly, if the automated system is upgraded or a cumbersome procedure replaced with a more streamlined one, users have to be persuaded that this new method is worth using – re-training is often more difficult than training. He also notes that being a parent is beneficial in dealing with the different personalities that need training.

In the situation where training is provided to the customer, a help desk or customer support facility is usually set up to assist users as they learn the system by experience. Unfortunately, customer support is also needed to provide a conduit for reporting problems from the field.

Customer support and maintenance prove to be a major part of one interviewee's work. His company's approach to customer problems is reactive in nature. Every problem reported is carefully noted, as is the solution. This company is lucky in that fixes to its software can be installed over a modem link and problems seem easy to fix. However, the solution is not broadcast to all customers, despite the mostly generic nature of the product; it is only issued to another customer if that customer also reports it. This involves close co-operation between the support personnel.

4.3.3 Interacting With Suppliers

Figure 12. Supplier Interaction

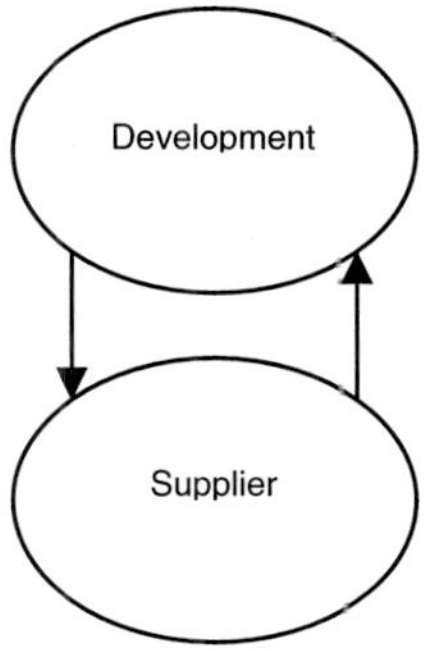

Supplier interaction ranges from the straightforward purchase of PCs and laptops to the commissioning of bespoke software sub-systems.

In one case, two software houses are employed to develop components that the interviewee integrates into the final product. The relationships with these suppliers are important as the software houses share the risk by using licensing as the method of charging. The importance of such relationships is stressed in Chavez, Tomabene and Wiederhold (1998). As well as software, hardware components such as "ruggedised" PCs are purchased. Advice is given on price negotiation:

> "If you respect their cash-flow position and pay them on time and stick to their credit ratings. ... When you're selling you want repeat business."

However, price should not be the main concern:

> "You have to make sure that the product you're getting is of suitable quality, is of the right quality, because, as I said, ruggedness is a huge thing in our industry and there's no point scrimping and saving for an item that's €50 cheaper but won't last in the field."

Another interviewee has responsibility for purchasing and adapting a complete software product. In other words this relationship places the interviewee in a customer role. Preference is given to products that are easy to configure and customise using scripting languages such as Visual Basic. Consideration for future growth plans is also a factor in choosing a vendor. It is noted that pitching requirements at a high level helps to reduce confusion.

At the other end of the process, when the components or the entire package is delivered, they have to be tested to ensure that they actually carry out the requirements. It is surprising that this interviewee has not developed a formal test suite to validate the requirements, as recommended by Weyuker (1998). However, a mutually beneficial relationship seems to have been established.

> "I'd say there were at least half a dozen features that we said were prerequisites that took a little work on their part and a lot of inspiration on our part in so far as we actually do things in a certain way and, based on procedural experience and journalism and all that, I felt that I had an idea of the way I wanted it to work and they thought: "Hey that's a good idea. Look, we'll help you develop that idea". When we got the thing working, our idea becomes part of product. So it benefits both."

Similarly, the GPS and RIFD software components seem to get tested as part of the integration process. Indeed, neither approach would merit the title "Procurement Oriented Requirements Engineering" (Maiden and Ncube 1998).

A further step in the process is required in both these situations. The component integrator has to examine the supplied documentation and rework it so that both sets of documents conform to the start-up company's formats.

The newspaper consultant has to learn how the system works with a view to training the staff. He also has to begin customising the software to match the editorial department's manual workflows. He notes that "real programmers" have a preference for working on new products and seem to have little or no interest in refining existing ones.

4.3.4 Interacting With Management

Figure 13. Project Management Interaction

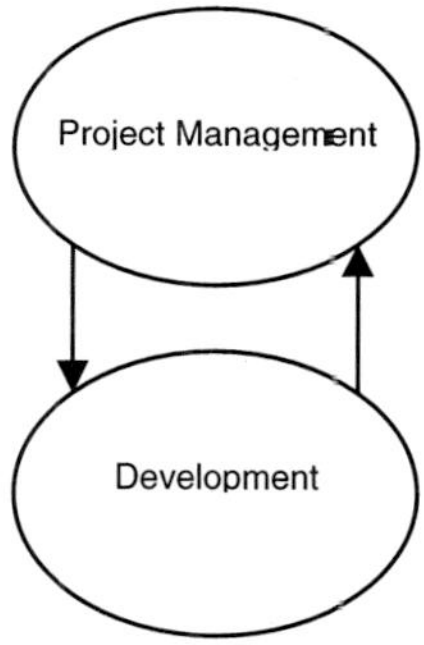

Software development is a team-based activity and as such needs to be planned, coordinated and tracked. Most of the interviewees are involved to a greater or lesser extent with project management activity.

Two are responsible for writing formal project plans. In both cases, the main component of the document is a work breakdown structure. One plan contains the inputs to the product and the external dependencies; the other contains estimates for the activities. Where the plan does not contain estimates, they are recorded using Microsoft Project.

Only one describes a formal tracking process – the use of earned value analysis. Interestingly, the start-up company's director brings up a point raised by Boehm and Huang (2003) when he stresses the importance of determining that the product is commercially viable before ensuring that budgets are adhered to during development.

Project management is a distinct activity from team leading. A situation is described where staff members are taken off the project (to deal with field problems for instance) without the project manager's consent.

> "That can be very difficult and sometimes, when you don't own the resources – either physical resources or people resources – it's very frustrating. We're given all the responsibility of delivering something without being given the full authority to do it."

However, as a skill, project management receives a ringing endorsement:

> "Project management skills are the most transferable skills of all – they apply to all industries"

Although the company director is in a situation where sub-contracting companies are involved, he only mentions planning in relation to the installation of the product. The impression is that the sub-contracting companies are sharing the risk so they are trusted to deliver on their part of the deal.

> "If we were to give ourselves our correct title, we'd really call ourselves more sub-system integrators than software developers because we're getting third party companies to design our software; we're buying hardware off a number of vendors and we're just coming up with different solutions for different customers."

The software test engineer stresses the planning needed for the shared lab resource. While all the engineers provide estimates for the projects they are planning to test, the whole schedule is thrown into chaos (a) if the development group is not ready in time or (b) a field problem needs to be reproduced in the lab. Setting up a customer-specific configuration can take several days.

Some interviewees mention estimation and they all seem to estimate activities based on their previous experiences. Interestingly, while one architect works out the development estimates for most projects in this fashion, some projects require the creation of prototype systems to define the work breakdown structure. She then calculates the testing and support overhead using standard formulae.

Those experienced in team leading situations stress the importance of communication.

> "To be honest: communicate with your staff; understand what the goal of the project is, what the end product is and ensure that everyone in the team knows that and their role in it."

They cite regular project meetings as being essential to building team morale and ensuring that everyone knows what is going on.

> "At least if you have regular meetings – it doesn't have to be every week you know – it can be once a fortnight or depending, but at least it gives everybody an idea of what's going on."

Another factor to consider in the role is the provision of feedback to the staff members. This is considered to be very important.

> "My own personal experience of that is if you give people a chance they'll come good. In a lot of these companies there's an ability to give negative feedback when there is really no need to give negative feedback. People look for feedback on a constant basis … My own philosophy would be to give positive feedback."

4.4 Summary

By the end of the pilot study, the interview checklist had been revised several times – c.f. Appendix A. The changes were informed by the literature and by the dynamics of the interviews themselves. The overall structure of the interview proved to be satisfactory and allowed the conversation to flow naturally.

Because of the small sample size and the wide spectrum of roles, no definite conclusions can be made from this investigation. However there are some interesting commonalities that are explored further in the main study.

All the interviewees agree that the best way to learn a skill is to combine practical experience with classroom training. This is highlighted in several ways. The person who had undergone an apprenticeship was full of praise for the block release structure; those who had pursued their studies via the Open University attributed much of the benefits of their courses to the fact that they had experience of the subject beforehand and were able to apply it immediately. Similarly, the overall feeling about professional training is that the courses must be scheduled to coincide with the application of the knowledge and that the student needs to have some experience beforehand.

A factor that has benefited careers is mentoring. It seems to have been where soft skills were initially developed. All those who completed graduate recruitment programmes approve of them. Even without a formal programme, mentoring in any guise is rated beneficial by those who experienced it.

For the experienced practitioner, it is noticeable that technical skills need to be supplemented with soft skills. As Mill (2002) points out: "the trend toward a more collaborative workplace has made it vital for all employees, including IT professionals, to have excellent soft skills with the most important ones being proficiency in verbal and written communication" (p.25). The experiences of the seven interviewees bear out the need for soft skills, highlighted by the amount of interaction their roles involve. However, what is equally obvious is that the formal training they have received has been lacking in interpersonal skill development.

Finally, Parnas' (1999) concerns about the title 'software engineer' seem to have been justified by this study. The two 'engineers' interviewed would, for their present roles, be more aptly described as technicians. Also, if Parnas warns us that a software engineer is not merely a good programmer, then it could be suggested that an architect is not an experienced good programmer. The two systems architects interviewed here would be better described as systems analysts (Downey 2006b).

The pilot study has been useful in showing the need to reduce the scope of the project to a single industry. By concentrating on people in one industry (problem domain) several variables, such as customer profile and quality expectations (Schein 1999) can be eliminated. By interviewing teams within a single company – i.e. by conducting a case study - a complete picture of the development process can be built up, allowing one company's process to be compared with another's. As will be shown in the next chapter, this is the strategy adopted. The pilot study also suggested what that application domain should be, as it is a telecommunications software company that employed the most mature development process.

CHAPTER FIVE

THE MAIN STUDY

5.1 Introduction

The main body of this study concentrates on software development in the telecommunications sector. A total of thirty-one people were interviewed across four different companies. The companies comprise the subsidiaries of two large (Fortune 500) North American-based corporations and a smaller European-based one. As a contrast, a very small (thirty employees) Irish indigenous company is included.

From six to nine people were interviewed in each site. Note that two people from one company were also included in the pilot study. The characteristics of the interviewees are summarised in the following tables.

Table 6 shows how the interviewees' actual job titles mapped onto the seven roles targeted for this study. These roles were chosen to cover the entire development cycle from requirements to installation. While it is obvious from this table that job titles are not standard across the industry, the amount of commonality is reasonably good. One of the interviewees is not listed in these tables. His role, a process architect in the project management domain, does not fit well into any category. However, his insights into project management have been included in the analysis.

All except two interviewees hold a primary-degree, while eight have Master's degrees. In total, twenty-one have engineering qualifications. This is shown in Table 7.

Table 8 gives as much of the person's career as was discovered during the interview. While their early experiences of mentoring and their efforts to keep up with their education were canvassed, no effort was made to capture their career paths in a comprehensive way.

Table 6. Actual Job Titles

Role	**Job Title**
Product Manager	
1	Product Manager
2	Product Engineering Manager
3	Product Manager
4	Technical Sales Manager
Project Manager	
1	Group Manager
2	Project Manager
3	Development Section Manager
4	Development Manager
Systems Architect	
1	Systems Architect
2	Systems Architect
3	Member of Technical Staff
4	Member of Technical Staff
5	Chief Technical Officer
Programmer	
1	Senior Software Engineer
2	Network Software Engineer
3	Senior Software Engineer
4	Software Developer
Tester	
1	Software Test Engineer
2	Test Group Manager
3	System Test Engineer
4	Lead Test Engineer
5	Test Engineer
6	Software Test Engineer
Technical Writer	
1	Technical Writer
2	Senior Technical Author
3	Technical Writer
Customer Support	
1	Product Support Manager
2	Technical Marketing Engineer
3	Customer Support Resource Manager
4	Customer Support Engineer

Table 7. Academic Qualifications

Role	**Qualifications**
Product Manager	
1	B.Eng. Computer Engineering
2	B.Sc. Electrical Engineering
3	B.E. Electrical Engineering
4	M.Sc. Physics
Project Manager	
1	B.Eng. Electronic Engineering
2	B.Eng. & M.Phil. Electronic Engineering
3	B.Tech. Electronic Engineering
4	M.Sc. Computer Science
Systems Architect	
1	B.Eng. Computer Engineering (unfinished M.Sc.)
2	B.E. & M.Eng.Sc. Electronic Engineering
3	B.Eng. Electronic Engineering, M.Sc. Computer Science
4	B.E. Electrical Engineering
5	M.Eng. Electronic Engineering
Programmer	
1	B.Eng. Electronic Engineering
2	B.Eng. Electronic Engineering
3	B.Eng. Electrical & Electronic Engineering
4	B.Ind.Eng. Industrial Eng, Grad Dip. & M.Sc. Comp. Sci
Tester	
1	Cert. in mechanical engineering. B.Sc. S/W eng (at night)
2	B.Tech. Electronic Production, Dip. Comp. Eng.
3	B.Sc. Maths, Physics.
4	B.Comm.
5	B.Eng. Electronic Engineering
6	B.Eng. Electronic Engineering
Technical Writer	
1	Diploma in Mainframe Computing
2	B.A. European Studies, Printing Diploma
3	B.A. Communications
Customer Support	
1	B.Eng. Electronic Engineering, M.Eng. Telecoms
2	B.Sc. Physics
3	B.Sc. Computer Science
4	Certificate in Electronic Engineering

Table 8. Partial Career Paths

Role	**Career Path**
Product Manager	
1	Programmer ▶ trainer ▶ product manager
2	Programmer ▶ product engineering manager
3	Programmer ▶ test ▶ customer support ▶ product mgr.
4	H/W design ▶ programmer ▶ technical sales manager
Project Manager	
1	Programmer ▶ group leader ▶ R&D mgr ▶ group mgr
2	H/W engineer ▶ programmer ▶ project manager
3	H/W test ▶ group leader ▶ R&D manager ▶ section manager
4	Programmer ▶ group leader ▶ development manager
Systems Architect	
1	Programmer ▶ group leader ▶ systems architect
2	Programmer ▶ project mgr ▶ systems architect
3	Programmer ▶ group leader ▶ member of technical staff
4	Programmer ▶ member of technical staff
5	Programmer ▶ customer support ▶ chief technical officer
Programmer	
1	Programmer ▶ group leader ▶ senior S/W engineer
2	Network S/W engineer (informal team lead)
3	Senior S/W engineer (informal team lead)
4	S/W developer (informal team lead)
Tester	
1	H/W test ▶ S/W test engineer
2	H/W test ▶ programmer ▶ S/W test ▶ test group manager
3	S/W test ▶ system test engineer (group leader)
4	Customer support ▶ lead test engineer
5	Programmer ▶ test engineer
6	H/W technician ▶ programmer ▶ S/W test engineer
Technical Writer	
1	Programmer ▶ technical writer (group leader)
2	Marketing ▶ senior technical author (informal team lead)
3	Technical writer
Customer Support	
1	Customer support ▶ product support manager
2	Programmer ▶ customer support ▶ technical marketing
3	Programmer ▶ customer support ▶ support resource mgr
4	H/W test ▶ network operator ▶ customer support engineer

5.2 Analysing the Interviews

Each interview was recorded onto a digital medium. During the interview, extensive notes were taken. As soon as possible after the interview, the longhand notes were written up into an interview summary document. To ensure accuracy and completeness, the interview recording was listened to and the summary document was corrected and augmented as appropriate.

At this point, the summary report was e-mailed to the interviewee who had editorial control over the document. Miles and Huberman (1994) call this step 'member checking' and point out that there may be drawbacks to the technique: "Such agreements can improve both the quality of data and the quality of final conclusions, but they also can result in truncated or distorted conclusions if someone has been given, and exercises, the right of censorship" (p.48).

The reasons for including member checking in this study are:

1. The interviewees are assured that neither their names nor the names of their companies are mentioned in the summary.
2. They have the opportunity to correct factual errors that were made when explaining something without access to reference material.
3. They can retract sensitive statements, such as opinions on company policy. It is this freedom that can remove some of the insights from the reports. Some of those interviewed in this study did retract statements relating to their organisation's culture.

Each summary report, once approved by its subject, was imported into the QSR Nvivo® software package. There, each sentence and paragraph was considered in order to identify 'chunks' of text that articulate particular concepts. If a new concept was identified, a new short, descriptive code was created and the 'chunk' of text filed under that code. If the concept had already been encountered, the text was stored with the other chunks under that concept's code. This is a process known as 'open coding', as its goal is to open up the data for analysis (Strauss and Corbin 1998).

Once all identified participants from a single company were interviewed, a report of that company was prepared. This is recommended by Eisenhardt (1989) who states that these "write-ups are often simply pure descriptions, but they are central to the generation of insight" (p.540). These reports were based on the codes identified and the interview findings were used to underpin the concepts presented. In order to prepare the reports, each relevant interview recording was revisited to get more detail about the chosen concepts and to elicit exemplary quotations. Because Irish telecommunications is a small community, these reports have not been published. It would be too easy to identify the organisation and, from that, it is a simple step to identify the individual contributors.

As the interviews proceed, the need to create new codes will diminish. The goal is to reach the stage when each new interview can be completely filed using existing codes. This state is called theoretical saturation (Strauss and Corbin 1998). Throughout the process of identifying open codes, higher order concepts, or axes, were being considered. The search for such logical groupings of the open codes is called 'axial coding'. Early attempts at axial coding can inform the interview instrument as potential insights can be probed in more depth in later interviews. This can be seen in appendix A where some interviewees had problems understanding what was meant by a particular skill; others described a methodology they used, while certain interviewees talked about training they had received. All three concepts were explored in later interviews.

Considering the data across roles and across companies should lead to common observations or characteristics of the industry. These observations were presented to industry experts for comment. Using different evaluators to interpret the findings is called 'investigator triangulation' (Patton 1987). This step adds confidence to the analysis process.

The techniques described above are informed by grounded theory. However, true grounded theory suggests that the researcher's prior experience and the existing literature should have no bearing on the research. As shown in chapter 1, the interview instrument draws heavily from the literature. But, once the data are gathered, analysis will proceed without the goal of supporting or disproving any pre-conceived hypotheses. Goldkuhl and Cronholm (2003) support this approach, noting that "a new theory should not only be grounded in empirical data… it also should be grounded in already existing theories" (p.12).

5.3 Preliminary Findings

Preliminary analysis of the interview data produced a series of observations that help to characterise the interviewees.

To obtain an extra measure of confidence, two industry experts – a consultant, with many years manufacturing and telecommunications software experience and a senior telecommunications software manager - were presented with the twenty-one observations listed below. Reassuringly, they declared that there was nothing in the list that they would disagree with. These experts spoke about the industry as a whole and their insights have been appended to the relevant observations. Although efforts were made to structure the interviews according to the list, some points were not discussed. These have been placed at the end of the list.

1. Prevalence of engineering backgrounds.
    a. Roughly two-thirds of the interviewees have engineering qualifications.
    b. Many cite their engineering background as the basis for their problem-solving skills.
    c. Engineers work in all roles, except technical writing.
    d. Engineers have an understanding of the telecommunications domain.

    The consultant expresses the view that engineers do not have formal problem solving skills, but do have good problem analysis skills. Rather than come up with innovative solutions to problems, engineers are good at applying or extrapolating existing knowledge. He also asserts that engineers think they are good at problem solving because they are engineers. Finally, he argues that engineers need training in formal problem solving techniques and tools.

2. Issues with management roles.
    a. Little formal management training.
    b. Many team leaders would not take the role if they had a choice.
    c. There is little sense of team identity among team leaders.
    d. The fostering of good group morale seems to be up to the individual leader's personal beliefs.

The team lead role is compared to the 'foreman' role in the construction sector and 'line leader' in manufacturing. It is cited by the consultant as the most difficult role in any industry. Many team leaders are in the situation where they have to assign work to staff, but do not carry out their appraisals - they have accountability without authority. This makes the team lead role a frustrating one (Womack, Jones and Roos 1990).

The problem of team leaders trying to carry out their roles without adequate training and without mentoring support has been addressed in the manufacturing world. There, team leaders meet regularly as a group with a senior management facilitator to discuss their issues and share experiences.

Team leaders need to understand what their spheres of influence are. The goal is to expand your sphere of influence if you wish to get on.

The senior manager concurs that engineers may not be well suited to managerial roles. He makes the point that engineers tend not to trust anyone else's work but their own, while a manager must trust subordinates to get tasks done. Another difficulty for newly promoted managers is coping with ambiguity – management decisions often need to be made without having the complete picture. The politics involved in management roles is also unattractive to engineers.

Companies can put the newly promoted manager under pressure by associating the role with status symbols such as company cars. In these circumstances, an engineer who finds the management role unpleasant or who cannot get to grips with it, will loose face if s/he steps down from the position. The senior manager has a policy of giving senior engineers exposure to management duties without the associated status in order to assess their aptitude before committing them to this sort of role.

3. Lack of business knowledge.
    a. Very few manage budgets.
    b. Contributions to costing are mainly confined to time and headcount estimates.
    c. There is a general lack of awareness of overhead costs – utility bills, engineer hours, etc.
    d. This trait is seen in both the indigenous and multi-national companies.

The consultant describes this as a shortcoming in terms of communication skills rather than a deliberate effort on the part of companies to suppress business awareness. No one is trained both in finance and in software, leading to a situation where the finance and software development departments do not communicate. This situation means that software people are not aware of costs or cost-benefits and finance people are not aware of the software development environment and its associated financial needs.

The senior manager approached this observation by asking: how many managers can read and understand a balance sheet? In the boom times market share, rather than cost overheads, was the main concern of managers. When the market collapsed, managers were required to know their breakeven costs. This manager feels that senior managers today have had to acquire these business skills.

4. Very similar background, for all except technical writers.
    a. Good at maths and science at school.
    b. Most entered third-level education straight after school.

The senior manager agrees that most software developers are very alike. He attributes this to the fact that people with engineering degrees and experience in the telecoms domain are readily available when the economy is doing badly. However, when things are good and there is competition for available workers, companies are forced to consider people without the necessary engineering background. The senior manager regards this as a good thing because different backgrounds bring different perspectives and fresh thinking. He also notes that meticulous developers always tend to park in the same spots, while effective trouble shooters not only park in different places, they work irregular hours and cannot be made to follow a process.

5. Interviewing skills.
    a. There is not a lot of training in evidence.
    b. A wide range of goals were expressed when asked: 'what do you look for in a candidate?'
    c. Some endorse 'gut instinct' as a basis for selection.

The lack of interviewing skills has been seen by the consultant across all industries. The decision whether to hire someone or not is made on gut instinct within twenty-five seconds – "I want you in my tribe". However, formal training would be useful, to ensure correct fit of potential candidates within the organisation. As Shapero (1985) states: "the most important management decision in the conduct of professional activities is hiring" (p.1).

The senior manager agrees that most companies have a very informal interviewing process. He makes the point that interviewing is a de-selection process initially – unsuitable candidates need to be ruled out at the earliest possible stage. This reflects a testing philosophy – prove that the product does not work.

The idea that recruitment initially involves a de-selection, or filtration, process is seen in Litecky et al (2004). They assert that candidates are short-listed for interview because of their espoused technical skills. However, final selection is based on their interpersonal skills that are assessed in a face-to-face interview.

6. Technical writing.
    a. This is different from creative writing and, as such, can be taught.
    b. There is a general distaste for this activity.
    c. Not a lot of training has been received. A specialised course on writing requirements was mentioned however.
    d. The use of templates appears helpful.

According to the consultant, the general lack of training or regard for technical writing vis-à-vis presentation skills is explained by the fact that no one reads the manuals and little regard is paid to project documentation. Managers prefer oral presentations rather than comprehensive documentation. In addition, the end user is often one single individual installing new software across an organisation, and needs on-line technical support during the commissioning phase, not abundant manuals.

When asked to explain why engineers dislike documentation, the senior manager made the distinction between technical and customer documentation. Customer documentation is seen as a chore that can easily be done by another function. Technical documentation is viewed as part of the development process and is a necessary evil.

The use of document templates is not only a good idea but a sign of a good engineering process.

7. Few have significant outside interests.
    a. Most try to avoid committees.
    b. Little commitment to serious sport or hobbies.
    c. Those in the GAA cite it as a great source of skills.

When asked why most of the interviewees seem to have few serious outside interests, the senior manager cited his own background as a new graduate in a new town. There, socialisation centred on the sports and social activities organised by the company. He also points out that technical workers tend to be wrapped up in their work.

This seems to be a general trend in professions. As Ramachandran and Rao (2006) note: "Employees who practice the same profession tend to band together into occupational communities, draw their identities from the work they do and proceed to share a set of values, norms and attitudes, which collectively form a part of the culture of that occupation." (p.198)

8. Presentation skills.
    a. Quite a good amount of training has been received.
    b. Some evidence of shyness from those in technical roles.
    c. Regular emphasis placed on knowing what you are talking about.

d. One application of this skill is the presentation of training materials.

When asked about why presentation skills seem to have been taught more than technical writing skills, the senior manager explained that managers have not the time to read long reports. The process of deciding whether to go ahead with a new product development was given as an example. The senior manager has to know what information is needed before making that decision. One of the questions asked in the example scenario was: who are the competitors in this market? If there are no competitors, this is a bad sign – it is likely that this market is not worth pursuing.

9. Night classes.
    a. Some have completed degrees at night, but that was done in their twenties, before they had family commitments.
    b. There is a general consensus that work and home should be separate.

In order to facilitate continuous learning and still retain a separation between work and home life, the consultant recommends changing the way we learn. He makes the point that it should be possible for anyone to find half an hour at work every day to devote to computer-based training courses. Thus learning can fit into the student's schedule rather than vice versa. Using the latest adaptive e-learning tools, these training courses would be adjusted to the companies' specific requirements.

While Ireland has sold itself as having a highly educated workforce, the senior manager is critical of the retraining opportunities available. He offers himself as an example. He has completed the course work and examinations but has been unable to get the time to do the thesis part of a Master's degree. This has been the case for most of that class. Indeed one of the interviewed systems architects also failed to finish the thesis.

Few worker-friendly retraining options are available. The senior manager recommends week-long blocks as modules that workers can take once or twice a year. In the final analysis, anyone who is promoted needs to be trained in the new skills required. He also notes that job hopping is not a major problem in Ireland. He also argues that there are schemes where the employee agrees to pay for the training if s/he leaves the company in the near future.

10. All of the interviewees have experience of the multi-national sector.

When multinational companies arrived in Ireland in the 1970's, they set up manufacturing facilities. These companies subsequently created R&D divisions in those facilities. Some of the manufacturing managers, such as the consultant, transferred to the R&D departments and brought with them techniques learned from manufacturing. Since then, R&D has become divorced from manufacturing – multinationals are setting up R&D facilities in Ireland but locating their manufacturing in lower-cost countries. Thus the management processes and the lessons learned from sophisticated use of cell-based production (cell = temporary, multi-functional team) developed in 'world-class' manufacturing facilities have never been transferred to R&D. Hence there exists in the software industry an ever increasing lag before implementing the latest 'world-class' processes.

This point is echoed by McIver Consulting (2004) when they note that "throughout the '90s, the skill capacity of managers at all levels has lagged behind best international practice" (p.10).

11. Importance of experience.
    a. Compensates for lack of formal training.
    b. Particularly obvious in new group leaders.
    c. Also seen in a systems architect who moved into a more sales-oriented role – he learned his sales technique on the job.
    d. General agreement that trial and error was the way most of their skills were honed.

This is endorsed in the literature with Shapero (1985) observing that: "the competent older worker is more useful than the competent younger worker and certainly a better bet than the unproven younger person" (p.18).

According to the consultant, it is the goal of multinational companies to remove expertise from processes – to reduce everything to small chunks – so that the process can be easily ported to cheaper countries.

Multinational companies seem to place no value on experience, preferring to hire new graduates rather than attract veteran developers. The senior manager makes the point that a person needs to get into a role that adds more value if s/he is to continue getting pay increases.

New senior technical roles, such as system architects, may not be required if the company is not growing. In these circumstances, there is little need for new architectures. There is also a need for the management team to control their cost base.

In the current job market, many senior technical people are on too high a salary. This is due to the dot com boom, where salaries were increased to unsustainable levels. The senior manager recommends the concept of variable pay, where the basic rate is quite low but supplemented with bonus schemes. He notes that American companies are good at this.

12. Influence of corporate culture.
    a. This is seen in the amount of process used and training received.
    b. It also dictates how other sites are regarded, in particular head-office.
    c. It may be a factor in limiting the scope for technical advancement – e.g., in the case of systems architects, either the absence of the full spectrum of R&D on-site, or lack of resources, reduces the amount of architectural research carried out.

The senior manager is critical of the cultural values that large corporations espouse. He feels that these values are used to attract new staff in the good times. However, values like caring for the workforce are soon forgotten when head office orders layoffs and closures. He notes that Irish people tend to be cynical about such corporate image making.

13. Very little supplier interaction.
    a. Some of the interviewees have to get quotations for lab equipment, but the actual buying of the items is handled by a purchasing department.
    b. Only one interviewee has had to review requirements and test plans for third-party software projects.
    c. A possible explanation for this is the use of Open Source software rather than bespoke third-party systems.

The senior manager discussed the issue of suppliers in terms of outsourcing developments to low wage economies. He expresses the view that whether off-shoring development is regarded as a threat or an opportunity is a matter of perspective. The ability to commission an Indian company to develop parts of a product cheaply, allied to the diminishing cost of hardware, means that small Irish companies can bring products to market quickly and cheaply.

However, the manager warns that the definition of these components, the domain knowledge, is at the core of the Irish company's added value. He also warns that any part of the customer relationship must be maintained by the parent company.

If part of the project is off-shored, then a great deal of flexibility is lost. To manage the off-shore facility a strong process is required. Relating to the amount of informal communication channels seen in this research project, the manager recommends that complete components be developed in the off-shore site. Functional divisions, such as locating a test facility off-shore are not advised.

The trend to using Open Source software is also acknowledged. However, the senior manager draws attention to licensing agreements. The inclusion of some Open Source components means that the finished product must also be freely available.

14. Few work in well defined, permanent teams.
    a. Ancillary functions, such as technical writing, testing and customer support seem to have good team identity, despite individuals being assigned to different projects.
    b. Systems architects, project managers and programmers seem to float between projects as they are needed.
    c. When 'matrix' structures are used, they seem only to apply to the programmers.

The consultant recommends that a course explaining how people work in teams should be tailored for each company. In this way, the team learns the particular rules of engagement for that company. By trying to understand the training as a team, the group learns how to work together. The consultant believes that this approach is better than instructor-led training.

The matrix management organisation has been perfected in manufacturing. The important aspect of the structure that R&D seems to lack is strong vertical leads. In manufacturing, small groups of specialists report to their permanent managers and are assigned individually to various projects. The result is that people become expert in one functional area, across an entire product line. The practice, as seen in some companies in this study, where programmers are pooled together as 'coding engines' is not recommended.

15. Tremendous informal cooperation between groups.
    a. Could be a uniquely Irish phenomenon – c.f. Trauth (2000).
    b. Technical writers need early access to code; they provide useful feedback in return.
    c. Programmers and testers cooperate to set up lab test systems.
    d. Customer support gets to see installations in the test lab. In return they gather live call traces on sites for use in generating realistic test traffic.
    e. Possible bugs are informally assessed between programmers and testers before bug reports are raised.
    f. Customer support can feed back informal conversations with customers to product managers.

g. Product managers get insights into how to answer requests for quotation (RFQs) from individual programmers.

Figure 14. Informal Communications Paths

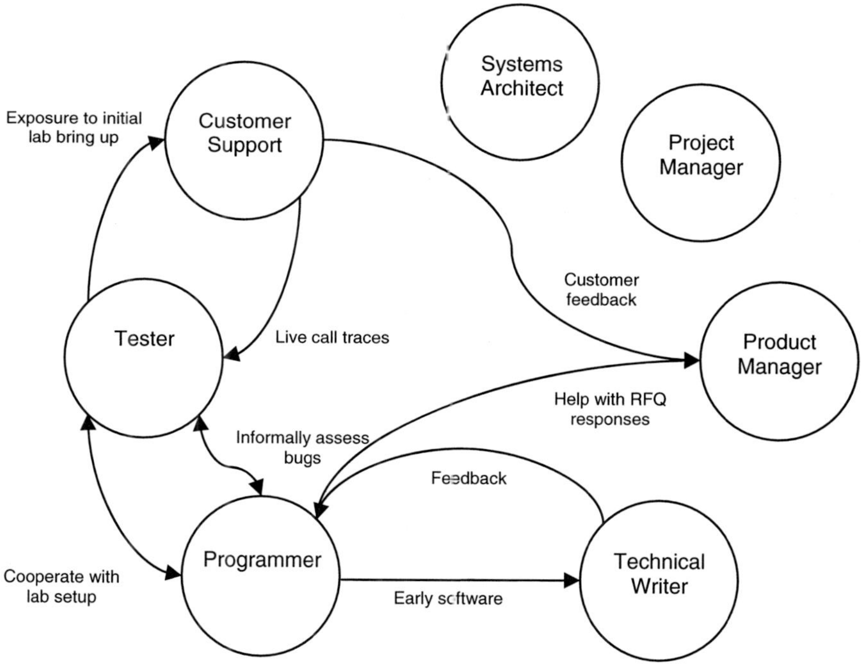

Figure 14 suggests that only the systems architects and the project managers communicate using well-defined, formal channels. Although formal communications paths also exist between the other parties, they are supplemented by unofficial transactions. The literature endorses the value of informal communication with Shapero (1985) declaring that "the most important source of work-related information for the professional (and probably for everyone else) is other people, and the most important channels are informal ones" (p.127). Sterne (2004) also describes this networking as "another core characteristic of software development in Ireland" (p.18).

However, the amount of informal cooperation observed in this study is viewed with caution by the consultant. Although it can be healthy if managed properly, it is symptomatic of immature management skills. It is likely that the team is trying to get the job done, in spite of the organisation. Managers tend not to like informal communications, because they are not in the loop.

The senior manager agrees that a real strength with Irish people is our willingness to communicate. He gives an example of a field-reported problem that was logged in the company's bug tracking system and assigned to a developer to fix. The person making the assignment rang the developer concerned so that s/he would have advance notice.

16. Mentoring.
    a. Endorsed by most.
    b. Warning # 1: The mentor must be suitable.
    c. Warning # 2: Goals must be set for the mentoring process and time scheduled for mentoring activities.

The first warning is echoed by Drucker (1999) when he argues that some people "are exceptionally talented as coaches and mentors; others are simply incompetent as mentors." (p.67)

17. Responsibilities differ between companies. Thus we see different levels of interaction between systems architects and the customer. Similarly, we see 'informal' team leaders and programmers involved in estimation for feasibility studies.

18. There is some evidence of job title confusion.

19. Few keep up with the trade journals.
    a. Those in customer-facing roles are inclined to keep up with industry developments.
    b. There are regular complaints that there is not the time to do so.
    c. The web is cited as being the most effective way to gather information.
    d. Promotional articles in journals are criticised.
    e. Books are cited as good reference material.

20. It is difficult to define roles.
    a. Many of the interviewees are team leaders – they are involved in the planning process.
    b. There are some surprising findings in terms of principal responsibilities – e.g. testers can spend the bulk of their time configuring lab systems; technical writers spend most of their time gathering the data needed for their documents.

21. Senior team members have more people interaction.
    a. Most of the interviewees have some form of management experience, whether formal or informal.
    b. People who opt for the technical career ladder are not necessarily free from management responsibilities.
    c. They also can have significant customer interaction.
    d. Given the trend towards component-based software engineering, it was surprising that very little supplier interaction was discovered.

5.4 Coding the Data

A total of 115 open codes were used to classify all the interview data. Reassuringly, the final series of interview reports fitted within these codes, demonstrating saturation. As Eisenhardt (1989) recommends, "researchers should stop adding cases when theoretical saturation is reached" (p.545).

The next stage in analysis is called 'axial coding'. This involves grouping the open codes around more sophisticated concepts, called axes. The initial attempt at this activity led to a hierarchy of codes that reflected the original data collection strategy. In other words, a hierarchy was produced that followed the triadic breakdown of social cognitive theory – person, environment and behaviour (Bandura 1986). This breakdown is shown in the following figures.

Figure 15. Top-level Breakdown

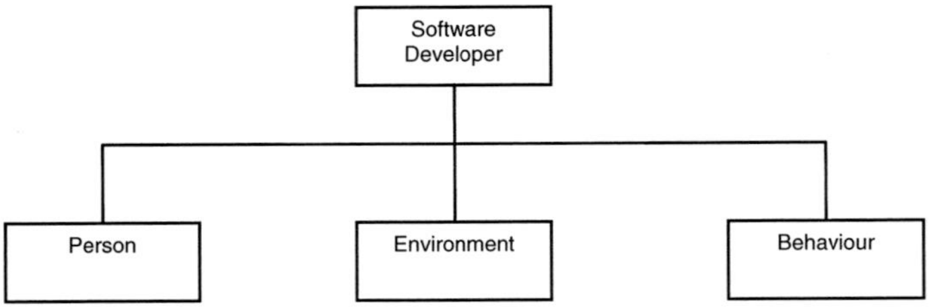

Figure 16. Breakdown of Personality

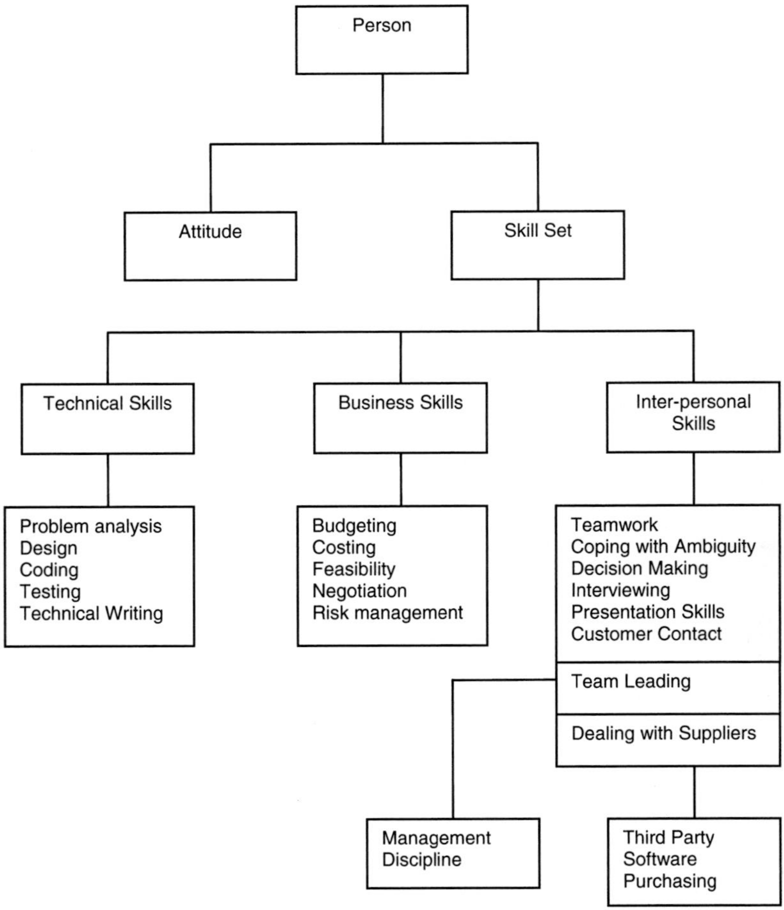

Figure 17. Breakdown of Behaviour

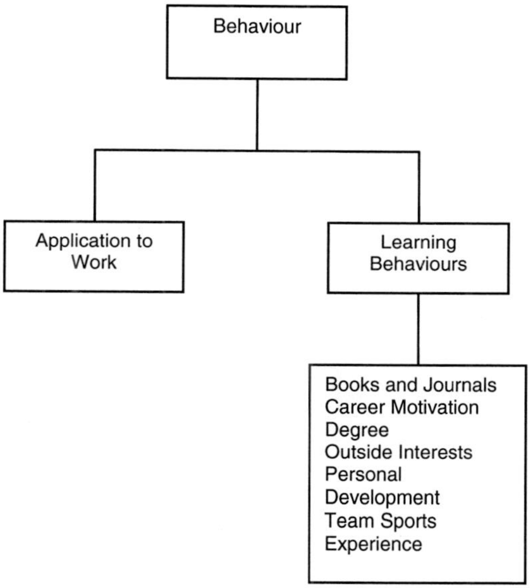

Figure 18. Breakdown of Environment

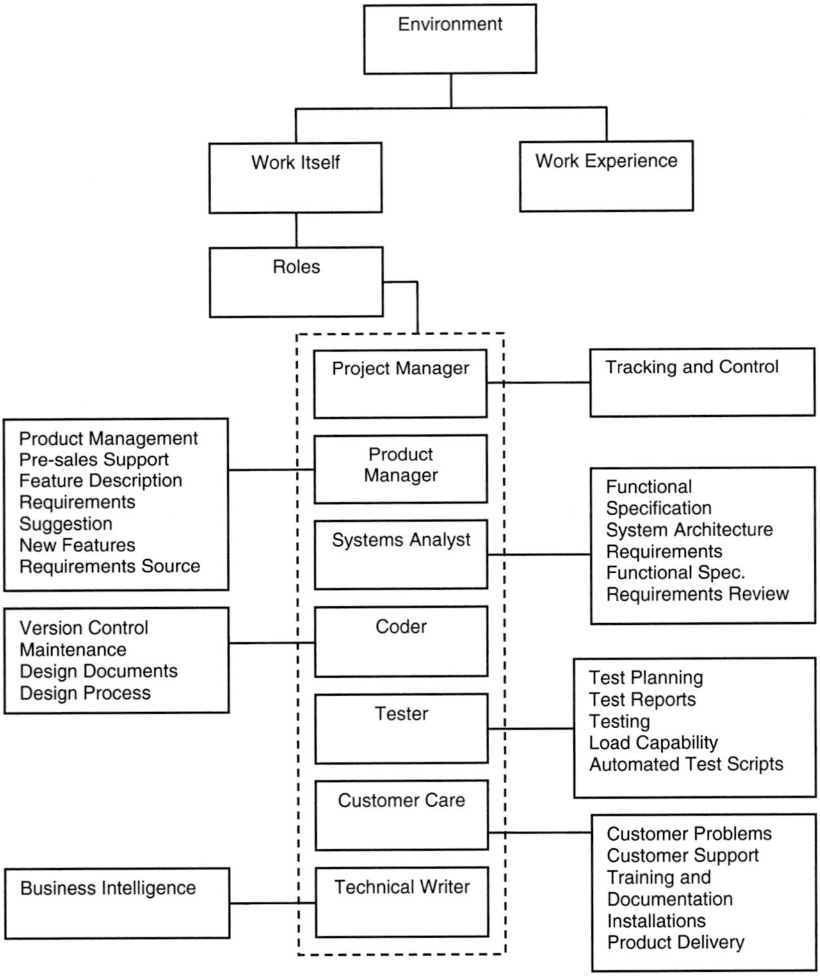

Thanks to the "What skills do you need?' question in the interview instrument (c.f. Appendix A), a list of skills is obtained. This list is informed by the literature and it is an interesting exercise to display this list across all the roles. Because Table 9 is based on the inputs of all the interviewees, each entry of the table needs to reflect whether all, some or none possessed this skill. Thus an entry can have five possible values as follows:

A : This is an important skill in all interviews.
B : This is an important skill for the majority, but not all, interviewees.
C : This is an important skill, but only for some interviewees.
D : The skill is a minor skill in some, but not all, interviews.
\- : The skill is not used in this role by any of the interviewees.

Table 9. Explicitly Canvassed Skills

	Product Manager	Systems Architect	Project Manager	Programmer	Tester	Technical Writer	Customer Support
Technical							
Problem Analysis	A	A	A	A	A	B	A
Design	C	A	C	A	B	B	C
Coding	-	A	C	A	B	-	D
Testing	C	C	C	A	A	B	B
Technical Writing	A	A	A	A	B	A	A
Business							
Feasibility	A	A	B	A	C	-	-
Costing	B	D	C	B	D	B	C
Planning / Risk Management	A	A	A	C	A	B	A
Negotiation	B	C	D	-	-	C	D
Budgeting	D	-	D	-	C	C	B
Interpersonal							
Coping with Ambiguity	A	A	A	A	A	B	A
Teamwork	C	C	C	B	B	B	A
Team Leading	C	D	A	C	C	B	A
Interviewing	C	A	A	B	B	A	A
Presentation Skills	A	A	A	B	B	B	B
Customer Interaction	A	A	D	C	D	D	A
Supplier Interaction	C	C	-	D	D	-	C

This table highlights skills common to all the roles. Specifically, problem analysis, technical writing, coping with ambiguity and presentation skills are needed in all disciplines. However, while planning and interviewing skills figure prominently in each column, is this because the role requires them, or is it because most (twenty-five) of the interviewees are, or have been, in managerial positions?

Indeed, this level of analysis highlights a very significant problem: What are the lines of demarcation for each role? Is it possible to define any of the roles, given the differences across companies? It appears that similar problems have been encountered by other researchers. As Shaw (2000) reminds us: "Despite intermittent attempts to identify specific roles, the distinctions remain unclear" (p.375). This difficulty has also been reported by Belbin (2000), who notes that the "old compartmentalized descriptions of jobs have begun to lose their relevance to the modern world. Jobs are increasingly becoming accretions: they are built up in serial layers of work activity in a continuous process where there are no hard and fast boundaries." (p.49)

To give some examples of this phenomenon, the interviews highlight the following issues:

1. The product manager and the systems architect provide the interface between the customer and the programming team. Between them, they define a precise set of requirements and assess both the technical and commercial feasibility of these requirements. However, if the product manager has an engineering background, s/he should be able to field technical questions from the customer and produce a set of testable and measurable requirements. In this case, the systems architect rarely, if ever, meets the customer face-to-face. On the other hand, if the product manager has a sales and marketing background, with limited technical knowledge, the systems architect will have to attend most of the customer meetings in order to answer the technical queries. S/he will also have to use prototypes or scenario modelling to elicit requirements from the customer. When attempting to define the skills needed for these roles, should we declare that both parties need the same skills sets?

2. Because this study concentrates on people in their thirties and forties, people at what Dalton, Thompson and Price (1977) call Stage III of their careers, many (twenty-five) have group leader experience. When they describe their roles, several of the skills identified relate to their leadership role – coordination, planning and motivation, for instance. Should these skills not be considered when defining the role or should they be included in order to characterise the added responsibility a senior person has?

3. Because the test group tries to simulate the target network for the new/enhanced product, the installation of new software in the test labs provides a useful guide to the customer support staff for their field installations. Sometimes, if customer support people are called away to address field problems, the test group can be called upon to install the product on-site. Does this mean that, to work in test, a person needs the skills of a customer support engineer?

4. Only one of the companies studied has a dedicated trainer on-site. It seems that customer training is assigned to people at random. In one company, for instance, the product manager has a background in training, so he is assigned the role. In others, customer support personnel and even the programmers who supply the underlying knowledge for the training materials are given the task. Given that almost anyone on the team can be placed in a training role, are presentation skills and some knowledge of andragogy (the study of adult learning (Knowles, Holton and Swanson 1998)) universal requirements?

5. The senior programmer is probably the most pervasive of the roles, with programmers being involved from the requirements elicitation stage all the way through to assisting the customer support personnel installing the product on site. They are expected to display customer-facing skills as well as being involved as informal team leaders. It would appear from the interview data that the role of the programmer encompasses all the other roles and suggests that a programmer really needs to be able to assist in any aspect of the development life-cycle.

6. The project manager/group leader role is also difficult to define. While most of those interviewed drew on their technical and

> domain knowledge to manage projects, it is argued in one company that generic project management skills are sufficient if the process is mature enough. However, Mintzberg (1998) warns us that managing "without an intimate understanding of what is being managed is an invitation to disharmony" (p.146). It is also important to remember that professionals work in a collegiate manner with their supervisors and each individual "has a need to receive some judgement or evaluation from respected others" (Shapero 1985, p.90). Also, as Winston (2004) maintains, "it is more beneficial to enhance the leadership potential of an engineer than to educate the nontechnical manager in technology" (p.412).

The situation, where every role seems to require all the skills, is reflected in the Standard Occupational Classification produced by the British Office for National Statistics (2000a; 2000b). In this taxonomy, project leaders, systems architects, programmers, testers and support engineers are all identified by the same code, 2132. Associated with this code are the following tasks (Office for National Statistics 2000a, pp.77-78):

- "examines existing software and determines requirements for new/modified systems through consultation with clients and staff;
- "undertakes feasibility studies of software solutions through specifying and costing functional details, equipment, staffing and operational procedures;
- "investigates, plans, designs and develops software solutions within stated constraints;
- "installs, implements and maintains the reliability and security of software systems as business functions;
- "writes operational documentation and provides subsequent support and training for users."

While it seems absurd on the surface that these diverse roles carry out the same tasks, the interview data shows precisely this situation.

5.5 Summary

This chapter introduces the participants to this study by listing their job titles, qualifications and part of their career paths. It then describes how the interview data is analysed before summarising the findings of the interviews and reporting on the thoughts of two industry experts who reviewed them.

The main point made in this part of the document is the discovery that individual roles are not clearly delimited, the boundaries of each role being distorted by three factors:

1. The person's history within the company. For instance, if a person is promoted from a technical role to a managerial one, s/he is also expected to provide consultancy relating to products s/he worked on in the past. Managers hired from outside the company would not be expected or able to make the same contribution.
2. The combination of technical and managerial roles. When promoted to group leader level, software practitioners are still expected to carry out technical work. It is difficult to distinguish between the skills needed for either role. This is particularly the case when the person's team leading duties are informal.
3. The skill sets of other team members. This is most obvious in the interaction between the product manager and the systems architect. The amount of customer-facing skills required by the architect is a function of the product manager's technical ability.

Because of the wide variety of responsibilities between people carrying out the same role and the extensive overlap between those with different roles, it is felt that attempting to associate skills with roles is a quixotic exercise.

However, the next chapter will present an alternative approach to the problem of relating knowledge and skills/abilities to roles, one that offers the potential for a far richer perspective than a simple role/skills mapping.

CHAPTER SIX

AN ARTEFACT-CENTRIC FRAMEWORK

6.1 Introduction

The main study, comprising four different companies, uncovered the fact that roles differ widely between companies (even between projects) and they also overlap significantly with other roles. This situation is shown in Table 9 (chapter 5), where the explicitly canvassed skills are displayed. How then can the research question be addressed if roles are not clearly defined?

Because the activities and the artefacts of the software development process are largely the same across all the companies, it was decided to revisit the interview data to see if an answer would emerge from the lifecycle information. Figure 19 shows the development cycle as elicited from the interview informants. This figure suggests that a project can be described either in terms of phases or artefacts.

Because the companies follow variations of the familiar 'V' model (Norris and Rigby 1992), it was clear that the study of project phases would simply explore well covered territory. However, changing the focus to the artefacts associated with the development process proved to be much more enlightening and leads to a conceptual framework where artefacts are central.

Figure 19. A Common Development Lifecycle Model

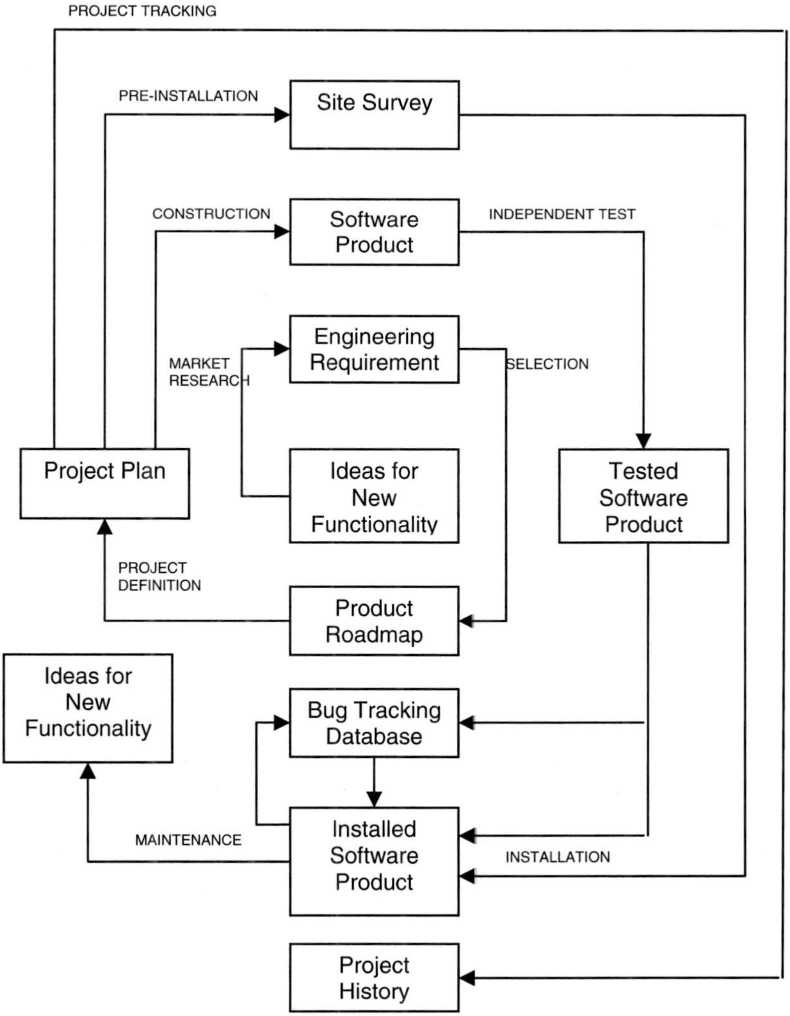

Artefacts have been studied in the software literature before. For instance, Cluts (2003) describes artefacts as the means of relating people and activity systems. Artefacts also hold the history of those relationships within them. Maurizio, Stamelos and Tsoukias (2002) are concerned with the attributes of software artefacts, arguing that these can be measured and these measurements used to support the decision-making process. A particular type of artefact, called a 'boundary object' is the focus for Mambrey and Robinson's (1997) study. Such objects "inhabit several intersecting social worlds *and* satisfy the informational requirements of each" (p.119).

For the purposes of this study, an artefact is considered to be a tangible entity, such as a document or a piece of code. Artefacts are used throughout a development project to embody stakeholder knowledge and contribute to the development process. No one member of the development team is involved in the creation of all the artefacts. Some are produced by other team members; some originate in other departments within the company and more are externally sourced – customer requests, for instance.

Early attempts at creating a conceptual framework for this project uncovered the difficulties in defining roles adequately. By replacing roles with artefacts, it becomes possible to develop a framework comprising two relationships: Firstly, although it is not possible to relate artefacts to individual roles, it is possible to identify the organisational function or functions that the artefact impacts on. As will be seen, most of the artefacts identified in this study are boundary objects, providing interfaces between the development team and other departments within the organisation, or between the organisation and external entities. Secondly, knowledge and skills/abilities (KSAs) are related to artefacts. The latter relationship has not been established by researchers in this area.

6.2 Artefact-based Analysis

Figure 20 shows each of the artefacts identified in the main study and how they relate to one another; appendix B describes the development lifecycle and the artefacts in more detail. While this diagram is a complex one, four distinct phases can be identified:

1. **Definition.** At the beginning of the project, much work is done to identify what exactly is being demanded by the marketplace. The culmination of this work is what is being termed here the engineering requirements document. This specifies the requirements in a testable and measurable format.

2. **Selection.** The products being developed by these companies can evolve in a variety of ways. Decisions must be made to choose the features that yield maximum revenue and provide the most customer satisfaction. As well as being commercially feasible, they must also be technically possible. All the factors influencing these decisions appear in feasibility reports. These reports contain input from sales and marketing people as well as technical contributions from the programming team. Once a feature is deemed feasible, it is placed on a product roadmap and scheduled to be developed as part of a release.
3. **Management.** Once a project release has been defined and the approval given to develop a set of features, the construction of the project is guided by the project plan. This consists of a schedule and a work breakdown structure. Some companies include mitigation and contingency plans to cope with identified risks. It should be noted that the definition and selection activities are carried out before the project officially exists.
4. **Construction.** The remainder of the project artefacts relate to the task of producing and installing the finished product. It must be emphasised that a commercial software product involves user manuals and training materials as well as working software.

Figure 20. All Identified Artefacts

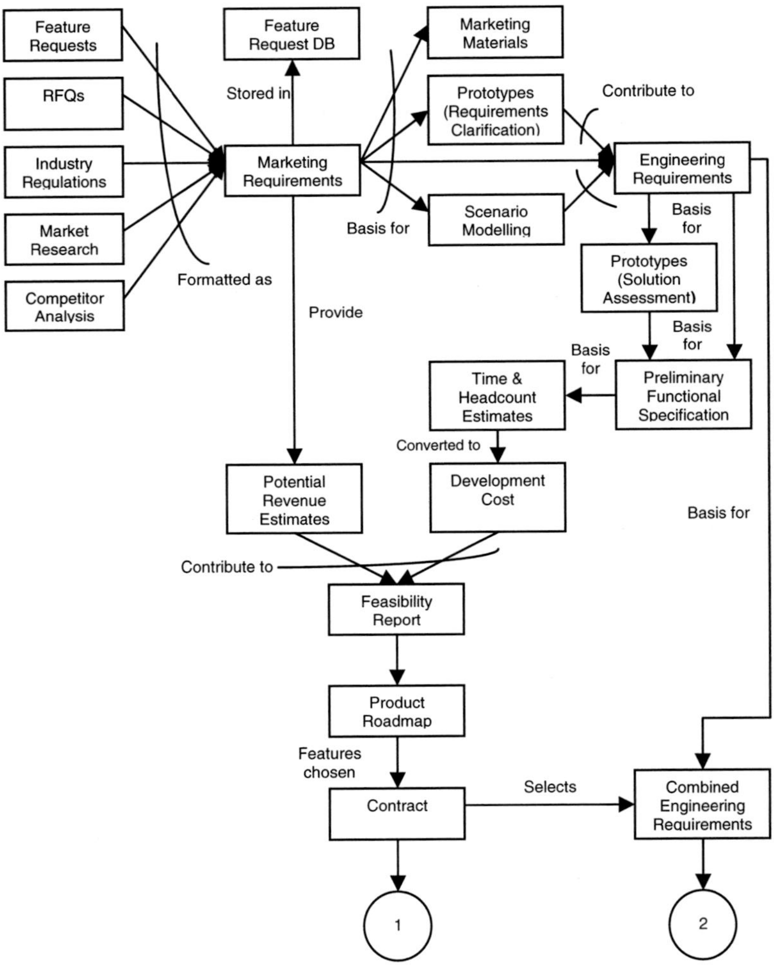

Figure 20 (cont.) All Identified Artefacts

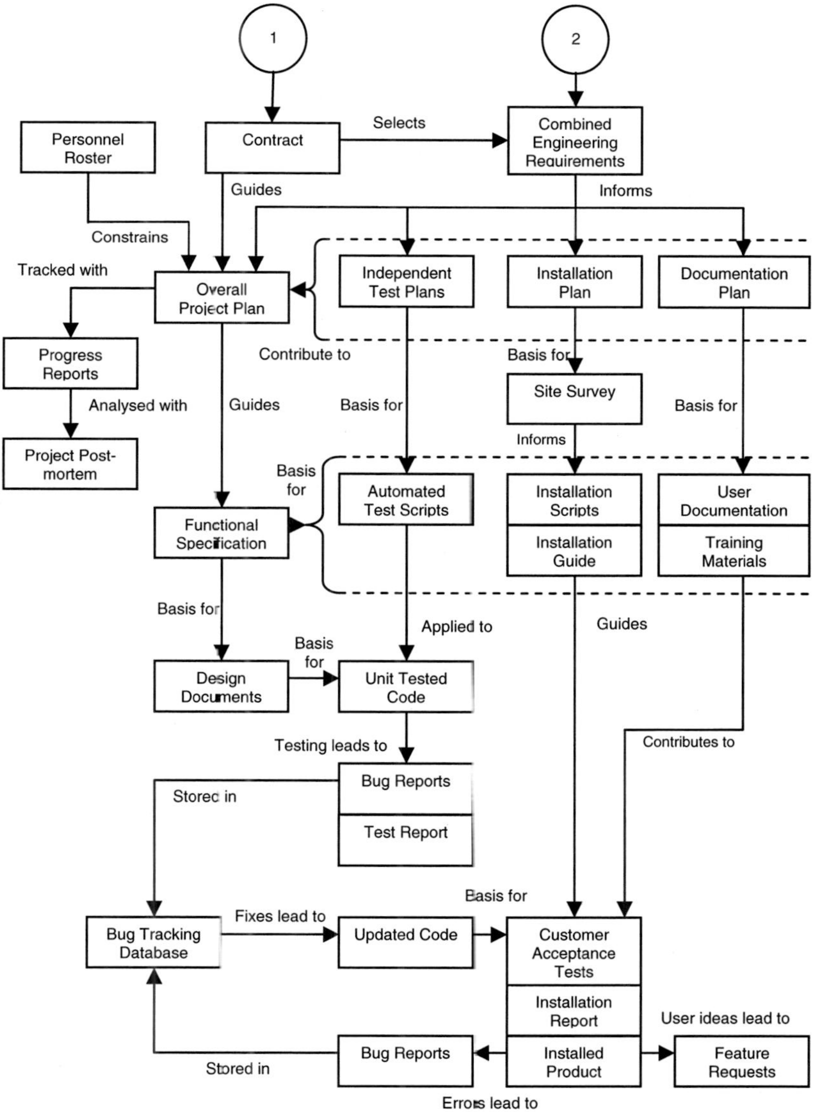

The four phases identified here prove useful when the open codes are revisited. Nearly half of the codes relate to artefacts and these can be located within the four phases. Using these artefact-related open codes to create new axial codes produces an entirely new structure for the environment branch of the hierarchy as shown in Figure 21 and Figure 22. This replaces the "Work Itself" breakdown shown in Figure 18.

Figure 21. Artefact-based Environment Breakdown

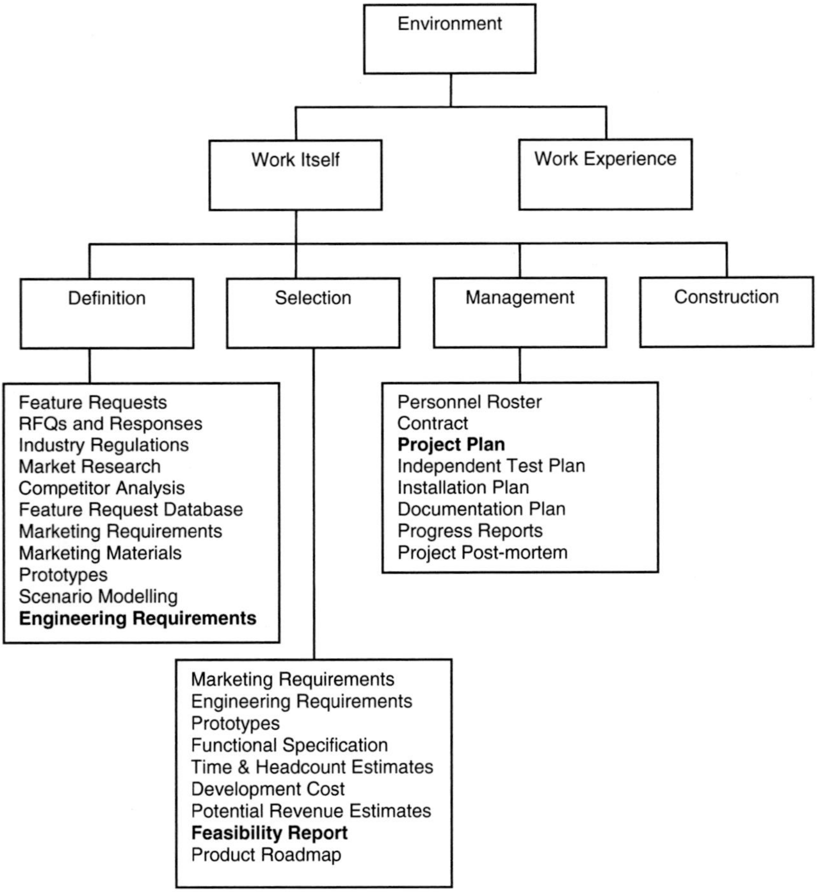

Figure 22. Artefact-based Breakdown of Construction Work

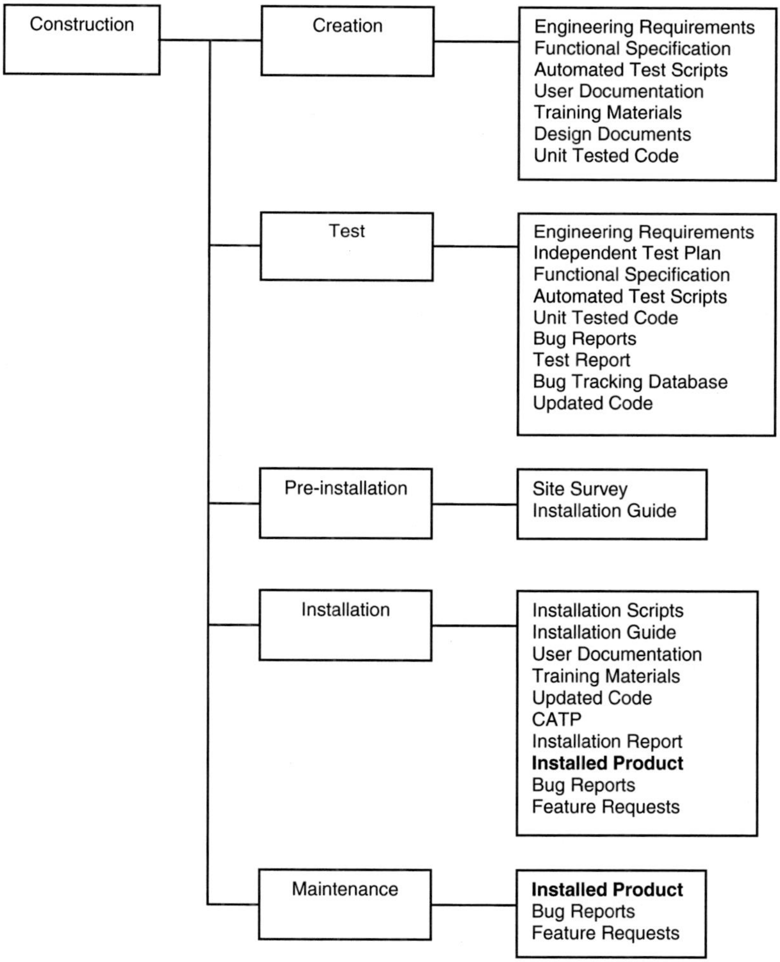

Having identified four phases to development, a more abstract picture of the artefacts and their interaction is possible. Figure 23 shows how the principal artefacts relate to one another. The engineering requirements document is the result of the definition phase; the feasibility report is the product of the feasibility study; the project plan is the principal management artefact and the installed product is the outcome of the construction phase.

Figure 23. The Principal Artefacts

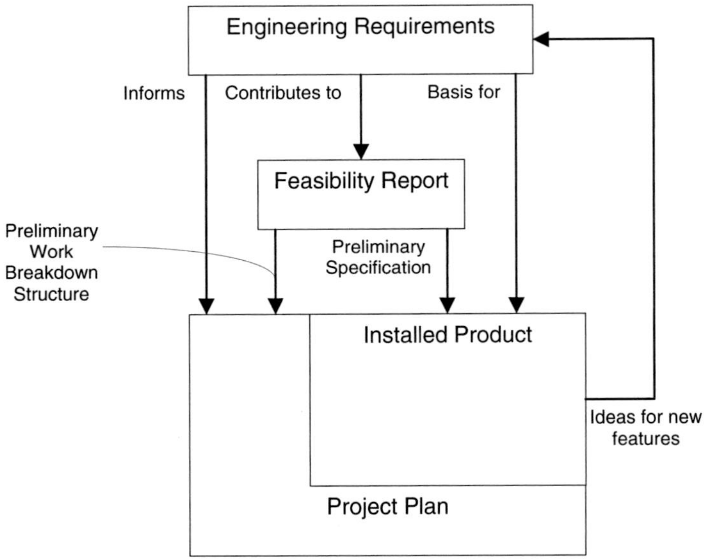

A noticeable feature of these key artefacts is the way so many different roles are associated with them. The project plan, for instance, is created by the project manager and receives input – such as time and headcount estimates - from architects, programmers, testers, technical writers and customer support personnel. It is also reviewed by the product manager. In effect, the artefact acts as a communications medium, allowing collaboration between parties, as well as supporting the decision-making process. In other words, the artefact functions as a boundary object, marking the interface between different organisational functions.

6.3 Relating Artefacts to Organisational Functions

The main study (chapter 5) has shown that it is the organisation and the individuals concerned who dictate which person works on what artefacts. Although it is not possible to formulate rules relating artefacts to individuals, a level of understanding is possible if attention is given to the organisational functions that are related via artefacts.

During the pilot study, it was noted that the development team has to interface with various functions in order to relate with the world outside the company. In Figure 8 (chapter 4) the developers have to deal with the sales and marketing function, the company's management, purchasing departments and the customer support function. However, Figure 8 suggests that the interface between developers and the other company functions is transactional and well defined.

We have seen from the main study that this is far from the case. It would be more useful to consider the corporate structure as a set of overlapping functions. It is clear from the interview data that the overlap between functions is accommodated by means of artefacts. Indeed, the interface between the company and its external customers is also facilitated through artefacts. This suggests that the bulk of the artefacts reside in overlapping areas, signifying that the software development process is truly a multi-functional team effort.

The term 'organisational function' has been chosen deliberately rather than department, as each company may have different organisational structures. Thus, for the purposes of this study, the organisational functions will be defined as:

1. **Management.** This includes project management and senior management. It also covers the finance and legal departments. Essentially, it is where the major decision-making activities take place.
2. **Front-end customer interface.** Here we find the product managers and the sales and marketing personnel. These people interact directly with the customer and with the marketplace.
3. **Back-end customer interface.** This is where the product is installed in the customer site. The installation and the subsequent maintenance of the product are under the control of the customer-support function.
4. **Development.** This area includes all personnel who contribute directly to the creation of the delivered product. That is: programmers, testers, technical writers and trainers.

Figure 24. Overlapping Organisational Functions

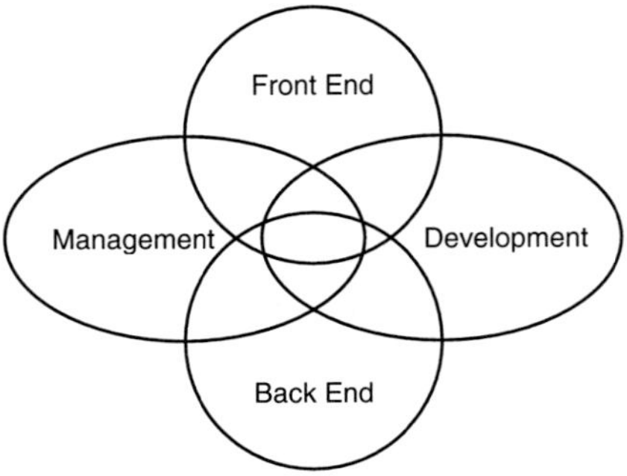

Locating artefacts within the organisation is achieved by studying the interview data and determining which actors are involved with each artefact. A person may be associated with a particular artefact if s/he designs and creates it, contributes data to it, reviews it or makes use of it to create another artefact or to make a decision.

To illustrate the process, the four principal artefacts identified in Figure 23 are analysed:

- **Engineering Requirements.** This is the responsibility of the systems architect, who is part of the development function. S/he is assisted by programmers, who are also in this function. The trigger for the engineering requirements is the marketing requirements document, which is produced by a product manager. This establishes an overlap between development and the front-end customer interface. Because the engineering requirements document informs the project plan, the management function is involved. Finally, because the requirements might contain aspects that affect the external interfaces of the product, the customer-support personnel need to review the document. This creates an overlap with the back-end customer interface. These relationships place the engineering requirements artefact firmly in the intersection of all the organisational functions.
- **Feasibility Report.** As this is the responsibility of product management, it involves the front-end customer interface function. As time and headcount estimates and technical feasibility input come from the architects and programmers, it

overlaps with the development function. Its purpose is to provide the basis for the go/no-go decision, made by the management function. There is no evidence in this study that the back-end customer interface is involved.

- **Project Plan.** This is the responsibility of the project manager in the management function. It depends for its time and headcount estimates and details of the work breakdown structure on both the development and back-end functions. It is also of concern to product managers, who need to be able to relay to potential customers what features are currently under development and when they are likely to become available. These overlaps place the project plan in the centre of all organisational functions.
- **Installed Product.** The installed product relates the back-end customer interface function with the customers themselves, providing a boundary with the outside world. It seems surprising that the development function is not involved with this artefact, as programmers and testers often accompany the installation team. However, the installed product is literally that which is installed in the customer site. It is the end product of the development lifecycle and is being used by the customer. If there are problems with the product, the bug report/code update mechanism is employed.

Table 10. Locating the Principal Artefacts

	Feasibility Report	Engineering Requirements	Project Plan	Installed Product
Front-End	x	x	x	
Management	x	x	x	
Development	x	x	x	
Back-end	x	x	x	x
Outside World				x

As can be seen from Table 10, the principal artefacts are all boundary objects. That is, they are positioned on the overlap between organisational functions or between the organisation and other organisations, such as customers. In contrast, a non-boundary object facilitates communication and collaboration between members of the same organisational function - an example being design documents that are of use within the development function only. At this point the remaining artefacts may be considered in terms of organisational functions. Figure 25 shows that most of these are also boundary objects.

Figure 25. Relating Artefacts to Organisational Functions

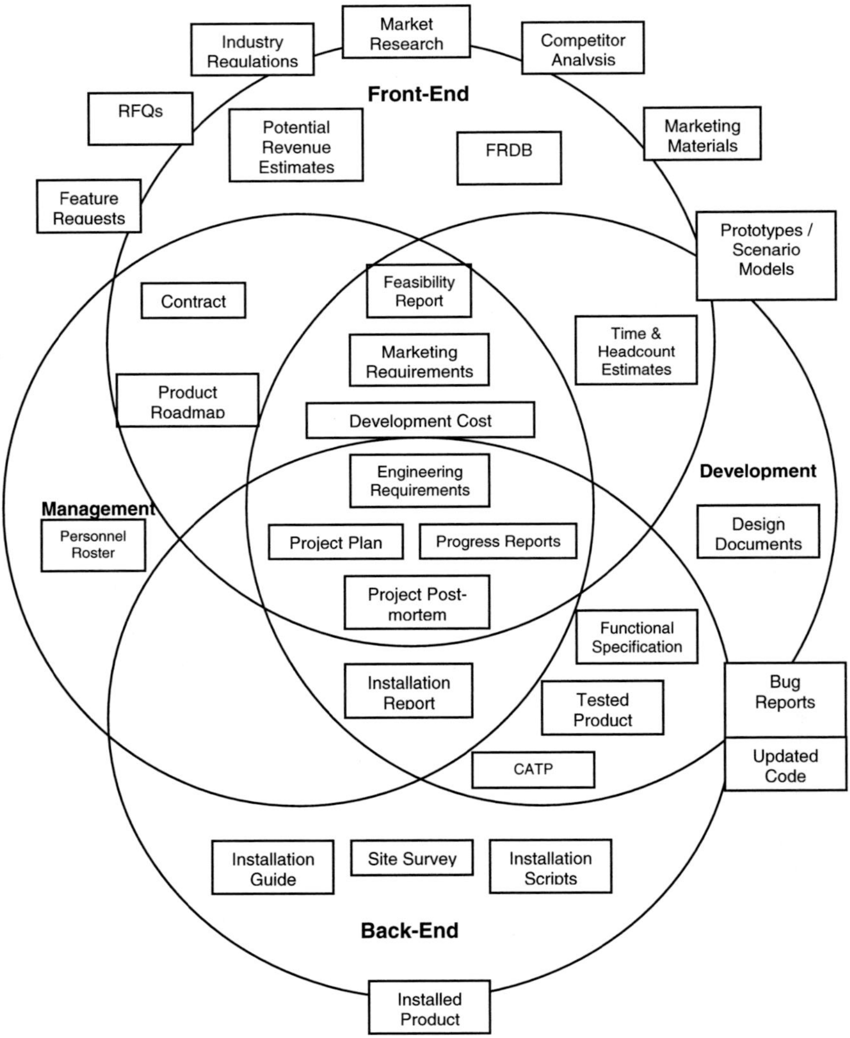

The position of the majority of artefacts on the boundaries between functions suggests that these artefacts provide a communications mechanism between functions, allowing the practitioners to collaborate. Study of the principal artefacts also shows how some of them contain data that is needed for decisions – such as the go/no-go decision – to be made. If knowledge, skills and abilities are now considered in terms of artefacts, it is likely that each artefact will require certain communications, collaboration and decision-support skills. However, before exploring this possibility, the concept of an artefact needs to be examined further.

6.4 Artefact Dynamics

Artefacts represent milestones achieved during the project. However, they need to be created in a particular order. For instance, in the development projects described during the interviews, the feasibility study cannot take place until the requirements are understood and the construction effort cannot proceed without a project plan. Thus one major artefact depends on its predecessors, suggesting that development proceeds in a linear fashion. However, for each artefact, a cycle of activity needs to take place:

1. A trigger event occurs. This could be an external stimulus or the review of another artefact.
2. The goals for the triggered artefact must be defined. This process involves gathering the necessary information – other artefacts, for instance – and may trigger the creation of intermediate artefacts (such as prototype systems) to assist in the definition process.
3. The concept to be contained in the new artefact must be synthesised.
4. This concept must be articulated by producing an artefact.

This cycle resembles Kurt Lewin's experiential learning model (Kolb 1984). The steps taken to learn something new from experience - where learning is defined "as a change in cognitive structure (knowledge)" (Lewin 1952, p.66) - involve having an experience, reflecting upon that experience, devising a course of action based on these reflections and then testing this course of action. The result of this experiment is analysed in order to refine understanding, i.e. it triggers another learning cycle.

Figure 26. Cyclical Development Model

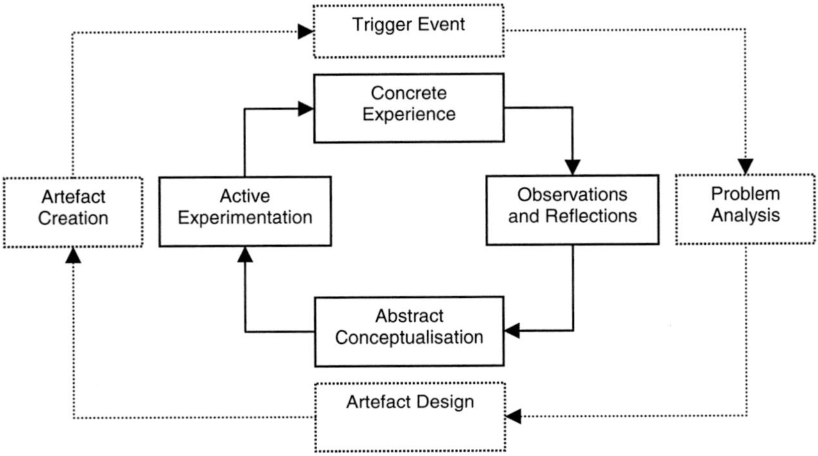

Similarly, the construction of an artefact involves some initial trigger; say a request from a customer for a new feature. Reflecting on the request, the practitioner may notice that several other customers have asked for similar functionality. S/he may also notice that the request is already on the product roadmap. In this case, the marketing requirements artefact already exists, so the course of action is to forward the requirements to the customer. If the customer finds these requirements lacking in some way, this triggers a possible revision of the marketing requirements.

Alternatively, if the request has not been seen before, analysis of the request can result in a variety of actions:

If the request is clearly understood, then the practitioner will be able to design a new marketing requirements artefact by paraphrasing the original request:

Figure 27. Creating the Marketing Requirements Artefact

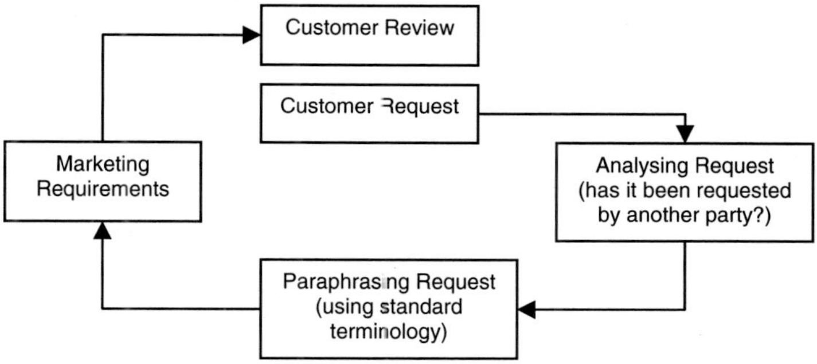

If the request is obviously unacceptable – i.e. it goes against the product strategy – a response to its originator must be framed, ideally pointing out how the product strategy will solve the problem in a different manner:

Figure 28. Creating a Customer Response

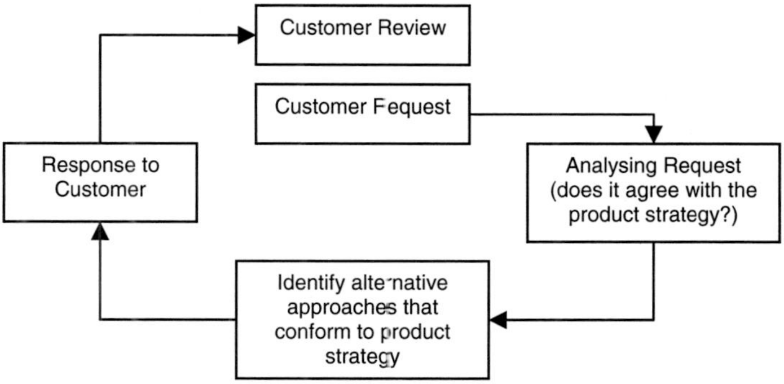

If the overall request looks interesting, but contains ambiguous elements, this will trigger a series of clarifying actions, such as producing a prototype and presenting it to the customer for feedback:

Figure 29. A Confirmation Loop

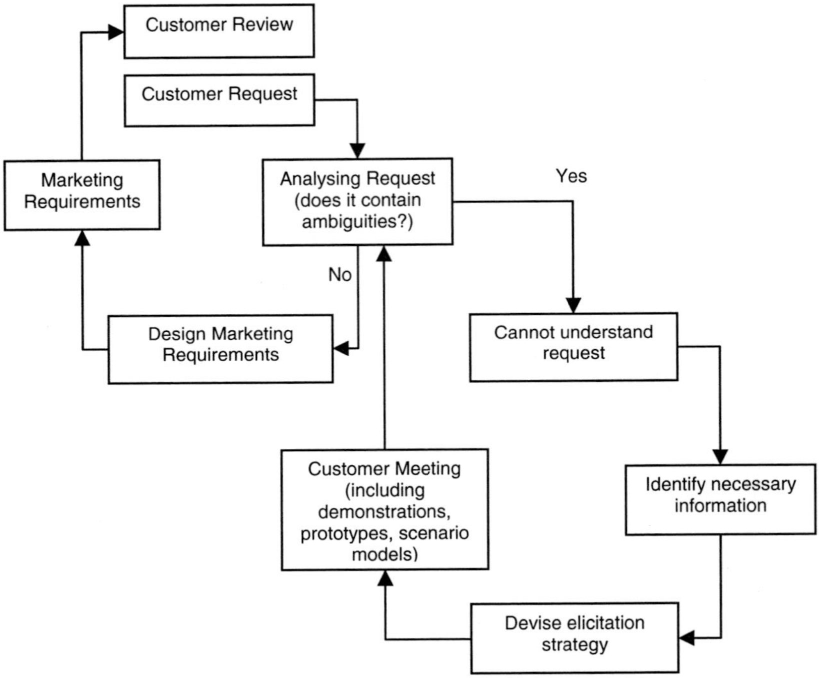

In terms of KSAs then, this cycle requires practitioners to:

- Evaluate the trigger event. This could involve simply recognising a trigger, such as a news story that in some way affects the company, or a scheduled review of a planned artefact, such as a design document.
- Gather information and build up the knowledge necessary to understand what is required of the target artefact. Sufficient information may be available from existing artefacts, but it might be necessary to create intermediate artefacts - such as the prototype system shown in Figure 29 - to obtain clarification.
- Design the artefact. This requires the creative, high-level skills needed to devise new concepts. Also required here are the decision-making and negotiation skills mainly associated with management but are required when investigating alternative

courses of action. For instance, detailed analysis of a particular requirement may show that the initial estimates were too optimistic. In this case, the design part of the cycle will have to conceive a solution to satisfy the requirements as well as calculating revised schedule estimates. The update to the project plan is triggered by a report from the programmer.

- Produce the artefact. These KSAs supplement the creative skills and include technical writing, prototyping, coding, testing, proof-reading, presentation and reporting.

Another way of looking at the lifecycle of an artefact is to consider it in terms of knowledge management. Demarest (1997) proposes a process where knowledge is embodied in the form of an artefact and disseminated throughout the organisation, as shown in Figure 30:

Figure 30. Knowledge Management Process

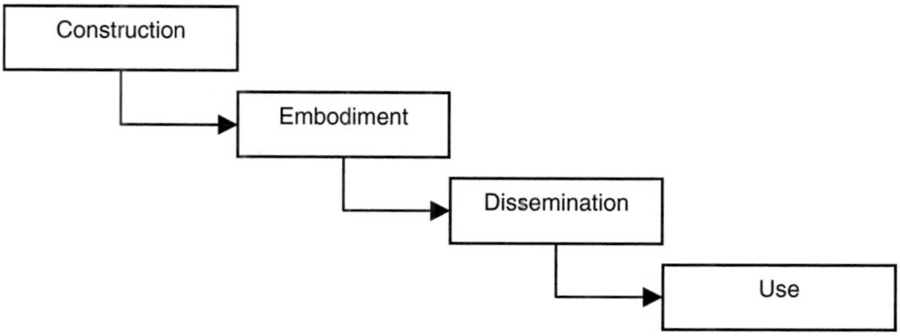

Although this process is not cyclical like the previous models, it is suggested that the use of an artefact will generate new knowledge that, in turn, needs to be organised and embodied into a new sort of artefact. Relating the steps in Figure 30 with the cyclical model of Figure 26 gives:

Table 11. Relating the Models

<table>
<tr><th>Cyclical Model</th><th>Knowledge Management Process</th><th>Learning Cycle</th></tr>
<tr><td>Trigger Event</td><td>Dissemination</td><td>Concrete Experience</td></tr>
<tr><td rowspan="2">Problem Analysis</td><td>Use</td><td rowspan="2">Observations and Reflections</td></tr>
<tr><td rowspan="2">Construction</td></tr>
<tr><td>Artefact Design</td><td>Abstract Conceptualisation</td></tr>
<tr><td>Artefact Creation</td><td>Embodiment</td><td>Active Experimentation</td></tr>
</table>

Thus the trigger event is the dissemination of some sort of knowledge and this is used to analyse the problem of creating the next artefact. The analysis and design of the new artefact is termed construction, which is defined by Demarest as "the process of discovering or structuring a kind of knowledge: how to sell a particular product to a particular market, for example, or how to diagnose a particular kind of customer problem" (p.376). The actual creation of the artefact maps onto embodiment.

An interesting feature of the knowledge management process is the way the management of these phases is considered separately from the knowledge itself. The cyclical development model views the creation and manipulation of management artefacts in the same way as product-related ones.

To summarise, these models illustrate the dynamic nature of artefacts. They begin after a trigger event, which may well be the dissemination of a previous artefact. The goals of the new artefact must be tied down and all necessary information gathered before it can be designed. The design is conceived and then articulated, or embodied, in the form of a tangible artefact. This artefact, in turn, must be disseminated and used to make decisions or base further artefacts on.

Thus, from a KSA perspective, an artefact should not be considered merely in terms of the skills needed to design it, but also in terms of the knowledge and the other artefacts that must be acquired before any sensible synthesis can take place. Having created, or embodied, the artefact, it must be made available to others on the project team and reviewed by them. Therefore, a single artefact draws on research, analysis, design, implementation and evaluation skills.

6.5 Relating KSAs to Artefacts

The research question seeks to relate KSAs with individual roles and the categorisation of skills/abilities under technical, business and interpersonal headings suits this perspective. However, considering KSAs in terms of the four phases of an artefact's lifecycle, brings the team into focus. This is a useful development as the three factors influencing team performance are: the task, the team and the individual (Adair 2003; Adair 2004). Team focus is achieved by highlighting the communication, collaboration and decision support skills intrinsic in the lifecycle of an artefact.

1. **Communication.** Obviously, information is conveyed via artefacts. This is particularly the case when the parties involved are not co-located. It should be noted that not all artefacts are produced by the development team. These artefacts may be produced by other organisations (such as industry regulators) or by other divisions within the same company (such as the finance and purchasing departments).
2. **Collaboration.** An artefact is not something that is created by a project stakeholder and never seen by anyone else. At its simplest, it is created by one party and acted upon by another. For more sophisticated artefacts, a myriad of people, from many different organisational functions, may be involved in its creation. Their product is then reviewed by interested parties and the insights from the review go to generating an improved version of the artefact.
3. **Decision Support.** The management team needs to decide on what courses of action to take. They must decide what features are worth investigating further, what features should comprise a release and what actions to take if a project is running behind schedule. Each of these decisions is informed by artefacts – feasibility studies and progress reports in these examples.

It should be noted that technical skills are still required and make up a fourth category in this new taxonomy. Each of these categories plays a critical role in particular phases. Because each artefact has a similar lifecycle, it is not surprising that each of the interviewees has a broadly similar skill set. While specific technical skills are role specific, the communication, collaboration and decision-support skills are required to deal with any artefact in a team environment.

Table 12 highlights the way the collaboration and decision-support skills are so important for dealing with trigger events and the gathering of data in the analysis stage. For instance, a noticeable feature of the interviews is the way teams are formed on an ad-hoc basis, often for the sole purpose of creating a single artefact, such as a feasibility report. The technical skills, those cited by the senior programmers and the systems architects as the most rewarding, are really only called for to synthesise and embody solutions. This suggests that the emphasis that is currently placed on technology-based skills is not equipping team members with the range of KSAs to deal with the entire artefact lifecycle.

Table 12. Relating KSAs to Artefact Phases

	Artefact Trigger	Artefact Analysis	Artefact Design	Artefact Creation
Communication				
Reading	x	x		
Listening	x	x		
Comprehension	x	x		
Writing				x
Presentation	x			x
Reporting				x
Collaboration				
Evaluation				
Document Review		x		
Code Inspection		x		
Problem Analysis		x		
Management				
Coordination	x	x	x	x
Teamwork	x	x	x	x
Team Leading	x	x	x	x
Negotiation	x	x	x	x

Table 12 (cont.). Relating KSAs to Artefact Phases

	Artefact Trigger	Artefact Analysis	Artefact Design	Artefact Creation
Decision Support				
Management				
Decision Making	x	x	x	x
Coping with Ambiguity		x	x	
Prioritisation		x	x	
Risk Identification		x	x	
Planning		x	x	x
Risk Management		x	x	
Business				
Estimation		x		
Budgeting		x		
Purchasing		x		
Logistics		x		
Technical				
Design			x	
Prototyping			x	
Coding			x	
Testing				x
Proof-reading				x

6.5.1 Knowledge

The different types of knowledge identified in this study – technical, product, market, domain, commercial and political – are important to all aspects of the artefact's lifecycle. Note that technical knowledge is only one of many displayed by the team. Indeed, looking at Table 13, the importance of product and domain knowledge is highlighted. The different types of knowledge can be described as:

- **Technical.** This contributes to design and programming ability. The person must be able to understand design representations and read existing programs. S/he needs to be able to take part in design discussions, recognising the terminology being used.

- **Product.** Someone with this knowledge has a 'black box' understanding of the product. S/he knows what it does and how to make it do these things. For instance, the customer support personnel need product knowledge in order to configure the system to do what the customer wishes. Similarly, technical writers draw on product knowledge to create their user documentation.

- **Domain.** This refers to the environment that the product works in. In this study, it refers to the telephony network. As one of the customer support engineers points out, 70% of the problems they deal with involve troubleshooting network related problems that often have nothing to do with their product.

- **Market.** This sort of knowledge is used to answer the question: What business need is our product satisfying? Because of deregulation and intense competition, customers are constantly trying to differentiate their service offerings from those of their competitors. This forces the vendors to devise new products that support such schemes. Being a truly global market, it is important to be aware of the different business cultures that must be dealt with.

"I notice in the Middle East that they're not so much interested in what you write down as whether they trust you or not. You build up a certain level of trust and, if you can maintain that trust, you'll get repeat business. If you lose that trust by not being compliant – no matter what you've written – but if you managed to build their trust verbally, then damage that and you're scuppered. In Europe and North American, it's what you write down that matters – you can say what you want, but what you write down is important … Of course, when you go to Asia, if you embarrass somebody or belittle them in some way, no matter how compliant or sophisticated the use of words you're going to use, they don't like to lose face over there, so trust in the Middle East, face in Asia and in Europe and North America it's whatever you write down and sign on the dotted line."

- **Commercial.** While market knowledge indicates what sort of product will sell, commercial knowledge will determine what customers are willing to pay for it. One of the companies studied finds it useful to offer the product at a very low basic cost. This is supplemented with licensing arrangements that makes further revenue dependent on the customer making a profit.

- **Political.** Politics plays its part both in the marketplace and in the vendor's own organisation. Large, 'tier one', customers will get more dedicated support and better commercial terms in return for the prestige of using them as reference sites. Similarly, the larger customers exert significant influence over the shape of the product roadmap. Within the company, the project manager has to compete for resources and make every effort to keep to the original schedule.

Table 13. Knowledge Requirements

	Technical Knowledge	Product Knowledge	Domain Knowledge	Market Knowledge	Commercial Knowledge	Political Knowledge
Feature Requests		x	x	x		
Requests for Quotation	x	x	x	x		
Industry Regulators	x		x	x		
Market Research		x	x	x		
Competitor Analysis						
Marketing Requirements		x	x			
Feature Request Database	x					
Marketing Materials		x	x			
Prototypes (Requirements)	x	x	x			
Scenario Modelling		x	x			
Engineering Requirements		x	x			
Prototypes (Solutions)	x	x	x			
Preliminary Functional Spec.	x	x	x			
Potential Revenue Estimates			x	x		
Time & Headcount Estimates	x					
Development Cost					x	x
Feasibility Report					x	
Product Roadmap					x	x
Contract		x		x	x	x
Combined Engineering Reqs.	x	x	x			

Table 13 (cont). Knowledge Requirements

	Technical Knowledge	Product Knowledge	Domain Knowledge	Market Knowledge	Commercial Knowledge	Political Knowledge
Personnel Roster						x
Overall Project Plan						x
Independent Test Plan		x	x			
Installation Plan		x	x			
Documentation Plan		x	x			x
Progress Reports	x					x
Project Post-mortem	x					x
Functional Specification	x	x	x			
Automated Test Scripts	x		x			
Site Survey		x	x			
Installation Scripts						
Installation Guide		x	x			
User Documentation		x	x			
Training Materials		x	x			
Design Documents	x	x	x			
Unit Tested Code	x	x	x			
Bug Reports	x	x	x			
Test Report		x	x			x
Bug Tracking Database	x					
Updated Code	x	x				
Customer Acceptance Tests			x			x
Installation Report		x	x			
Installed Product			x			

The skills/abilities identified in the study can also be considered in the same way:

6.5.2 Communications Skills

Artefacts need to be understood so that their contents may be used. Thus the creators of an artefact must present their designs in an accessible manner, so that the users of the artefact can make sense of their work. In Table 14 several of the artefacts appear not to involve any of these skills. This will be explained by the skills descriptions, where ‘reading’, for instance, is only highlighted when the practitioner has to decipher a communication written in poor English.

- **Reading.** This might seem like an obvious skill, but in this highly-regulated, global industry, some specialised reading skills are required. The development team has to deal with industry regulations that are written in legalistic terms and are difficult to understand – often drawing on the reader's coping with ambiguity strategies. The product managers and systems architects have to make sense of requests for quotations (RFQs) that may be written by customers who do not have English as a first language.

- **Listening.** Poor English also makes verbal communication difficult. It requires immense concentration to understand everything that is being said in some customer meetings. Interestingly, none of the customer-facing interviewees were fluent in languages other than English.

- **Comprehension.** Because of the difficulties with the customers and standards bodies mentioned above, it is not surprising that making sense of their various requests is difficult. The use of demonstration systems and prototypes can help to clarify customer requirements, but the details of communications protocols often only become clear when the product is plugged into the target network. Being able to retrieve live call traces from existing customers is very helpful in this effort. The review process appears to aid artefact comprehension.

- **Writing.** The technical writers insist that technical writing is not the same as creative writing and can be taught. For the other team members, the use of templates is regarded as helpful in this effort. Writing does not seem to be as highly regarded as oral presentations, judging by the lack of writing training in comparison with presentation skills training. Also, the interviewees tend to downplay their writing skills if templates are available for their work.

- **Presentation.** These skills seem to be very important in large companies. There, managers seem to prefer an oral presentation to a written document. It takes less time and allows the manager to clarify issues immediately. In other words, they are listeners rather than readers (Gabarro and Ritter 1980; Drucker 1999). This probably explains why so many of the interviewees have received training in this area.

- **Reporting.** This is a form of writing skill. While technical writing involves describing designs or procedures, reporting is about presenting the facts as they occurred. Thus progress reports, bug reports, test reports and installation reports need to provide as much detail as possible in order to allow their readers take action. Thus a progress report should flag if something is behind schedule; a bug report should give enough detail to allow the bug be reproduced; a test report should be enough to decide whether to ship or not and the installation report will indicate how difficult it will be to get payment from the customer. It could be argued that reporting should be identified as a decision-support skill. However, while the reports are used in decision-making, the creation of reports involves disseminating knowledge and draws upon communication skills.

Table 14. Communications Skills Requirements

	Reading	Listening	Comprehension	Writing	Presentation	Reporting
Feature Requests	x		x	x		
RFQs	x		x	x	x	
Industry Regulators	x		x			
Market Research						
Competitor Analysis						
Marketing Requirements	x	x	x	x	x	
Feature Request Database						
Marketing Materials		x	x			
Prototypes (Requirements)		x	x		x	
Scenario Modelling		x	x		x	

Table 14 (cont.). Communications Skills Requirements

	Reading	Listening	Comprehension	Writing	Presentation	Reporting
Engineering Requirements				x		
Prototypes (Solutions)						
Preliminary Functional Spec.				x		
Potential Revenue Estimates						
Time & Headcount Estimates						
Development Cost						
Feasibility Report				x		
Product Roadmap						
Contract					x	
Combined Engineering Reqs.				x		
Personnel Roster						
Overall Project Plan				x	x	
Independent Test Plan				x		
Installation Plan						
Documentation Plan				x		
Progress Reports	x	x	x		x	x
Project Post-mortem		x	x	x		x
Functional Specification			x	x		
Automated Test Scripts						
Site Survey				x		
Installation Scripts						
Installation Guide				x		
User Documentation		x	x	x		
Training Materials	x	x	x	x	x	
Design Documents				x		
Unit Tested Code				x		
Bug Reports						x
Test Report						x
Bug Tracking Database						x
Updated Code						x
Customer Acceptance Tests				x		
Installation Report						x
Installed Product						

6.5.3 Collaboration Skills

Software development requires the contributions of a multi-disciplinary team. The skills needed to coordinate their efforts will be similar no matter what artefact is involved. While management skills are called for at all four phases of the artefact's lifecycle, evaluation skills are needed during the artefact analysis stage.

6.5.3.1 Evaluation

- **Document Review.** Most of the key artefacts in a software development project are documents, such as the requirements document, the feasibility report and the project plan. These need to be critically reviewed before the project is allowed to continue. The review process is also useful to give ancillary groups advance warning of an impending project. As one of the test group leaders notes, reviewing the requirements document is interesting, but it is when the functional specification comes up for review that the test group needs to start planning – a requirements document is no indication that a project will proceed.

- **Code Inspection.** These are not widely carried out. There is a feeling in some companies that these are only needed for training purposes, to ensure that new recruits are performing adequately. The larger companies take code inspections very seriously, insisting that a certain amount of errors are detected at each one. Systems architects can maintain understanding of the overall product architecture by regularly reviewing code.

"It mightn't be to review the code on a line-by-line basis to find bugs as to review the code to understand the structure of what's developed at a high-level. So that, if there's a feature that comes in, you may have to propose that we can do the feature in a particular way and largely it's impossible to do that effectively if you don't have a reasonable understanding of how the thing is structured."

- **Problem Analysis.** Every one of the interviewees has had to deal with problems – deciding on the potential revenue of a feature, assessing the significance of an identified risk or trying to find the most convenient route to a customer site. Only one interviewee used a formal technique – the Kepner/Tregoe method

(1981); the rest described problem analysis as the process of breaking down the problem into smaller pieces. A forensic approach is recommended when dealing with field problems – identify the symptoms and think about the problem. The goal is to narrow down the problem and to eliminate suspects.

> "Sometimes, in cases of high customer pressure, you have to be seen to be doing something and sitting back thinking about it does not reassure a customer. Sometimes you have to have one person jump into the debugger - run a lot of commands - just to keep them from calling in a manager."

Another type of analysis is the location and assessment of Open Source software. Many of these companies make extensive use of this resource.

> "You're trying to find an Open Source library or something to do it. You find a lot of Open Source Java stuff – there's no point re-inventing the wheel. You find libraries for everything. … We've been fairly successful. I think we've benefited more than we've lost. I suppose you wouldn't use them if they were causing you a loss, but they allow you to get a lot of functionality going quickly."

6.5.3.1 Management

- **Coordination.** The various managers and group leaders have to coordinate the efforts of their teams. Coordination appears in the interview instrument's "What skills do you need?" checklist under team leading.

- **Teamwork.** An advantage of focusing on artefacts is that the multi-disciplinary aspects of the development process are highlighted. A notable feature of the companies studied here is the amount of informal communication between groups. However, in some of the companies, it is noticed that programmers tend to work alone until their parts are ready for integration and that product managers and systems architects tend to 'float' between ad-hoc groups that are formed for a specific purpose, such as a feasibility study.

- **Team Leading.** The "What skills do you need?" section of the interview instrument lists planning, coordination and motivation under the team leading heading. While the project manager and the various programming, test, documentation and support groups have formal leadership positions in the hierarchy, the product manager needs to coordinate the activities of systems architects, programmers and customer support personnel in order to get mini-projects complete. These are the requirements definition and feasibility studies as well as the installation of generic, off-the-shelf products that require no extra development.

- **Negotiation.** The most obvious need for negotiation skills is when dealing with customers. The product managers and the sales force will debate pricing and delivery issues as well as the product roadmap. However, within the company, the project manager has to negotiate for staff to work on the project and sell revised schedules to senior management. S/he will also have to make sure that the documentation, test and support groups are available to carry out their parts of the project.

Table 15. Collaboration Skills Requirements

	Document Review	Code Inspection	Problem Analysis	Coordination	Teamwork	Team Leading	Negotiation
Feature Requests							x
RFQs					x	x	
Industry Regulators							
Market Research	x						
Competitor Analysis	x						
Marketing Requirements			x				
Feature Request Database							
Marketing Materials			x				
Prototypes (Requirements)							
Scenario Modelling							
Engineering Requirements	x		x	x			
Prototypes (Solutions)			x				
Preliminary Functional Spec.							
Potential Revenue Estimates			x				
Time & Headcount Estimates							

Table 15 (cont.). Collaboration Skills Requirements

	Document Review	Code Inspection	Problem Analysis	Coordination	Teamwork	Team Leading	Negotiation
Development Cost			x				
Feasibility Report	x		x				
Product Roadmap							x
Contract							x
Combined Engineering Reqs.	x		x				
Personnel Roster							
Overall Project Plan	x		x	x	x	x	
Independent Test Plan	x		x	x	x	x	
Installation Plan	x		x	x	x	x	
Documentation Plan	x			x	x	x	
Progress Reports			x				
Project Post-mortem					x	x	
Functional Specification	x		x				
Automated Test Scripts							
Site Survey	x		x				
Installation Scripts			x				
Installation Guide	x		x				
User Documentation							
Training Materials							
Design Documents	x		x				
Unit Tested Code		x					
Bug Reports		x	x	x			
Test Report							
Bug Tracking Database							
Updated Code		x	x				
Customer Acceptance Tests							
Installation Report	x						
Installed Product			x				

6.5.4 Decision Support Skills

Decision support skills are called for mainly during the analysis and design parts of the artefact lifecycle. The most important decisions are made by those within the management function. Decision support varies between organisations. Several factors need to be considered (Kolb, Rubin and McIntyre 1974):

- In the organisation's hierarchy, the tasks carried out at the lower levels are inclined to be technical in nature, highly structured and often programmable. "At the executive board level, by comparison, interpersonal, as opposed to technical factors, assume greater importance. In other words, as decisions become less routine and programmable, the relationships between people involved in the decision-making process become more important" (p.42).
- Due to the complexity of the organisation, no single employee has access to all the information needed to make a decision. "As a result of this interdependency the communication process assumes primary importance in organizations" (p.42)
- In many groups gathered to make a decision, there is often a reluctance to share all the important details and people are inclined not to be as open as they should.
- Organisations consist of many departments and a decision to change something in one department may have knock-on effects in others. "To be effective, an organization must develop (implicitly or explicitly) a problem-finding mechanism that can integrate potentially conflicting problem priorities" (p.43).
- "Organizations are sociotechnical systems and a decision that alters the technological system has an impact on the social system and vice versa" (p.43).

As well as gathering and analysing data, the decision making process "depends upon individual member characteristics, such as their motives, values, and perceptions; upon group characteristics such as group norms and leadership styles; and upon organizational characteristics, such as intergroup competition and communication patterns" (p.47).

There are four types of decision models (Kolb et al. 1974):

1. **Autocratic.** You make the decision yourself based on information available or easily found.
2. **Consultative.** You share the problem with relevant subordinates, but retain the final decision rights for yourself.

3. **Group.** You share the problem with relevant subordinates as a group. Together you attempt to reach consensus on the solution.
4. **Delegated.** You delegate the problem to a subordinate (or group) and s/he has the responsibility for solving the problem.

6.5.4.1 Management

- **Decision-making.** Throughout the project, decisions must be made. Should we develop this feature? Should we investigate its feasibility first? Which course of action best suits the product strategy? Several interviewees noted that many of the more important decisions tend to get made at higher levels of management, such as the go/no-go decision based on the feasibility report and the decision to ship the product having read the final test report.

- **Coping with Ambiguity.** In many cases, decisions have to be made without all the pertinent facts. A project manager may, for instance, be committed to a deadline before s/he has had a chance to develop a detailed schedule or negotiate enough people to work on the project. Only two interviewees, a technical writer and a customer support engineer, state that ambiguity is not an issue. The others seem to have found ways of coping with it, with one mentioning that the review process is a good way of resolving these issues. One of the systems architects defined his role as removing ambiguity from requirements.

- **Prioritisation.** This skill is seen in ordering the product roadmap and assigning bugs to programmers to fix. In situations where there are fewer resources available to cover all options, an order must be placed on the work. The difficulty with prioritisation is that different customers have different concerns and, within the company, effective resource use will alter priorities.

- **Risk Identification.** During the investigations into the feasibility of the product, most risks are identified. There could be issues with new technologies, unskilled staff or the availability of third-party tools or components. If the market is unstable, the decision to pursue a particular direction may be incorrect. Risk identification offers the first step in coping with ambiguity.

- **Planning.** All the work must be planned, although how formal the planning process is depends on the company. Formal project management skills seem to be lacking in most of the companies studied. An important observation is the amount of planning required outside the formal project plan. For instance, before a project is ever approved, much work can be done in preparation and those participating in these efforts need to be coordinated.

"However, given the nature of the business, quite a lot of work can already have been put into a certain project before it becomes official. So, for various reasons, you may not sit down and go: 'to hell with the customer, we could give it to him three months after we get a PO [purchase order]'. You may actually realise that there may be a benefit in actually getting it out by a certain date. So, if three months comes and goes before that particular date, you may actually have to kick a lot of it off internally, prior to a PO; prior to it being official."

- **Risk Management.** This is what happens to the identified risks. Risks can vary in the magnitude of their impacts and the probability of their occurrence. The management of risk involves the identification of the risk, followed by an estimation of its likelihood – high, medium, low – and its impact on the project – small, medium, large. For each risk, a contingency or mitigation plan needs to be put in place. Then, during the project, the risks have to be constantly assessed. As time goes by, some risks will no longer be relevant and new risks will appear.

6.5.4.2 Business

- **Estimation.** This skill seems to be required by all parties to the development project. The bigger companies mention formal estimation strategies such as Function Point and Wide-band Delphi analysis. However, the general consensus is that estimates are based on experience.

- **Budgeting.** A surprising discovery in this study is how few people, including group leaders, manage a budget. Those who do seem to be responsible for estimating their travel, training and equipment needs for the next financial period. However, few of these are concerned with actual monetary amounts.

"Costing you typically do resource-wise. If we're buying boards – if we need boards for a project or we need to buy equipment for a project –

that's obviously a cost. But then, once you identify resources, there is a specific overhead associated with each resource and that would be as much costing as we would do. We would hand that resourcing information over to our finance people and they would actually deal with that. For tracking cost, we would typically track effort, people's effort – earned value and things like that".

- **Purchasing.** This was seen only in the installation phase when flights and hotel accommodation have to be provided. Buying new equipment and hiring new staff was not mentioned in any of the interviews.

- **Logistics.** The customer support people and the product managers are concerned with this area. They are tasked with getting computer hardware to the customer site. This involves dealing with shipping companies, overcoming importation procedures and ensuring that the product can be sold legally in that country. Another concern is the availability of parts and technical support for the hardware in the customer country. If the customer is to receive a generic product, it is often better to get the machines shipped directly from the manufacturers to the customer. The software will be installed at a later date.

Table 16. Decision Support Skills Requirements

	Decision Making	Coping with Ambiguity	Prioritisation	Risk Identification	Planning	Risk Management	Estimation	Budgeting	Purchasing	Logistics
Feature Requests	x									
RFQs	x									
Industry Regulators	x	x								
Market Research										
Competitor Analysis										
Marketing Requirements										
Feature Request Database										
Marketing Materials										
Prototypes (Requirements)										
Scenario Modelling										
Engineering Requirements					x					
Prototypes (Solutions)	x									
Preliminary Functional Spec.	x			x						
Potential Revenue Estimates				x			x			
Time & Headcount Estimates							x			
Development Cost										
Feasibility Report	x	x								
Product Roadmap	x		x							
Contract			x							
Combined Engineering Reqs.										
Personnel Roster										

Table 16 (cont.). Decision Support Skills Requirements

	Decision Making	Coping with Ambiguity	Prioritisation	Risk Identification	Planning	Risk Management	Estimation	Budgeting	Purchasing	Logistics
Overall Project Plan		x			x	x	x	x		
Independent Test Plan					x					
Installation Plan					x					
Documentation Plan					x				x	x
Progress Reports	x									
Project Post-mortem										
Functional Specification										
Automated Test Scripts										
Site Survey										
Installation Scripts										
Installation Guide										
User Documentation										
Training Materials										
Design Documents										
Unit Tested Code										
Bug Reports					x					
Test Report	x									
Bug Tracking Database										
Updated Code										
Customer Acceptance Tests	x									
Installation Report										
Installed Product	x									

6.5.5 Technical Skills

These are skills specific to particular types of artefacts and are used in their design and creation phases. Technical skills were highlighted during the interviews in relation to only a small number of artefacts, specifically those relating to software construction.

- **Design.** In the pilot study, an interviewee, trained in graphic design, argued that design is a transferable skill. In the software development context, program architecture and design are the activities requiring this skill. However, the technical writers also have to design their documents to follow the company's style guides and to instruct their readers logically. It could be argued that the project schedule has to be designed, coordinating staff and tasks.

  In this study, the Unified Modelling Language appears to be widely used for program design, with real time software being described using Z.100 SDL notation. It was noticed, during the interviews, that few of the programmers really follow any design methodology.

- **Coding.** When the final deliverable is a software-based product, coding is expected to be an important skill. What is surprising is the amount of code that is written that is not part of the shipped product. Obviously, the testers are coding automated test scripts, but the customer support people will often have to create simple scripts to manipulate data on the customer's machines. Indeed, in one company, the development manager took on the task of writing installation scripts. Coding seems to be a rewarding part of the job, with several of the systems architects still writing code.

- **Testing.** Ideally, there should not be a dedicated test group. One tester declared that having a test team reflects a fundamental flaw in the programming process. Certainly this study highlights a lack of appreciation for the theory of testing.

- **Proof-reading.** This skill is highlighted by the technical writers whose work needs to be grammatical and correctly spelled. Reviewing each others' documents and proof-reading them at home are techniques that can improve the error detection rate.

Table 17. Technical Skills Requirements

	Design	Coding	Testing	Proofreading
Feature Requests				
RFQs	x			
Industry Regulators				
Market Research				
Competitor Analysis				
Marketing Requirements				
Feature Request Database	x			
Marketing Materials				
Prototypes (Requirements)		x		
Scenario Modelling				
Engineering Requirements				
Prototypes (Solutions)		x		
Preliminary Functional Spec.	x			
Potential Revenue Estimates				
Time & Headcount Estimates				
Development Cost				
Feasibility Report				
Product Roadmap				
Contract				
Combined Engineering Reqs.				
Personnel Roster				
Overall Project Plan				
Independent Test Plan				
Installation Plan				
Documentation Plan				
Progress Reports				
Project Post-mortem				

Table 17 (cont.). Technical Skills Requirements

	Design	Coding	Testing	Proofreading
Functional Specification	x			
Automated Test Scripts	x	x		
Site Survey				
Installation Scripts		x		
Installation Guide				
User Documentation		x		x
Training Materials				
Design Documents	x			
Unit Tested Code		x	x	
Bug Reports	x	x	x	
Test Report				
Bug Tracking Database	x			
Updated Code	x	x		
Customer Acceptance Tests				
Installation Report				
Installed Product			x	

6.6 Summary

The analysis in this chapter is required because of the difficulties encountered in defining individual roles. To create a framework that addresses the research question, two relationships need to be considered: how artefacts are located in the organisational context and how knowledge and skills/abilities (KSAs) are related to phases of the artefacts' lifecycles. While this arrangement does not lead to the original goal of mapping KSAs to roles, it does provide a means of identifying the KSAs needed to develop software and the organisational functions that are involved in the effort.

The lifecycle of an artefact is central to this framework. Artefacts are triggered; their goals are set and relevant data gathered; their contents are designed and embodied in artefact form. Given this perspective, it is not surprising that most of the artefacts identified in this study are boundary objects, facilitating communication and collaboration between organisational functions and between the organisation and the outside world. They also serve to support the decision-making process.

The artefact-centric framework has produced a new taxonomy of knowledge and skills/abilities. The interview instrument classified KSAs as technical, business and inter-personal. Now, the artefact-centric taxonomy contains communication, collaboration, decision-support and technical skills as well as the different types of knowledge – technical, product, domain, market, political and commercial.

Figure 31. The Artefact-centric Framework

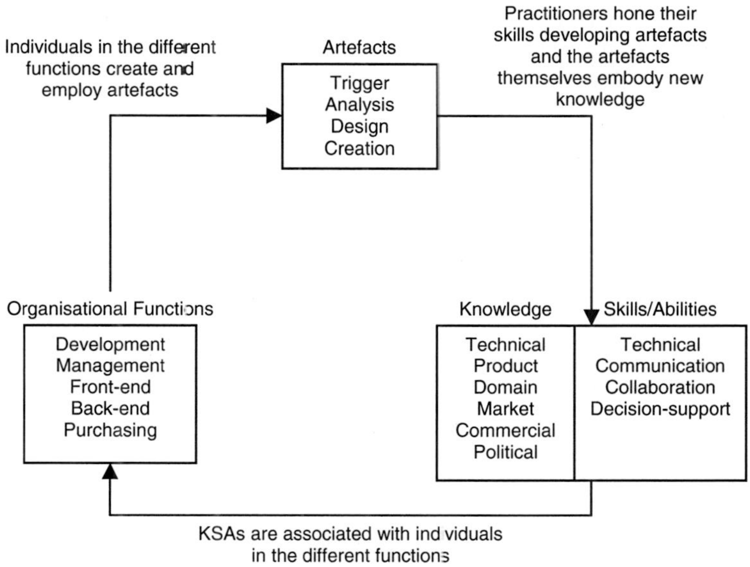

CHAPTER SEVEN

AN APPLICATION OF THE FRAMEWORK

Having invented a framework that establishes relationships between artefacts and organisational functions and between KSAs and artefacts, what application does it have? This research project has encountered difficulties with defining roles and it is suspected that individual organisations also have similar problems. If the artefact-centric framework is effective in circumventing this problem, then it should be able to assist companies in providing job descriptions for their workers. These job descriptions would be of tremendous use during recruitment campaigns.

In order to determine if the artefact-centric framework would be useful in preparing job advertisements, sample adverts for some of the roles studied in this project were taken from on-line recruitment websites. Many of these adverts lack a clearly defined job description. The following sections will present each advert together with a corresponding artefact-centric version.

The artefact-centric descriptions will contain two parts: a job description and a list of the skills required. Because some of the adverts are extremely vague, some 'reading between the lines' is required. Thus a short interpretation of the advert will be included in each section.

The artefact-centric framework gives the creators of job descriptions an awareness of:

- The entire software development lifecycle. Being aware of all the artefacts in the process encourages recruiters to define the scope of the role in a broader manner than if they concentrate on the job title alone.
- The multi-disciplinary nature of the development process. Because so many of the artefacts require contributions from other team members, the need for teamwork and communications skills is brought to the fore. It also identifies the organisational

functions the role interacts with, highlighting the need for a wider perspective than a mere technical one.

7.1 Project Manager

Figure 32. Original Project Manager Advert

*"**Requirements***

- *Degree in Electronic Engineering, Computer Science or Mathematics with a first class or second class honours grade 1 qualification.*
- *5 years software design experience with some team lead experience.*
- *Ability to work with a team of specialists and provide leadership, motivation and coherence.*
- *A track record of participation in the commercialisation of complex system products.*
- *Experience of software quality systems and software project planning.*
- *Familiarity with GUI development and networking.*
- *Familiarity with Linux would be an advantage.*"

The most significant feature of the project manager advert shown in Figure 32 is the total absence of a job description. Indeed, it is difficult to know what skills – technical or managerial – are required. Because there is so little detail, the artefact-centric job description is based entirely on the interviews with project managers conducted during the study. The first steps to take are the identification of the artefacts and the phases of their lifecycles the project manager is typically involved with.

In an ideal world, the project manager would come on board after the requirements have been clarified and a detailed feasibility study has been carried out. Unfortunately, it is often the case that the project manager is tasked with a very vague assignment – implement the latest version of a particular communications protocol, for instance. While the specification provided by the standards body should contain all the necessary details, these requirements must be translated into software functionality – i.e. a functional specification needs to be written. Similarly, the need to support emerging standards is vital to business in the telecommunications market. In other words, a feasibility report is unlikely to have been written. This implies that the project manager has to generate time and headcount estimates from scratch.

Table 18. Artefact lifecycle phases involving a Project Manager

Artefact	**Trigger**	**Analysis**	**Design**	**Creation**
Marketing Requirements	x			
Engineering Requirements	x			
Functional Specification	x			
Time & Headcount Estimates	x	x	x	x
Development Cost	x	x	x	x
Feasibility Report	x			
Project Plan		x	x	x
Independent Test Plans	x			
Documentation Plan	x			
Installation Plan	x			
Test Report	x			
Installation Report	x			
Progress Reports	x	x	x	x
Design Documents	x			
Unit Tested Code	x			
Bug Tracking Database	x			
Project Post Mortem		x	x	x

Thus, Table 18 shows the project manager generating time, headcount and cost estimates as well as making use of them. Whether or not a project manager has to drive the requirements gathering and feasibility work, the main artefact all project managers are concerned with is their project plan. This will contain a work breakdown structure and an ever-evolving schedule. It should contain detailed risk analysis and it will be informed by other contributors, such as technical writers (documentation plan), testers (independent test plan) and customer support personnel (installation plan).

Progress will be tracked using reports from individual developers, as well as final test reports and the installation report. In turn, the project manager must report on overall progress to senior management. Once the project is complete, the project manager needs to summarise the experience by producing a project post-mortem. Some companies hold such reviews at several stages in the project.

> "They would be held for projects at different stages. You would have one after the lock-down process. You would have one at the design completion stage and you'd have one at the ready-for-deployment stage. So there would normally be at least three. At each one you'd look at what happened between the last review and the present one and, based on the outputs of that, then process change may happen."

The project manager role is an extremely pervasive one, involving contact with all the other development roles, as well as the sales, finance and legal departments. In some cases, the project manager will engage with the customer, either during the requirements negotiations or the installation of the software. A job description reflecting this profile is given in Figure 33.

Figure 33. Artefact-centric Project Manager Description

Job Description

- *The project manager's primary responsibility is the creation and maintenance of the project plan artefact.*
- *This artefact draws on the product roadmap, the combined engineering requirements document, the preliminary functional specification and the time and headcount estimates produced during the various feasibility studies. The project manager is expected to evaluate critically all of these artefacts.*
- *The project manager must ensure that an adequate set of testable and measurable requirements are in place and that an agreed set of software solutions have been investigated. If not, s/he must work closely with senior designers to ensure that the work breakdown structure for the project can be developed.*
- *Parts of the final product will be supplied by third-party vendors. The project manager contributes to the creation of contracts with these suppliers. S/he also provides clear requirements and tracks their progress as closely as that of the in-house team.*
- *The project manager provides both written and verbal reports to senior management throughout the project.*
- *At the completion of each project, a post-mortem document is written by the project manager in order to improve the development process.*

Skills Required

- *Project management skills. Team leading, coordination, negotiation, prioritisation, planning, risk management, estimation, budgeting and the ability to cope with ambiguity.*
- *Strong technical, market and product knowledge is needed along with an awareness of commercial and political issues.*
- *Evaluation and analysis skills. The product manager has to base the project plan on earlier artefacts. S/he must be able to assess critically both technical and commercial documents.*
- *Both written and verbal communication skills are tested in this role. The project manager must create a cogent project plan and be able to defend the decisions contained within it. S/he must also ensure that work assignments are clearly understood as well as ensuring that all stakeholders are updated on progress.*

7.2 Product Manager

Figure 34. Original Product Manager Advert

> ***"Responsibilities:***
>
> - *Market research.*
> - *New product development.*
> - *Bring new products to the market.*
> - *Manage the existing product portfolio.*
>
> ***Key Skills:***
>
> - *Third level marketing/business qualification or equivalent work experience and/or postgraduate CIM Qualification.*
> - *Experience of working in the software industry.*
> - *Knowledge of basic LAN/WAN technologies.*
> - *Experience of working in the education sector.*
> - *Excellent communication, influencing and negotiation skills.*
> - *Attention to detail, and ability to see the big picture."*

This company could have saved a lot of time and simply advertised for Super(wo)man. This person appears to carry out the market research, develops new products, markets these products and manages the existing product line (whatever that entails). S/he will also have the contradictory traits of paying attention to detail while also being able to see the big picture. While "communication, influencing and negotiation skills" are mentioned, there is no indication to whom these skills are applied. Similarly, what details must we pay attention to – technical product details, or personal details of clients?

A more realistic description for this role may be obtained by focusing on the artefacts a product manager will work with. As with the previous example, the description draws heavily from the telecommunications interviews. Product managers tend to work mostly at the front-end customer interface, with some contributing at the back-end as well.

Table 19. Artefact lifecycle phases involving a Product Manager

Artefact	Trigger	Analysis	Design	Creation
Feature Requests	x	x	x	x
RFQs	x			
Industry Regulations	x			
Market Research	x			
Competitor Analysis	x			
Feature Request Database		x	x	x
Marketing Requirements		x	x	x
Engineering Requirements	x			
Potential Revenue Estimates		x	x	x
Feasibility Report	x			
Product Roadmap		x	x	x
Contract	x	x	x	x
Project Post Mortem		x		

The product manager's principal artefact is the product roadmap. This determines the evolution of the product. According to the interviewees, sales are often made on the basis of what is planned for the product, rather than on its current functionality. The product roadmap is a very dynamic artefact, changing to reflect the marketplace. The product manager obtains insight into the market mainly from the existing customer base. These customers submit feature requests for consideration. Another good indicator of demand is the request for quotation (RFQ) process, where potential customers tender for equipment. If several of these (or a single large operator) requests a particular feature, the roadmap may be changed to accommodate this. In the telecommunications sector, industry regulatory bodies have a profound influence on what vendors need to support. Business intelligence gathering, in the form of market research and competitor analysis are also useful.

A first step on the way to a product roadmap is a marketing requirements document. This describes a feature request, or a market demand, in terms customers understand. Marketing requirements often evolve into promotional literature. If a given feature is deemed likely to advance the product, the product manager needs to assemble an ad-hoc team to determine its feasibility. Sales and marketing people will assist in determining potential revenue estimates, while the systems architect will assess technical feasibility. The team will produce a feasibility report. If the idea is both technically and commercially feasible, the feature will be included on the product roadmap.

Product managers often act as the customer's point of contact within the company. In cases where a customer wishes to purchase an off-the-shelf product, the product manager may assist in specifying the product and drawing up the contract. S/he may work with the customer support people to purchase computer equipment and get the product installed on the customer site. This exercise is also useful in getting further access to the customer and ideas on how to develop the product further.

Based on these insights, the product manager role may be summarised by the description given in Figure 33.

Figure 35. Artefact-centric Product Manager Description

Job Description

- *The product manager is primarily responsible for the creation and maintenance of the product roadmap. This artefact must clearly articulate the product strategy for our LAN/WAN technologies both within and outside the company.*
- *The product manager gathers new feature ideas from existing customers, potential customers, market research, competitor analysis and the development team. The product manager describes these ideas in a consistent fashion by creating marketing requirements documents.*
- *The product manager works with sales, marketing, finance and software personnel to assess a feature's technical and commercial feasibility.*
- *The product manager works closely with the project managers and the customers to decide how best to define new releases of software. These release definitions will determine development timelines and how flexible the change request process is.*
- *The product manager defines the various product configurations and options that are available and ensures that each customer receives exactly what was ordered.*
- *The product manager will monitor reports from the development team in order to keep customers apprised of progress.*

Skills Required

- *The product manager must have excellent product, market, political and commercial knowledge. S/he must also have enough technical insight and domain knowledge to communicate effectively with software developers.*
- *Being a global market, the product manager will draw on excellent listening and comprehension skills as s/he will have to deal with a wide range of nationalities and perspectives.*
- *The product manager creates informal teams to carry out evaluation and feasibility studies. This requires sound project management skills, including team leading, coordination, decision-making, negotiation and planning.*
- *The product manager will express the product strategy using the marketing requirements and product roadmap artefacts. Thus strong writing skills together with a professional presentation technique are called for. The product manager must be a persuasive negotiator, convincing customers to buy in to the product strategy.*

7.3 Architect

Figure 36. Original Architect Advert

> *"As part of a small tightly knit team, using cutting edge technology you will Design/Architect, Implement and Deploy Internet based software solutions, from the ground up, using .net, windows forms, xml & c#.*
>
> *You should be able to implement OO based solutions and have good problem solving skills, along with excellent interpersonal skills and the ambition and energy to assist a small start up company become a global leader in their sector!*
>
> *You will be an EC Citizen, already living in Ireland, with native level fluency in English and educated to 3rd level in IT.*
>
> *Consistent performers can expect stock options in the company.*
>
> *Skills & Experience required:*
>
> *You should have strong software development experience with a minimum of 2 years using:*
>
> - *.net*
> - *c#*
> - *xml*
> - *VB*
> - *windows forms*
> - *web based development"*

Based on this advert, the company wants a programmer, not an architect. However, mention that it is "a small start up company" suggests that the role will be a lot more extensive than that presented here. Potential interviewees would be wise to probe what requirements and feasibility processes are in place. They should also inquire about who creates the documentation and training artefacts. It also seems likely that this company does not have an independent test group or a dedicated customer support organisation.

To create a more detailed description, knowledge of the systems architect role gleaned in Downey (2006a) is used to identify the artefacts and the phases of the artefact lifecycle the architect is involved with. Table 20 lists the artefacts a systems architect in the telecommunications sector may be expected to work with. Initially, the architect will be asked to generate detailed, measurable and testable engineering requirements from marketing requirements generated by the product managers. Thus, the marketing requirements document acts as a trigger for the architect's subsequent work.

Table 20. Artefact lifecycle phases involving a Systems Architect

Artefact	**Trigger**	**Analysis**	**Design**	**Creation**
Marketing Requirements	x			
Prototypes		x	x	x
Scenario Modelling		x	x	x
Engineering Requirements		x	x	x
Functional Specification		x	x	x
Time & Headcount Estimates		x	x	x
Development Cost	x	x		
Feasibility Report	x	x		
Design Documents	x	x		
Unit Tested Code	x	x		
Bug Reports	x	x		
Feature Requests	x	x	x	x
Project Post Mortem		x		

Marketing requirements are often quite vague and need clarification. To obtain this, the systems architect may ask to meet the customer directly. Clarification is possible in a question or answer session, but more effective results can be obtained by creating simple prototypes or by carrying out scenario modelling – working through use cases, for instance. While the goal of this exercise is a technical one – the creation of the engineering requirements artefact – the architect must demonstrate interpersonal and team working skills. However, the people the architect has to interact with for this exercise are not fellow developers, but sales and marketing personnel as well as customers. A further complication is that everyone in the customer site does not have the same concerns, for instance:

> "One customer includes the management, the marketing, the business, the hands-on operations staff and they all have different requirements and operations feed into how usable the system is; marketing how flexible it is; top-level management, does it close all the fault windows; etc."

Another artefact the architects get involved with is the feasibility report. Essentially, their responsibility is to assess technical feasibility. If an architect is satisfied that a solution to the requirements is possible, s/he must contribute time and headcount estimates to the finance and project management people, in order to arrive at the development cost estimate. Thus, architects need to have some appreciation of business realities and understand the way development is financed. Again, the architect is called on to display good interpersonal and team working skills, but this team has different perspectives from the market-driven team of the requirements phase.

> "I've done a few feasibility studies here in terms of adopting a certain technology or taking in a piece of third-party code when we could develop it ourselves – that type of thing. That's a technical feasibility study as opposed to a business feasibility study."

Typically, the systems architect provides technical leadership during what McConnell (1993) terms the construction part of the project (design, code and test) - although some of the interviewees do implement part of their products themselves. Their contributions would be seen in document and code reviews as well as in advice given during the analysis work of the construction artefacts.

Finally, the architect may offer consultancy to the customers in order to tailor the product to meet their needs better. This back-end interaction with the customer may suggest ideas for new features, which the architects will feed back to their marketing people.

This profile of the systems architect shows how the role is significantly more demanding than the line "strong software development experience" suggests. Knowing the artefacts and the other people who contribute to their lifecycles, a clear job description is possible, as shown in Figure 37. This description draws on both our overall knowledge of the architect role, as well as details from the original advert.

Figure 37. Artefact-centric Architect Description

Job Description

- *The architect will work with the sales and product management functions to agree customer requirements and to assess the feasibility of any proposed solution from a technical perspective.*
- *As part of the requirements definition process, the architect will be expected to produce realistic prototypes and scenario models of proposed solutions.*
- *The main contributions to feasibility will be sensible time and headcount estimates and the identification of possible risks associated with proposed solutions.*
- *S/he is responsible for creating engineering requirements documents, functional specifications and high-level design/architectural documents.*
- *The architect also takes part in the coding, testing and installation of the product in an advisory/technical lead role.*

Skills Required

- *As part of the requirements definition role, the architect will be called upon to deal directly with our international customers. This will require significant listening and comprehension skills, as well as the ability to present prototypes and use-case scenarios in an engaging manner.*
- *The architect works with a team of developers to produce Internet-based software products. However, the architect will also become part of ad-hoc, self-managing teams, created to identify particular requirements and to assess project feasibility.*
- *The company uses object-oriented design, requiring that the architect has competence in these techniques.*
- *The architect must be proficient in the C# and Visual Basic programming languages and familiar with .net, windows forms and web based development. Knowledge of the XML protocol is also needed.*
- *As this is a start up company, requirements will be quite fluid until the exact market niche is located. Thus the architect must be able to cope with ambiguity and be prepared to re-plan and re-evaluate designs at short notice.*
- *The architect is expected to take a lead role in development, requiring excellent communication and team leading skills.*

7.4 Programmer (Software Developer)

Figure 38. Original Programmer Advert

*"**Requirements:***
Experience with Software Engineering
*3-4 Years **Java Lifecycle Development** experience*
*Experience with OOA **Design Patterns, UML***
*Experience with related Technologies such as **XML***
*Database experience including **Sybase***
*Knowledge/Experience of **Telecoms, 2G, 3G**, ATM/IP*
Configuration and Build Management processes (Clearcase/ANT etc)
Experience with development on Unix and Windows platforms"

While this advert clearly expresses the technologies the company is involved with, the job seeker has no idea which of these technologies are used as tools and which will be developed by the company. S/he also has no clear idea of what the job entails. In the study of the telecommunications software domain, it was found that the programmer role is the most pervasive, particularly in the case of senior people. This role can require a great deal of customer interaction, both at the front-end and back end.

Programmers may feature all through the software development lifecycle. They may assist the systems architect in defining testable and measurable engineering requirements, perhaps by creating prototype systems. They may also help in the production of the functional specification by evaluating parts of proposed solutions. In this effort, the programmer may be in direct contact with the customer and will have to appreciate the business concerns of sales and marketing people, including the product manager.

Table 21. Artefact lifecycle phases involving a Programmer

Artefact	Trigger	Analysis	Design	Creation
Prototypes		x	x	x
Scenario Modelling		x	x	x
Engineering Requirements		x	x	
Functional Specification		x	x	
Time & Headcount Estimates		x		
Design Documents	x	x	x	x
Unit Tested Code	x	x	x	x
Progress Reports		x	x	x
Bug Reports	x			
Updated Code		x	x	x
Feature Requests	x	x	x	x
Installed Product		x		
Project Post Mortem		x		

Once the project has been approved, the programmer is assigned particular features to implement and will carry out design, code and test activities. The artefacts created in these phases are reviewed by the systems architect and peer programmers. In turn, the programmer is expected to review other construction artefacts.

Once the product has been tested by the programming team, it is handed over to the independent test team and the programmers stand by to address bug reports. Usually, some of the programmers move onto other projects at this point and the remaining ones have to field problems associated with other people's code. This situation becomes more demanding when the product is installed at a customer site. Now, one or two programmers may be asked to accompany the installation team and deal with any software problems that may arise. Several of the interviewees cited these visits as cathartic learning experiences.

Thus the programmer can be involved in all aspects of the development cycle and all the organisational functions. A realistic job description can be seen in Figure 39.

Figure 39. Artefact-centric Programmer Description

Job Description

- *Programmers review the engineering requirements document and contribute to the functional specification by experimenting with alternative potential solutions.*
- *Programmers contribute time and headcount estimates to the project plan for their portions of the development effort.*
- *The programmer will produce a detailed design document using object oriented design techniques, including use cases and design patterns.*
- *Once the design has been reviewed, the programmer will produce a unit-tested suite of code. A professional development environment is provided including version control and automated builds.*
- *The programmer will provide information to the technical writing group as a basis for their documentation.*
- *The programmer will assist the independent test and the customer support teams in diagnosing problems and providing updated code to address any bug reports.*

Skills Required

- *A programmer needs to have reasonable product and domain knowledge in order to contribute usefully to the requirements review.*
- *Detailed technical knowledge is also needed to evaluate alternate solutions and to design, code and test software.*
- *A programmer must be capable of estimating how long any assigned task is likely to take.*
- *Strong object-oriented design skills are essential in this role.*
- *Coding is carried out in Java under the UNIX operating system. Ability in Perl and shell scripting is also useful.*
- *A programmer needs to have a good knowledge of the theory of testing in order to produce comprehensive unit tests.*
- *Strong writing skills are required to produce clear design documents. Also, contributions to the end-user documentation need to make sense to the documentation people who have less technical understanding.*
- *Given the amount of interaction with other roles – project managers, architects, testers and customer support personnel – good communication and teamwork skills are essential.*

7.5 Summary

This chapter shows how the artefact-centric framework can offer practical assistance to organisations by facilitating better job descriptions in their recruitment adverts. This is achieved by specifying the people they want to hire in terms of the artefacts they will be expected to contribute to. Because the artefact-centric framework also highlights the fact that many of the artefacts are boundary objects, the multi-disciplinary nature of the work is brought to the fore. For potential candidates, the nature of the work they are invited to apply for is much clearer.

As can be seen from the sample adverts, some companies have a very poor understanding of what sort of knowledge and skills/abilities they need for their organisations. Considering the importance of hiring good staff (Weinberg 1971; Shapero 1985; DeMarco and Lister 1999), an effective means of describing the role required is essential. Although it has been shown from this project that generic roles are not possible to define, each organisation should be able to define what roles mean in their own context.

The artefact-centric framework provides such a means. An organisation needs to identify the key artefacts in its development process and locate them in terms of the company's organisational functions. It then needs to define its current staff in terms of their contributions to each artefact. This exercise should identify gaps in the team profile or areas where emphasis is weak. By understanding what the roles and responsibilities are, employers are in a position to define clearly what sort of additional staff they are looking for.

It should be noted that the examples given in this chapter have not been validated by human resource professionals. Indeed, this application of the artefact-centric framework would make an ideal subject for an action-research project, where a company's process would be described in terms of artefacts and each team member's work defined in relation to those artefacts. It is hoped that such an exercise would reveal gaps in the necessary skill sets and provide a basis for either training or recruitment.

CHAPTER EIGHT

IMPLICATIONS FOR NATIONAL SKILLS POLICY

Forfás is the national policy advisory board for enterprise, trade, science, technology and innovation in Ireland. Its report responding to Ireland's skills needs (Forfas 2003) and the later Enterprise Strategy Group's analysis of how Ireland can maintain its strong position in the global economy (Enterprise Strategy Group 2004) list areas where skills need to be developed:

1. Soft skills, with emphasis on managerial skills, "including the ability to work on a team; communication and influencing skills; and leadership and coaching skills" (Forfas 2003, p.87).
2. Sales and marketing. Irish industry "must develop, and be supported in growing, its capabilities in market intelligence, international sales promotion, sales and strategic management" (Enterprise Strategy Group 2004, p.xv).
3. Technology and research skills – "building technological and applied research and development (R&D) capability, to support the development of high-value products and services" (Enterprise Strategy Group 2004, p.xii).
4. Business skills – "it is necessary to improve skills in the ICT sector in business areas such as selling, marketing, product management, entrepreneurship and business strategy" (Forfas 2003, p.29).

The Forfás report is mainly concerned with how graduates can be equipped with appropriate skills for the future. However, the insights gained in this project from the study of senior practitioners offer a different perspective. If Forfás is correct in its recommendation that Ireland's economy needs to add more value and develop a presence along the entire value chain (Enterprise Strategy Group 2004), then the key skills needed for the future are the ones that add more value.

It can be argued that senior practitioners, by virtue of their higher pay, add more value to their organisations than entry-level ones. Therefore, the skills that they possess are likely to correspond with those that Forfás have identified.

Examining the Forfás recommendations in the context of the interview data shows strong support for the first two factors. The following sections will discuss each in turn.

8.1 Managerial and Soft Skills

It was noted in the interviews that poor communications skills – such as presentation skills – relate to the mainly introverted people working in the software sector.

> "It's not a favourite part of my job. Personality-wise I tend to be, and I guess a lot of engineers tend to be, more introverted than extroverted. It's not so bad getting up in front of your colleagues or your immediate team, but you get a lot of upper levels of management – senior management and directors – coming over here and, while they're over here, [the boss] likes to showcase what we're doing here, so he likes to get the teams to come in and talk through some stuff."

Although twenty-five of those interviewed have managerial experience, few are comfortable in the role and several complained about lack of training and support. Some of the interviewees argue that you are either a natural leader or you are not. As such, some management tips can be picked up at courses, but a person cannot be trained to be a manager:

> "I haven't done any training on management and I don't think it's made any difference to be honest. I'm not a huge fan. For some of the newer managers, there was a formal programme put in place. I believe you can pick up some stuff alright – I might be being a bit harsh there – but I think you're either suitable for being a manager and born to have management skills or you're not."

This perspective may indeed have merit. As reported by Hackman and Oldham (1980), decades of research have failed to identify the key attributes of a good manager and management training is not very effective because:

- It is not very clear what a manager needs to be taught

- It is difficult to get supervisors to transfer their learning from the training setting to the actual work environment
- The behavioural style of managers is largely a function of the types of people they have reporting to them. Diligent workers may inspire a considerate, participative style, while incompetent reports may inspire a structured, directive and bureaucratic style.

Judging by the interviews, a combination of training and mentoring support seems to be effective for managers. According to Blanton, Schambach and Trimmer (1998), the organisation needs to provide an "updating climate" for these skills to develop. It needs to provide support for advanced degrees, training, technical literature and professional activities, as well as supervisor support – performance feedback, career counselling, opportunities and rewards for updating and goal setting.

The company with the best updating climate is the one where team leaders are the most comfortable. As one points out: It is "hard to be a bad manager here". However, the impression given by the other companies is that very little formal training and mentoring is available for new team leaders. Some have been on short front line management courses that are rated highly. However, one erstwhile team leader embarked on a two-year night class in order to come to grips with the role. Another leader feels that he built up his team leading ability by watching other managers in action. This reinforces the point made by DeMarco (2001) that managers rarely get groomed. They might be sent on management courses that teach abstractions but they rarely have a "facilitator" and they do not get encouraged to work with their "co-learners".

The problems with developing the necessary skills for leadership roles are compounded by a general distaste for this type of work. One of the multinationals suffered from a noticeable problem in getting senior people to take on management roles. For instance, one team leader applied for his current position because he was afraid of who might get the job otherwise. A system architect was adamant that he did not want a managerial role on the basis that it would take him from his technical roots and turn him into a "paper pusher". These findings differ from an earlier study of Irish subsidiaries of U.S. multinationals (McGovern 1998) where professional staff were found to seek advancement by self-promotion and "being pushy".

Given the general situation where team leaders are not adequately trained and supported, it is not surprising that their understandings of good practice differ. Because management skills have, for the most part, been gained through personal trial and error, the interviewees' conceptions of good management technique differ significantly. Some are task focussed leaders, managing the work rather than the people. These managers recommend a good information flow and the provision of clear direction. They argue that technical staff tend to be professional in their attitude. Thus motivation is not an issue – people do their jobs.

In contrast, other interviewees focus on the individual, being concerned with keeping up morale and giving praise and words of encouragement. An important part of the role is to listen to problems. Apparently, if team members articulate their problems, they can often see the solutions themselves. An effective way to foster a sense of ownership is to involve the team in the planning and estimation process.

Discipline does not seem to be a problem for either type of manager. The interviewees argue that this is due to the individuals' need to achieve. People with high achievement motivation are inclined to work alone and prefer to take personal responsibility for their success or failure (Kolb et al. 1974).

An interesting aspect of one project manager's role is that she has no technical input to the project. She feels that she is able to contribute to a team-member's appraisal by examining the metrics gathered during the project. This approach is condemned by Weinberg (1971). He argues that too many managers rate their staff by what they appear to do. The advice Weinberg gives is to ensure that the front line group leaders regularly review code and build up a true picture of the worth of each team member.

One of a manager's responsibilities is taking part in the recruitment process, specifically interviewing potential candidates. Given the literature's agreement on the importance of good professional staff (Weinberg 1971; Shapero 1985; DeMarco and Lister 1999), it is disturbing that such a variety of answers are given to the question: "what do you look for when you interview someone?" This is especially true in light of the amount of training received.

Despite trying to follow the guidelines given on courses, some of the interviews admitted that "gut instinct" is probably the best way to choose candidates.

> "I was a terrible interviewer at the beginning. I was trying to be fair – hold back all subjective decisions and make the decision objectively. It's insane! I hired a person who turned out terrible. You know what they say: When the person comes in the door and you know in the first two minutes, or one minute, or five seconds, or whatever? Go with it!"

As can be seen from the above examples, management skills are required for senior software practitioners. Also, "the standard of management in Irish firms will have to improve as more sources of competition appear" (Sterne 2004, p.292). However, it appears that insufficient preparation has been given to the role, with people being thrust into management positions that they are not comfortable with. It appears that training and mentoring help in grooming the new manager but the experiential learning factor has been dominant in shaping the managers in this study.

It is grounds for concern that so few programmers wish to take on a managerial role. It is also disturbing that there is such a wide divergence in their understanding of what the role entails, in particular their understanding of the interview process. While this research endorses the Forfás position that we must develop these skills, it remains to be seen how this should be done. Training appears to offer limited benefits with mentoring support for on-the-job experiential learning being more useful. Reifer (2004) also makes the point that academic programmes "need to prepare software professionals to assume management roles" (p.13).

8.2 Sales and Marketing Skills

The artefact-centred framework really highlights the amount of customer interaction involved in developing commercial software. Customer requirements must be understood and choices have to be made in order to produce products with the most widespread appeal and the highest revenue potential. In the telecommunications environment, when the product is tested, it must be installed at the customer's site.

In order to understand requirements, the practitioners need to have in-depth knowledge of the telecommunications business and its networks, as well as the company's own product lines. Students can be trained to understand the telephony networks and can build up a reasonable level of domain knowledge before entering the workplace. However, detailed insights into the business models used and the products being developed have to be acquired in the work environment. Companies tend to keep their business practices and details of their products (such as known bugs) confidential.

Reflecting the fact that the telecommunications industry is a global one, understanding what the customers require is difficult. Although English is the lingua franca of this domain, many potential customers do not have English as a first language. Thus requests for quotations (RFQs) are often difficult to decipher and customer meetings require a great deal of concentration to understand what is being asked. Another problem with the requirements definition process is actually determining the requirements – often customers phrase their requirements in terms of solutions.

Given this potential for confusion, the use of demonstration systems and prototypes helps vendors in this sector to clarify their understanding of the requirements.

Deciding on how to proceed involves assessing the feasibility of each proposed development. This involves more than simply estimating the potential revenue versus the likely development cost. Some initiatives may be required simply to stay in the marketplace – support for a new protocol version or a feature that a competitor has put on the market, for instance.

Even in cases where a single customer is willing to pay the development costs, it might be better not to proceed; as such a move may compromise the product strategy or the product's architecture. Being able to convince the customer that an alternative solution – one that does not distort the product so much – will meet their needs is a key skill.

Technical knowledge of software development and knowledge of the product's existing architecture are needed to arrive at development estimates. The general opinion from those interviewed in this study is that developments that resemble previous work tend to be estimated accurately, while estimates for unfamiliar features can be untrustworthy. The better the practitioners understand the solution, the more accurate will be the estimates. The use of prototypes to assess potential solutions is regarded as helpful. However, as one company points out, there is roughly a 10%

success rate in responding to RFQs, so the amount of work done to determine likely development times needs to be curtailed.

Although not explicitly mentioned in the Forfás reports, a vital part of the customer relationship is the installation and maintenance of the product in the field. The products that telecommunications equipment vendors sell are entities in a network. Thus they must inter-work with equipment from other companies. For the people tasked with installing the system, this involves having strong domain knowledge of the surrounding network entities. As one customer support engineer reports, almost 70% of their work is tracing network problems, most of which have nothing to do with their own products.

Being a global market, actually getting the equipment and the necessary personnel to site involves an appreciation of the logistics involved. Travel arrangements need to be made and the equipment must be shipped to the site in the most convenient way possible. Political considerations also play a part. Some computer vendors (or their governments) will not allow their equipment to be sold in certain countries. These restrictions mean the software must be ported onto machines that are not constrained in this fashion in order to satisfy the customer's order without breaking any laws.

Just like the management skills discussed in section 8.1, it appears from this study that customer-facing skills are built up by experience. It seems that product managers and systems architects who have a technical training need to learn how to deal with customers and their own sales and marketing people. For product managers who come from a business background, they need to develop their product and technical knowledge. The impression given by these interviews is that no training is given – the expectation is that you either sink or swim.

> "Last year, in the first six months of the year, I spent more than 120 days on the road, on sales visits. Very quickly, when you give a presentation – either it works or it doesn't – and you know from the feedback from the audience whether it's actually suitable to the audience or not, or whether the message is being transmitted in the right way – you suck it and see. It's a task of revising the message on a particular topic enough times until it actually works."

Similarly, many of the interviewees cite being sent on site to assist with installations as cathartic experiences, especially when it happens early in their careers. This approach suggests that people need to develop solid interpersonal skills before entering the workplace.

In summary, the sales and marketing skills needed by software practitioners are based on market, domain and product knowledge. These skills centre on communications – being able to understand others and impart your understanding to them. In the case of feasibility work, decision-making and negotiation skills are also required.

Although not obviously associated with sales and marketing skills, the people involved in requirements definition, feasibility and installations have to be managed. Despite not being subject to a formal project plan, these activities need to be regarded as mini-projects, with their own schedules and resources. This suggests that management skills are also needed in the customer-facing roles.

8.3 Technology and Research Skills

Probably the most surprising observation of this study is the lack of high-end technology research that is employed. This became very obvious during the interviews with systems architects. It would be reasonable to assume that someone called a 'systems architect' is responsible for the overall architecture (both hardware and software) of a computer system. In any given sector, an in-depth knowledge of that problem domain would also be expected, reflecting the view that systems architecture is "a result of technical, business and social influences" (Bass et al. 2003).

Bass et al (2003) list the activities involved in systems architecture as: creating a business case, understanding the requirements and creating the architecture. That architecture must be communicated to the stakeholders and evaluated before a system is implemented. During construction of the system, the systems architect must ensure that the implementation conforms to the architecture.

The Guide to the Software Engineering Body of Knowledge (IEEE Computer Society 2004) does not have a knowledge area devoted to architecture. Instead, it places "architectural structures and viewpoints, architectural styles, design patterns, and, finally, families of programs and frameworks" (p.1-4) into the Software Design knowledge area. This suggests that Software Design should be the system architects' focus. However, based on the activities listed by Bass et al (2003) above, we would also expect them to be concerned with Software Requirements and to have some part in directing the Software Construction effort.

From these descriptions, the role of the systems architect seems similar to that of a building architect. Indeed, both the Massachusetts Institute of Technology and Carnegie Mellon University have taught design using the studio techniques of building architects (Kuhn 1998). If this model is correct, systems architects should spend a great deal of time with customers, trying to understand their concerns. As it was put by Lawson (1980): "The vast majority of the artefacts we design are created for particular groups of users. Designers must understand something of the nature of these users and their needs" (p.5). Having identified the requirements, the architect should construct the overall architecture of the product, addressing all the non-functional requirements, such as performance, maintainability, scalability, security and reliability.

Companies in the telecommunications sector provide their programming staff with both managerial and technical career ladders. Senior software developers can choose between advancing via a management career (the first step being a team leader role), or the more technical focus of the systems architect.

However, this picture of a systems architect differs from that described by the architects interviewed in this study. To define what these interviewees actually do, the interview reports were analysed using open coding and the method of triples in order to produce the following definition (Downey 2006b, p.7):

> "The systems architect is a technical expert with experience of the company's products and the industry in general. S/he works with product management to refine customer requests into a set of engineering requirements that are possible to implement. S/he will identify possible implementations that satisfy the requirements and assess their feasibility in terms of time schedules and headcount. Architects sometimes remain with a project through construction, writing the functional specification and contributing to the design, code and test activities as a technical lead, an advisor or in a hands-on development capacity. After product delivery, architects may provide additional consultancy as well as training to end-users."

From this definition it is clear that there are marked similarities between this role and that of a systems analyst in the management information systems field. This can be seen by comparing the above definition with that developed by Misic (1996, p.35):

> "A systems analyst is a problem-solving specialist who works with users and management to gather and analyze information on current and/or future computer-based systems. With this information, the systems analyst, working with other MIS personnel, defines the requirements which are used to modify an existing system, or to develop a new system. The systems analyst identifies and evaluates alternative solutions, makes formal presentations, and assists in directing the coding, testing, training, conversion, and maintenance of the proposed system."

An explanation for this discrepancy between what a systems architect actually does and what s/he might be expected to do relates to the fact that all the interviewees are working on mature products. Thus the features that are being developed enhance existing functionality rather than radically change the underlying architecture. The nature of telecommunications work facilitates this sort of progression – new versions of protocols are supported and new billing techniques are catered for. Also, telecommunications products tend to have long shelf lives, meaning that products can still be commercially viable for decades after their initial launch.

This lack of architectural work is not surprising in the multinational sector. McGovern (1998) has commented on a 'glass ceiling' effect due to Irish subsidiaries not being exposed to the full spectrum of research and development. What is surprising is that the same lack of architectural work pertains in the Irish indigenous company. This company spent some two years developing the initial product, funded by venture capital. Now it is trying to recoup its investment by selling it to as many customers as possible. Investment in the next generation architecture is non-existent. This philosophy is seen in their feasibility assessments:

> "If you get something that's very desirable in the marketplace and it's easy to do, it will be top of the list. Whereas if it's something that's very desirable in the marketplace but it's difficult to do, then you just have to go on the long finger a bit, because it's going to suck up too many resources."

The senior manager who reviewed these findings notes that India has a policy of educating enormous numbers of people in software related subjects. These are generally two-year sandwich courses that are of dubious quality. However, he warns that any work assigned to an Indian facility must be carefully specified. If the specification is wrong, the implementation will reflect the error exactly. This philosophy of producing people well equipped for low-level technical work seems to suit the multinational sector well, where the leading-edge technologies are confined to head office.

This presents Irish educational policy makers with a dilemma: to satisfy the current needs of the multinational sector, we need a large cohort of graduates capable of carrying out low-level design, code and test activities; to prepare for a time when the multinational sector moves its operations to lower-wage economies, we need people who are skilled in architectural matters and advanced technologies. Even now, it appears that graduates are often over-qualified for the work available.

Another factor to consider is the amount of Open Source software that is being used. Instead of developing every component of a system from scratch, Open Source modules are adapted to suit. A similar approach is seen in the pharmaceutical industry, where they have coined the phrase "search and development" to explain how a research group "constantly screens the scientific sector for new modules and product ideas, which are then developed in cooperation with partners" (Schwarz Pharma 2006). Thus an increasingly important skill is finding and integrating useful software rather than developing it from first principles. Indeed, Trauth et al (1993) identified "a new type of IS professional. This individual will possess traditional IS skills but will be focussed on integration rather than systems development" (p.299).

8.4 Business Skills

Another noticeable finding in this study is the lack of business skills used by the interviewees. None of the interviewees knew how much an engineer-hour cost and very few of the managers actually manage a budget. Those that do seem to work in terms of tangible quantities such as headcount, training courses, travel arrangements and specific items of equipment, rather than monetary amounts. Being so unaware of the costs of running the company, front-line managers have little incentive to make local economies.

Having said that, one business skill that is required of all the practitioners is the ability to estimate how long a given piece of work will take to complete. Despite the use of formal techniques, such as wide-band Delphi and function-point analysis, most of the estimates provided are based on personal experience. This type of estimation uses time as a measurement, not money.

Another widespread responsibility is the identification of risks. While many of the practitioners are constantly looking out for potential pitfalls, very few companies seem to manage risk properly.

> "Sometimes risks get highlighted and they get discussed and they get escalated and it comes back down that it's something we're just going to have to live with for the time being and, if it happens, we're all going to scramble around and do what we can. So, quite often, you highlight risks and you try to work them and that happens: It just comes back down and we're not going to spend the money and that's it."

The two managers who reviewed the findings offer two opposing explanations for this lack of financial awareness. One argues that the lack of business knowledge relates to the early days of software when market share was the main driving force. Today companies are becoming more concerned with breakeven costs. While it was the case that few managers could understand a balance sheet, business awareness is increasing. Certainly there is little evidence of this at the front-line management level.

The other viewpoint is that finance people do not understand software either and the two communities are incapable of talking to each other. However, if a company assembles a multi-functional team that can visit customers and elicit their requirements; create computer-based solutions to those requirements and can install the systems on site, what is to stop this group setting up its own company to compete with its former employer? It may be due to a lack of business skills.

Indeed it would be fair to say that none of the interviewees exhibits an 'entrepreneurial/creativity' self-concept, or 'career anchor' as Schein (1990) describes it. This is consistent with Igbaria et al (1991), who found that less than five percent of IS practitioners displayed an entrepreneurial orientation. Therefore, the lack of business skills seems to be coupled with a lack of business acumen. From a Forfás perspective, it seems unlikely that many software developers will choose to set up their own businesses.

8.5 Summary

In this chapter, the interview findings are used to review the Forfás recommendations for future skills needs. This project endorses the immediate need for soft and managerial skills. It also highlights how useful customer-facing skills are.

If the status quo is to be maintained then high-end technical skills and business skills are wasteful, leading, in the former case, to over-qualified staff members. However, if Ireland is to move toward the ends of the value chain, then inventors and entrepreneurs will be required. For those simply seeking employment in this sector, these skills are not in demand.

It has been suggested that a person's 'career anchor' will influence their choice of work. Thus someone displaying general managerial competence may be a better manager than someone who has received extensive management training. Similarly, someone with an entrepreneurial/creativity anchor is more likely to set up a business venture than someone with technical/functional competencies. Although managerial career anchors have been found to be more prevalent than technical ones in the IT world (Igbaria et al. 1991), neither managerial nor entrepreneurial ambitions are in evidence among the majority of this study's participants. If the Irish government wishes to see more indigenous software companies, it might be advised to get entrepreneurs interested in software development rather than encouraging software developers to set up their own businesses.

CHAPTER NINE

CONCLUSIONS

The knowledge and skills/abilities (KSAs) needed by the different members of a software development team is the question that this research project set out to address. In order to target the research so that a single researcher could gain useful insights, the project was focused along personnel, industry, company and geographical lines. These restrictions provide the exact research question that the project sought to explore: what are the knowledge and skills/abilities needed to carry out the senior roles in the Irish telecommunications software industry.

Researchers in the software engineering sector have been more concerned with technical questions than skills-related ones. Although there have been suggestions to improve software engineering education (Hilburn 1997; Kuhn 1998; Tomayko 1998; Parnas 1999; Hilburn and Humphrey 2002; Parnas and Chik-Parnas 2005), little empirical research has been carried out on the actual skills required. By comparison, extensive skills research has been undertaken in the IS field (Trauth et al. 1993; Lee et al. 1995; Misic 1996; Sawyer et al. 1998; Shi and Bennett 1998; Sumner 2001; Noll and Wilkins 2002). However, these practitioners are concerned with using technology to solve problems within their organisations, whereas commercial software houses seek to create products for sale outside the organisation. For this reason, applying the IS findings to a software development environment may not be justified.

Given the lack of existing research in this area, it was decided to carry out a qualitative study, where established practitioners would be interviewed to assess the skills they require. In accordance with the methodology literature (Patton 1987; Eisenhardt 1989; Miles and Huberman 1994; Yin 1994; Strauss and Corbin 1998; Lethbridge et al. 2005), a semi-structured interview instrument was created based on social cognitive theory (Bandura 1986; Downey 2005) and validated using a pilot study (Lethbridge et al. 2005).

Although it was not necessary to adapt Bandura's theory for this study, the personal (skills set, attitude), behavioural (learning behaviours, application to work) and environmental (work itself, work context) attributes used represented a novel application of the theory that provided useful insights during the data elicitation stage. Subsequently, the pilot study served to refine the instrument and suggested that telecommunications would be a good industry to explore further. Certainly, the interviewees from that industry appeared to have the best development processes.

This study is a multiple-case embedded study (Yin 1994) where project teams from four telecommunications software development companies were interviewed. Analysing the data from the four sites using Grounded Theory coding techniques (Strauss and Corbin 1998) revealed a significant problem with the goal of determining what KSAs are needed for each role: Roles in this sector are not clearly defined. There are no lines of demarcation and roles differ widely across companies. They also overlap to such an extent that every role needs to employ virtually every skill. Organisations such as Forfás (2003), the British Office of National Statistics (2000a) and the SFIA Foundation (2008) seem to have also encountered this problem, but have surmounted it by either relating the skills they identified to the ICT sector as a whole or by attributing the same responsibilities to a myriad of job titles.

Given this obstacle, the interview data were revisited in an effort to establish a common thread across the informants. This exercise uncovered commonality between the companies' development processes. It was also noted that the different organisations based their development work around similar artefacts. These artefacts became the focus of the study.

Although it proved impossible to make a general association between artefacts and individual roles, it is possible to relate artefacts to organisational functions. This exercise uncovered two interesting aspects of artefacts: Firstly, the majority of artefacts are boundary objects, serving as interfaces between organisational functions and between the organisation and its customers. Secondly, it highlights the multi-disciplinary aspect of the development team – working in software development involves interaction with many different types of non-technical people.

Initially, artefacts were considered as items that needed to be created. In other words, the KSAs involved are those needed to construct the artefact.

However, thinking in terms of artefacts leads to the realisation that each artefact has a lifecycle and that this lifecycle is similar for all the artefacts encountered. Thus some sort of trigger event – a customer request, a news item, the availability of another artefact – establishes the need for a new artefact. Then information must be gathered to base the artefact on – what are the requirements for the artefact and what information is needed before it can be created? Only then can the new artefact be designed. Whatever knowledge is to be embodied in the artefact must be organised in such a way that it can be disseminated to the target audience – customers, management or other team members.

Viewed in this light, it becomes clear why so many skills are common to all roles. While the design of the artefact requires specialist, technical skills, the organisation of the artefact requires similar skills no matter what it is. Thus communication skills are important when trying to identify the trigger event and when disseminating the new concepts. Team members need to cooperate in the gathering and analysis of data. This aspect of the process also highlights the need for collaboration with different functions within the organisation and with members of customer organisations. Finally, the dissemination of knowledge in the form of an artefact is the basis for many of the decisions made during the software development process.

Thus the decision to explore the software development artefacts in more depth has produced a useful taxonomy of skills/abilities, organising them under technical, communication, collaboration and decision-support headings. The idea of an artefact embodying knowledge (Demarest 1997) recognises the fact that there are many types of knowledge and, like the technical skills, different knowledge types are required for different artefacts. The interview data revealed a total of six different types: technical, product, domain, market, commercial and political.

In summary, the artefact-centric framework relates artefacts to organisational functions and KSAs to artefacts. This mechanism provides insight into the skills needed to develop software in the telecommunications sector and suggests a new classification of the skills/abilities required. This taxonomy, together with the different types of knowledge identified, highlights the need for generic soft skills and a wide knowledge base for practitioners in this area.

Where do these insights fit into the software development body of knowledge? The software engineering discourse pays little attention to personnel matters. When it does, it suggests improvements to the third-level engineering curricula and it promotes efforts to establish software engineering as a profession (Ford and Gibbs 1996; Wernick 1996; Jackson 1998b; Gotterbarn 1999; Holmes 1999; McConnell and Tripp 1999; Speed 1999; Raccoon 2001; Holmes 2002; Saur 2005; Wing 2005). The artefact-centric framework can contribute to both strands.

A newly qualified programmer will have little appreciation for the amount of artefacts that exist beyond those relating to the installed software product. Even then, s/he may regard a software product as simply executable code. Also, the educational system encourages students to work alone, because of the difficulty in evaluating individual contributions to team performances (Harrisberger, Heydinger, Seeley and Talburtt 1976). So the practice of developing only part of the product will be a new experience.

Even the most junior programmer will have to understand the engineering requirements and functional specification documents. The first work assignment is likely to be a very small part of the project, but even the smallest piece of production code involves artefacts that the novice may not be aware of.

Software practitioners are expected to be able to estimate how long any given task will take. This estimate will be combined with all the others to generate the project plan. Up until now, estimation was not an issue – assignments had deadlines, which the students did not help to set.

The first artefact produced by a programmer is likely to be a detailed design document. This will be reviewed by other programmers and the newcomer has to learn how to accept this type of criticism. Even writing code may be difficult for the graduate. S/he must learn about the development environment, the use of templates, coding standards, version control and build tools. Having to adapt to a standard coding style and to accept criticism at the code inspection are further steps on the way to becoming a fully-fledged programmer. As Seely-Brown and Duguid (1991) put it, the "central issue in learning is *becoming* a practitioner not learning *about* practice" (p.48).

Preparing the unit-tested code artefact is also difficult for the newcomer. Firstly, s/he has to understand the theory of testing and then has to design and run tests that may involve the development of test harnesses or the use of in-house tools. Finally, s/he will have to decide if this piece of code is ready for integrating into the system.

If this particular module has a strong user-interface component or otherwise affects the product's external operation, the programmer will have to contribute to the documentation suite and the training materials. This may involve providing a written description of the functionality or informal conversations with the documentation and training people.

Problems with this code may surface during independent testing and installation. The new programmer must be able to debug problems that are manifested at a system level. This requires reasonable product knowledge. This knowledge is also necessary if it is decided to include the programmer with the installation team. Being called upon to help out with the installation will force the programmer to consider the whole product and not just one component.

Thus, even at the first stages of their career, programmers are exposed to things they are generally not prepared for. These can be considered under two headings:

1. Decision making
    a. The programmer is expected to estimate how long any development task s/he might be assigned will take.
    b. The programmer must decide if any artefact s/he produces is fit for dissemination.
2. Communication
    a. The programmer has to resolve ambiguous requirements by intelligently probing the systems architect for details.
    b. S/he has to convey design information in document form and to defend it in a review situation.
    c. S/he has to convey the external impact of the code to non-technical people.
    d. S/he must interface code to other modules and negotiate a shared understanding with fellow programmers.

Looking at the interview data, we see that senior programmers have a sphere of influence that touches every artefact in the process. Therefore, the undergraduate needs to learn about the existence of these artefacts, if nothing else. The cyclical development model may provide a way of achieving this. Weinberg (1971) argues that we should learn how to read programs before we start writing them. Expanding this argument, we should learn how to evaluate and use an artefact before creating one.

Turley and Beiman (1995) consider having a broad perspective to be a characteristic of an exceptionally good software engineer. To develop this sort of viewpoint, undergraduate students should learn how to read a requirements specification in a critical fashion. Similarly, they need to understand what a high-level functional specification contains. Having understood the meanings of these artefacts, the student can then identify what use they have.

Because they will have to contribute to the project plan, students need to understand what the plan contributes to a project. They need to appreciate the need for estimates, the identification of risks and dependencies in the schedule and how their contribution to the project exists as part of a work breakdown structure.

Contributing to other people's artefacts rather than creating them yourself may surprise newly qualified graduates. The undergraduate needs to understand how user documentation and training materials are prepared. This understanding will help the new programmer to describe functionality in a non-technical fashion.

If Weinberg is correct, then the undergraduate needs to review code before writing any. In this manner, the student learns what styles are easy to understand and will be encouraged to write maintainable code. Lessons from the extreme programming community (Beck 2000) suggest that the first artefact the student should produce is a test plan for some existing code; the second artefact will then be a bug report. The bug report is an interesting artefact because, for it to have any use, it needs to be disseminated to other people in the team.

A further exercise to broaden the student's perspective is the review of a feasibility report. While a basic understanding of commercial feasibility may be useful in the future, being able to assess technical feasibility will be crucial. Learning the factors that contribute to a design's technical feasibility will encourage the student to consider competing designs and to choose the most appropriate one.

On graduation, a student should at least have been introduced to each artefact in the artefact-centric framework. S/he should know what information is to be found in each and how s/he will be expected to contribute to them. S/he will realise that commercial software development is a team activity and will have learned how to disseminate artefacts that are clearly understandable. S/he will also appreciate that the goal of the exercise is to make money for the company, so lower-cost alternatives are often better than technically interesting ones.

Thus, such a curriculum would identify the trigger artefacts and teach students how to analyse them critically. It will only expose the student to the synthesis of the more technical artefacts. However, the cyclical model will require that these synthesised artefacts are clearly presented and disseminated to the rest of the group.

In terms of the software engineering discourse's second personnel concern, one of Ford and Gibb's (1996) criteria that define a mature profession is continuous professional development. Vroom (1964) makes the observation that for "most people the range of possible [career] alternatives from which to choose is greatly limited by the restricted range of information which they have concerning the world of work" (p.76). Based on the interview data, software practitioners appear to have a limited perspective of the commercial aspects of the development process.

This suggests that software developers should be encouraged to pursue circumferential career paths, where the employee seeks assignments in other areas in order to build up a better picture of how the entire organisation works (Schein 1990). Dalton, Thompson and Price (1977) endorse this activity as providing a sound basis for stages III and IV of a career.

The lack of inter-disciplinary integration appears to be a general problem with organisations. As Grant (1996) points out: "the wider the scope of knowledge being integrated (and hence, the greater the diversity of the individuals involved), the lower the level of common knowledge, and the more inefficient the communication and integration of knowledge" (p.380). The multi-disciplinary nature of professional software development, with all its potential career alternatives, is highlighted by bringing artefacts to the centre. Aside from its technical responsibilities, a development team will have to interact with groups both within and outside the company. For instance, this study has identified the following:

Outside the Company:

- Existing customers
- Potential customers
- Business intelligence agencies
- Regulatory bodies
- Equipment vendors
- Shipping companies
- Partner companies
- Competitor companies

Within the Company:

- Sales and marketing people
- Finance people
- Legal people
- Purchasing staff

Although there is an acknowledgement that the changing face of technology is having an impact on career paths as we know them (Trauth et al. 1993; Calitz, Watson and Kock 1997), the only formal means of pursuing different careers within software development appears to be the two-track career path. This has been encountered in the current study and also in the literature (Bailyn and Lynch 1983; Igbaria et al. 1991; Tan and Igbaria 1993; Andrews and Niederman 1998; McGovern 1998; Joseph, Ang and Slaughter 2005). However, the artefact-centric framework encourages us to look outside the development team and to see potential career advancement in a multi-disciplinary way.

For instance, one of the principal artefacts in this study is the feasibility report. This involves input from the systems architects and programmers, who determine technical feasibility and provide time and headcount estimates; the finance department who converts those time estimates into monetary amounts; while the product manager and the sales and marketing people work together to estimate potential revenue.

It seems an obvious progression for the systems architect to build up the necessary financial skills to provide actual costings for the development effort. A further progression would be to acquire the necessary market and commercial knowledge to estimate the potential revenue of the proposed product. Being able to understand the entire feasibility process will make this person much more effective in a future managerial role.

Similarly, as the software industry develops in low-wage economies, the 'build or buy' decision (Boehm 1981) becomes crucial, with more companies deciding to sub-contract their software development. Now the process becomes one of developing exact requirements and comprehensive test plans – what Maiden and Ncube (1998) term "Procurement-oriented Requirements Engineering". The practitioner needs to build up a certain amount of legal expertise to negotiate proper contracts. S/he will also have to understand the cost implications of the buying decisions and be able to justify them, using terminology that accountants understand such as returns on investment and net present values.

A further example is that of the requirements document. This draws on extensive domain knowledge, with both the product managers and systems architects needing to appreciate the customers' business models and to understand what their concerns are. Understanding of customer concerns has been seen at both ends of the development process. Some of the interviewees cite initial visits to customer sites as cathartic learning experiences. Also, one of the systems architects notes how dealing with a potential customer involves more than satisfying their technical people; finance and marketing departments have to be convinced as well.

Thus a person's career can develop along lines other than managerial or technical. Customer-facing roles are available for those who want to increase their exposure to the problem domain, while legal and financial progression is also possible. It is important to stress that these career paths will not necessarily lead to a software practitioner becoming an accountant or a lawyer. By learning the language of these other professions, the technical person can better span the boundary between the development team and the outside world. Thus, because certain artefacts exist on this boundary, the interfaces between the two worlds are clearly marked.

This project has drawn extensively from the skills surveys carried out in the IS computer personnel research arena (Trauth et al. 1993; Lee et al. 1995; Misic 1996; Sawyer et al. 1998; Shi and Bennett 1998; Sumner 2001; Noll and Wilkins 2002). Has the artefact-centric framework anything to contribute to this discourse? In an effort to justify the use of the IS studies, data from this project was used to define the role of the systems architect, as seen in the Irish facilities studied (Downey 2006b). This definition proved to be comparable to Misic's definition of a systems analyst (Misic 1996). While it must be acknowledged that this comparison may only be valid for architects working in subsidiary companies, it does suggest that the artefact-centric framework could provide a useful basis for further computer personnel research. Particularly when the IS practitioners have even more difficulties in defining roles – having to ask the basic question: "who is the IT workforce?" (Kaarst-Brown and Guzman 2005).

Given its potential to contribute to both the IS and software engineering personnel discourses, the artefact-centric framework may act as a bridgehead between these two related disciplines. Certainly both would have a lot to gain. Studies by the IS researchers have covered the areas of how personality affects practitioners in different roles (Moore 1991), what factors influence turnover (Trauth 1999; Agarwal and Ferratt 2000; Meland, Waage and Sein 2005), career orientation (Igbaria et al. 1991; Igbaria and Baroudi 1993) and general job satisfaction (Igbaria, Parasuraman and Badawy 1994). On the other hand, software engineering researchers have much to suggest on the topic of professionalism and certainly, it would be useful to have their ideas on engineering education including into the IS model curriculum (Gorgone, Davis, Valacich, Topi, Feinstein and Longenecker 2003).

Finally, the research presented in this thesis provides a different perspective on the findings of the Irish government advisory bodies' reports (Forfas 2003; Enterprise Strategy Group 2004). The central message from these reports is that the Irish economy needs to add more value and develop a presence along the entire value chain. To achieve this, educational institutions are advised to produce graduates with higher skill levels. Because this research project focuses on senior practitioners – ones who justify their higher pay by adding more value than entry-level practitioners – it is uniquely placed to comment on the skills needed to add extra value. As shown in chapter 8, senior practitioners require management as well as sales and marketing skills – endorsing the government bodies' findings. However, this chapter also suggests that the current organisational structures require neither business nor high-order technical research skills. In other words, if the status quo remains, it would be pointless to develop skills in the last two areas. Unfortunately, if the multinational sector relocates to lower-wage economies, the Irish software industry will have to create its own organisations and carve niches in the marketplace with new, original products and services. In this scenario, not only will business and research skills be called for, but people with entrepreneurial career anchors will be needed as well (Schein 1990).

9.1 Future Research

Knowledge and skills/abilities are required to get things done in an organisation. Therefore, any insights into what KSAs are actually needed is useful. The artefact-centric framework may provide a starting point for any organisation interested in establishing what it requires of its people. A conclusion from this project is that many of the skills/abilities applied by the informants are generic ones – communicating, collaborating and providing input into the decision-making process. This idea of commonality is also alluded to by some of the interviewees, who note that both project management and design are transferable skills.

This insight would be tremendously useful for educators and trainers if it could be shown to really apply. Obviously, further study in the software sector would be needed to add confidence to these findings, but if similar studies were conducted in other project-based industries, where the artefacts are radically different – such as building construction or movie-making – would the same generic skills come to the surface? Would knowledge divide up under the same categories?

If project management is truly a transferable skill, can we state that projects themselves are all basically the same? Do all project workers have to demonstrate the same core set of skills, augmented by a specialised knowledge base and technical skill set? Because university faculties and organisational functions are all divided according to these specialised KSAs, how can the skills needed to become an effective project team member be learned?

It would be interesting to explore the advantages and disadvantages of teaching generic project skills in schools, or in universities, or in the workplace. Indeed, it might be argued that these skills can only be acquired through experiential learning (Kolb 1984). Certainly the informants in this study acquired many of their non-technical skills through trial and error. If these are truly generic KSAs, then they should apply to blue-collar as well as to white-collar teams.

Given the emergence of distributed, virtual teams (Steinfield 2002), the importance of team formation is of critical interest to researchers and practitioners. Understanding how teams communicate and collaborate remotely may be facilitated by studying the artefacts that these teams use to communicate. How can these be adapted to facilitate the flow of information and understanding among the team?

If attempts are made to replicate this study, then the interviews would need to bring artefacts to the fore. It can be seen in the skills tables of chapter 6 that there are holes in the data. Because the interviewees were prompted to explain what they did in terms of project phases, a full picture of each artefact did not emerge. The interviewer should ask the participants about their roles as before, but probe in more detail when an artefact is mentioned. The researcher would determine what phases of the artefact lifecycle they participate in, as well as identifying who else is involved with the artefact. Which KSAs are employed in each phase could be elicited with the help of a checklist.

If the goal is to confirm the findings of this study, then a questionnaire survey may be applicable. The forty-three identified artefacts could be presented one at a time and the respondents asked to identify what phases of the artefact lifecycle they contribute to. For each phase they work on, the types of knowledge (six) and skills/abilities (twenty-eight) that they brought to bear must be canvassed. For a senior programmer, who deals with most of the artefacts, this may prove to be a tedious exercise. The researcher also needs to provide concise descriptions of each artefact as terminology differs between companies. Scope needs to be provided to allow the respondent describe other artefacts, ones that were not uncovered in this project.

If studies replicating this project endorse its findings, then the whole subject of KSAs in the project context will have a useful artefact-centric framework to base further work on.

REFERENCES

Adair, J. (2003). *The Inspirational Leader: How to Motivate, Encourage and Achieve Success*. London, Kogan Page Ltd.

—. (2004). *The John Adair Handbook of Management and Leadership*. London, Thorogood Publishing Ltd.

Agarwal, R. and T. W. Ferratt (2000). *Retention and the Career Motives of IT Professionals*. ACM SIGCPR conference on Computer personnel research, Chicago, Illinois, ACM Press.

Andrews, A. and F. Niederman (1998). *A Firm-Level Model of IT Personnel Planning*. ACM SIGCPR conference on Computer personnel research, Boston, Massachusetts, ACM Press.

Bailey, J. L. and G. Stefaniak (1999). "Preparing the Information Technology Workforce For The New Millennium." *ACM SIGCPR Computer Personnel* **20**(4): 4-15.

Bailyn, L. and J. T. Lynch (1983). "Engineering as a life-long career: its meaning, its satisfactions, its difficulties." *Journal of Occupational Behaviour* **4**(4): 263-283.

Bandura, A. (1986). *Social Foundations of Thought & Action: A Social Cognitive Theory*. Englewood Cliffs, New Jersey, Prentice Hall.

Bass, L., P. Clements and R. Kazman (2003). *Software Architecture in Practice*, Addison-Wesley.

Beck, K. (2000). *eXtreme Programming eXplained: Embrace Change*, Addison-Wesley.

Belbin, R. M. (2000). *Beyond the Team*. Oxford, Elsevier Butterworth-Heinemann.

Birk, A., G. Heller, I. John K. Schmid, T. Von Der Masser and K. Muller (2003). "Product Line Engineering: The State of the Practice." *IEEE Software* **20**(6): 52-60.

Blanton, J. E., T. Schambach and K.J. Trimmer (1998). "Factors affecting Professional Competence of Information Technology Professionals." *ACM SIGCPR Computer Personnel* **19**(3): 4-19.

Boehm, B. and L. G. Huang (2003). "Value-Based Software Engineering: A Case Study." *IEEE Computer* **36**(3): 33-41.

Boehm, B. and R. Turner (2003). "Using Risk To Balance Agile and Plan Driven Methods." *IEEE Computer* **36**(6): 57-66.

Boehm, B. W. (1981). *Software Engineering Economics*. Englewood Cliffs, New Jersey, Prentice-Hall.

Boehm, B. W., M. H. Penedo, E. D. Stuckle, R. D. Williams and A. B. Pyster (1984). "A Software Development Environment for Improving Productivity." *Computer* **17**(6): 30-44.

Brooks, F. P. (1972). *The Mythical Man Month*, Addison Wesley.

—. (1986). *No Silver Bullet - Essence and Accidents of Software Engineering*. Information Processing 86, Elsevier Science Publishers B.V.

Calitz, A. P., M. B. Watson and G. de V. de Kock (1997). *Identification and Selection of Successful Future IT Personnel in a Changing Technological and Business Environment*. Proceedings of the 1997 SIGCPR Conference on Computer Personnel Research, San Francisco, ACM Press.

Carnegie Mellon Software Engineering Institute (2008). Capability Maturity Model Integration. **2008:** *http://www.sei.cmu.edu/cmmi*.

Chavez, A., C. Tornabene and G. Wiederhold (1998). "Software Component Licensing: A Primer." *IEEE Software* **15**(5): 47-53.

Cheng, M.-I. and A. R. J. Dainty (2005). "What makes a good project manager?" *Human Resource Management Journal* **15**(1): 25-37.

Cluts, M. M. (2003). *The Evolution of Artifacts in Cooperative Work: Constructing Meaning Through Activity*. ACM SIGGROUP 2003, Florida, USA, ACM Press.

Coffey, A. and P. Atkinson (1996). *Making Sense of Qualitative Data*, Sage Publications.

Colwell, B. (2002). "Near Misses: Murphy's Law Is Wrong." *IEEE Computer* **35**(3): 8-12.

Cook, S. D. N. and J. Seely-Brown (1999). "Bridging Epistemologies: The Generative Dance Between Organizational Knowledge and Organizational Knowing." *Organizational Science* **10**(4): 381-400.

Curtis, B., W. E. Hefley and S.A. Miller (2001). *People Capability Maturity Model (P-CMM)*. Pittsburgh, Carnegie Mellon, Software Engineering Institute.

Dalton, G. W., P. H. Thompson and R. L. Price (1977). "The Four Stages of Professional Careers - A New Look at Performance by Professionals." *Organizational Dynamics* **6**(1): 19-44.

DeMarco, T. (2001). *Slack - Getting Past Burnout, Busywork and the Myth of Total Efficiency*, Dorset House.

DeMarco, T. and T. Lister (1999). *Peopleware: Productive Projects and Teams*, Dorset House.

Demarest, M. (1997). "Understanding Knowledge Management." *Journal of Long Range Planning* **30**(3): 374-384.

Dijkstra, E. W. (1969). *Structured Programming*. Software Engineering Techniques, Rome, Italy, Nato Science Committee.

—. (2001). "The End of Computing Science?" *Communications of the ACM* **44**(3): 92.

Downey, J. (2005). *A Framework to Elicit the Skills Needed for Software Development*. 2005 ACM SIGMIS CPR Conference, Atlanta, Georgia, ACM Press.

—. (2006a). The Knowledge, Skills and Abilities Required for Telecommunications Software Development: An Artefact-centric Framework (PhD Thesis). *Computer Science and Information Systems*. Limerick, University of Limerick: 310.

—. (2006b). *Systems Architect and Systems Analyst: Are These Comparable Roles?* 2006 ACM SIGMIS CPR Conference, Claremont, California, ACM Press.

Drucker, P. F. (1999). "Managing Oneself." *Harvard Business Review* **77**(2): 64-74.

Eisenhardt, K. M. (1989). "Building Theories from Case Study Research." *Academy of Management Review* **14**(4): 532-550.

Enterprise Strategy Group (2004). Ahead of the Curve: Ireland's Place in the Global Economy. Dublin, Forfas.

Fitzgerald, B. and D. Howcroft (1998). "Towards Dissolution of the IS Research Debate: From Polarisation to Polarity." *Journal of Information Technology* **13**(4): 313-326.

Fleishman, E. A. (1975). "Towards a Taxonomy of Human Performance." *American Psychologist* **30**(12): 1127-1149.

Ford, G. and N. E. Gibbs (1996). A Mature Profession of Software Engineering, Carnegie Mellon University: 1-94.

Forfas (2003). Responding to Ireland's Skills Needs, The Fourth Report of the Expert Group on Future Skills Needs. Dublin, Forfas: 24-33, 86-94.

Gabarro, J. J. and J. P. Ritter (1980). "Managing Your Boss." *Harvard Business Review* **58**(1): 92-100.

Galbraith, J. R. (1973). *Designing Complex Organizations*. Reading, Massechusetts, Addison-Wesley.

Gartner (2008). The Gartner Group. **2008:** *http://www.gartner.com*.

Goldkuhl, G. and S. Cronholm (2003). *Multi-grounded theory - Adding theoretical grounding to grounded theory*. 2nd European Conference on Research Methods in Business and Management, Reading, England.

Gorgone, J. T., G. B. Davis, J. S. Valacich, H. Topi, D. L. Feinstein and H. E. Longenecker (2003). "IS 2002: Model Curriculum and Guidelines for Undergraduate Degree Programs in Information Systems." *The Database for Advances in Information Systems* **34**(1): 52.

Gotterbarn, D. (1999). "A Positive Step Towards A Profession: The Software Engineering Code of Ethics and Professional Practice." *Software Engineering Notes* **24**(1): 9-14.

Graham, I. (2003). "The Compleat Requirements Analyste." *IEEE Software* **20**(6): 99-101.

Grant, R. M. (1996). "Prospering in Dynamically-competitive Environments: Organizational Capability as Knowledge Integration." *Organization Science* **7**(4): 375-387.

Hackman, J. R. and G. R. Oldham (1980). *Work Redesign*. Reading Massachusetts, Adison-Wesley.

Harrisberger, L., R. Heydinger, J. Seeley and M. Talburtt (1976). *Experiential Learning in Engineering Education*. Washington D.C., American Society for Engineering Education.

Hart, C. (1998). *Doing a Literature Review*. London, Sage publications Ltd.

Hatton, L. (1998). "Does OO Sync with How We Think." *IEEE Software* **15**(3): 46-54.

Herzberg, F., B. Mausner and B. B. Snyderman (1959). *The Motivation To Work*, John Wiley & Sons Inc.

Hilburn, T. B. (1997). "Software Engineering Education: A Modest Proposal." *IEEE Software* **14**(6): 44-48.

Hilburn, T. B. and W. S. Humphrey (2002). "Teaching Teamwork." *IEEE Software* **19**(5): 72-77.

Hofstede, G. (1984). *Culture's Consequences*. London, Sage Publications.

Holmes, N. (1999). "Software Engineering: To Be or What To Be?" *Software Engineering Notes* **24**(3): 81-83.

—.. (2002). "To See Ourselves As Others See Us." *IEEE Computer* **35**(1): 142-144.

IDA Ireland (2008). Business Sectors/ICT/Software. Dublin. **2008:** Industrial Development Authority summary on employment in the Irish software sector.

IEEE Computer Society (1998). *IEEE Recommended Practice for Software Acquisition*. New York, IEEE Inc.

—. (2001). *IEEE Standard for Software User Documentation*. New York, IEEE Inc.

—. (2003). *IEEE Guide Adoption of PMI Standard: A Guide to the Project Management Body of Knowledge*. New York, IEEE Inc.

—. (2004). *Guide to the Software Engineering Body Of Knowledge*. Los Alamitos, California, IEEE Computer Society, Los Alamitos, California.

Igbaria, M. and J. J. Baroudi (1993). "A Short-Form Measure of Career Orientations: A Psychometric Evaluation." *Journal of Management Information Systems* **10**(2): 131-154.

Igbaria, M., J. H. Greenhaus and S. Parasuraman (1991). "Career Orientations of MIS Employees: An Empirical Analysis." *MIS Quarterly* **15**(2): 151-169.

Igbaria, M., S. Parasuraman and M. K. Badawy (1994). "Work Experiences, Job Involvement, and Quality of Work Life Among Information Systems Personnel." *MIS Quarterly* **18**(2): 175-201.

Irish Computer Society (2008). Irish Computer Society Website. **2008:** *http://www.ics.ie*.

Jackson, M. (1983). *System Design*. Englewood Cliffs, New Jersey, Prentice-Hall, Inc.

—.. (1998a). "Defining a Discipline of Description." *IEEE Software* **15**(5): 14-17.

—.. (1998b). "Will There Ever Be Software Engineering?" *IEEE Software* **15**(1): 36-39.

Jackson, N. and P. Carter (2000). *Rethinking Organisational Behaviour*. Harlow, Essex, Pearson Education Ltd/Prentice Hall.

Jacobson, I., G. Booch and J. Rumbaugh (1999). *The Unified Software Development Process*. Reading, Massachusetts, Addison Wesley.

Jones, C. (2003). "Variations in Software Development Practices." *IEEE Software* **20**(6): 22-27.

Joseph, D., S. Ang and S. Slaughter (2005). *Identifying the Prototypical Career Paths of IT Professionals: A Sequence and Cluster Analysis*. 2005 ACM SIGMIS CPR Conference, Atlanta, Georgia, ACM Press.

Kaarst-Brown, M. L. and I. R. Guzman (2005). *Who is "the IT Workforce"?: Challenges Facing Policy Makers, Educators, Management, and Research*. 2005 ACM SIGMIS CPR Conference, Atlanta, Georgia, ACM Press.

Keane, B. (2005). Attitudes and Experiences within the Indian and Irish Software Communities. *Computer Science and Information Systems*. Limerick, University of Limerick.

Kepner, C. H. and B. B. Tregoe (1981). *The New Rational Manager*. Princeton, New Jersey, Kepner Tragoe, Inc.

Knowles, M. S., E. F. Holton and R. A. Swanson (1998). *The Adult Learner*. Woburn, MA, Butterworth-Heinemann.

Kolb, D. A. (1984). *Experiential Learning: Experience as the Source of Learning and Development*. Englewood Cliffs, New Jersey, Prentice Hall.

Kolb, D. A., I. M. Rubin and J. M. McIntyre (1974). *Organizational Psychology: An Experiential Approach*. Englewood Cliffs, New Jersey, Prentice-Hall Inc.

Kuhn, S. (1998). "The Software Design Studio: An Exploration." *IEEE Software* **15**(2): 65-71.

Larman, C. and V. R. Basili (2003). "Iterative and Incremental Development: A Brief History." *IEEE Computer* **36**(6): 47-56.

Lawson, B. (1980). *How Designers Think*. London, The Architectural Press.

Lee, D. M. S., E. M. Trauth and D. Farwell (1995). "Critical Skills and Knowledge Requirements of IS Professionals: A Joint Academic/Industry Investigation." *MIS Quarterly* **17**(3): 313-340.

Lehman, M. M. (1998). "Software's Future: Managing Evolution." *IEEE Software* **15**(1): 40-44.

Lemon, N. (1973). *Attitudes and Their Measurement*. London, B.T. Batsford Ltd.

Lethbridge, T. C., S. E. Sim J. Singer (2005). "Studying Software Engineers: Data Collection Techniques for Software Field Studies." *Empirical Software Engineering* **10**(3): 311-341.

Lewin, K. (1952). *Field Theory in Social Science: Selected Theoretical Papers*. New York, Tavistock Publications.

Lhermitte, M. (2004). Ernst & Young European Attractiveness Survey, Ernst & Young: 28.

Litecky, C. R., K. P. Arnett and B. Prabhaker (2004). "The Paradox of Soft Skills versus Technical Skills in IS Hiring." *Journal of Computer Information Systems* **45**(1): 69-76.

Maguire, T. (2004). How to Capture Data: Methods, integrity, difficulties and possible solutions. Limerick, Unpublished. **2004:** *http://www.ul.ie/phdforum/TerryMaguireFeb2004_files/frame.htm.*

Maiden, N. A. and C. Ncube (1998). "Acquiring COTS Software Selection Requirements." *IEEE Software* **15**(2): 46-56.

Mambrey, P. and M. Robinson (1997). *Understanding the Role of Documents in a Hierarchical Flow of Work*. ACM SIGGROUP 1997, Phoenix, Arizona, ACM Press.

Martinez-Solano, L. E., M. Giblin and E. Walshe (2005). Knowledge Intensive Service Activities in the Irish Software Industry: Country Report for the OECD KISA Project, 2002-2005. Galway, OECD**:** 75.

McConnell, S. (1993). *Code Complete*. Redmond, Washington, Microsoft Press.

McConnell, S. and L. Tripp (1999). "Professional Software Engineering: Fact or Fiction?" *IEEE Software* **16**(6): 13-18.

McGovern, P. (1998). *HRM, Technical Workers and the Multinational Corporation*, Routledge.

McIver Consulting (2004). Synthesis Report / Literature Review on Aspects of Training of those at Work in Ireland. Dublin, FAS Expert Group on Future Skills Needs: 49.

Meland, H., R. P. Waage and M. K. Sein (2005). *The Other Side of Turnover: Managing IT Personnel Strategically*. 2005 ACM SIGMIS CPR Conference, Atlanta, Georgia, ACM Press.

Miles, M. B. and A. M. Huberman (1994). *Qualitative Data Analysis*. Thousand Oaks, California, Sage Publications.

Mill, S. (2002). "Become an Indispensable Asset." *Computing Canada* **28**(2): 25.

Mintzberg, H. (1998). "Covert Leadership: Notes on Managing Professionals." *Harvard Business Review* **76**(6): 140-147.

Miranda, E. (2002). "Planning and Executing Time-Bound Projects." *IEEE Computer* **35**(3): 73-79.

Misic, M. M. (1996). "The Skills Needed by Today's Systems Analysts." *Journal of Systems Management* **47**(3): 34-40.

Misic, M. M. and N. L. Russo (2000). "Reading between the lines: an examination of systems analysis and design texts." *The Journal of Systems and Software* **50**(1): 65-73.

Moore, J. E. (1991). Personality Characteristics of Information Systems Professionals. *Proceedings of the 1991 conference on Computer Personnel Research*. Athens, Georgia, ACM Press: 140-155.

Morisio, M., I. Stamelos and A. Tsoukias (2002). *A New Method to Evaluate Software Artifacts Against Predefined Profiles*. ACM SIGSSEKE, Ischia, Italy, ACM Press.

Myers, G. J. (2004). *The Art of Software Testing*. Hoboken, New Jersey, John Wiley & Sons, Inc.

Nichols, R. G. and L. A. Stevens (1957). "Listening to People." *Harvard Business Review* **35**(5): 85-92.

Noll, C. L. and M. Wilkins (2002). "Critical Skills of IS Professionals: A Model for Curriculum Development." *Journal of Information Technology Education* **1**(3): 143-154.

Norris, M. and P. Rigby (1992). *Software Engineering Explained*. Chichester, England, John Wiley & Sons.

Office for National Statistics (2000a). *Standard Occupational Classification - Volume 1*. London, The Stationary Office.

—. (2000b). *Standard Occupational Classification - Volume 2*. London, The Stationary Office.

O'Malley, E. and C. O'Gorman (1997). *The Irish Indigenous Software Industry: An Application of Porter's Cluster Analysis*. Dublin, National Economic and Social Council.

Ovum (2008). Advising on the commercial impact of technology and market changes in telecoms, software and IT services. **2008:** *http://www.ovum.com*.

Parnas, D. and L. Chik-Parnas (2005). "Goals for Software Engineering Student Education." *ACM SIGSOFT Software Engineering Notes* **30**(4): 6-8.

Parnas, D. L. (1999). "Software Engineering Programs Are Not Computer Science Programs." *IEEE Software* **16**(6): 19-30.

Patton, M. Q. (1987). *How to Use Qualitative Methods in Evaluation*. Newbury Park, California, SAGE Publications, Inc.

Raccoon, L. B. S. (2001). "Definitions and Demographics." *Software Engineering Notes* **26**(1): 82-91.

Ramachandran, S. and S. V. Rao (2006). *An Effort Towards Identifying Occupational Culture among Information Systems Professionals*. 2006 ACM SIGMIS CPR, Claremont, California, ACM Press.

Reifer, D. J. (2004). "Catching the Brass Ring." *IEEE Software* **21**(3): 12-14.

—. (2005). "Educating Software Engineers: An Industry Viewpoint." *ACM SIGSOFT Software Engineering Notes* **30**(3): 8-9.

Roper, M. (1994). *Software Testing*. Maidenhead, England, McGraw-Hill.

Ryan, A. M. and N. T. Tippins (2004). "Attracting and Selecting: What Psychological Research Tells Us." *Human Resource Management* **43**(4): 305-318.

Saur, J. (2005). "Project Management (Here we go again!)." *ACM SIGSOFT Software Engineering Notes* **30**(4): 8.

Sawyer, S., K. R. Eschenfelder, A. Diekema and C. R. McClure (1998). "Corporate IT Skill Needs: a Case Study of BigCo." *ACM SIGCPR Computer Personnel* **19**(2): 27-41.

Schein, E. H. (1990). *Career Anchors: Discovering Your Real Values*. San Diego, Pfeiffer & Co.

—. (1999). *The Corporate Culture Survival Guide*. San Francisco, Jossey-Bass.

Schenk, K. D., N. P. Vitalari and K. S. Davis (1998). "Differences Between Novice and Expert Systems Analysts: What Do We Know and What Do We Do?" *Journal of Management Information Systems* **15**(1): 9-50.

Schwaber, K. (1997). *SCRUM Software Development Process*. Business Object Design and Implementation: OOPSLA '95, Austin, Texas, Springer-Verlag Telos.

Schwarz Pharma (2006). Search and Development. **2006:** *http://www.schwarzpharma.com/?node_id=126*.

Seely-Brown, J. and P. Duguid (1991). "Organizational Learning and Communities-of-Practice: Toward a Unified View of Working, Learning, and Innovation." *Organization Science* **2**(1): 40-57.

SFIA Foundation (2008). Skills Framework for an Information Age. **2008:** *http://www.sfia.org.uk*.

Shapero, A. (1985). *Managing Professional People: Understanding Creative Performance*. New York, The Free Press.

Shaw, M. (2000). *Software Engineering Education: A Roadmap*. 22nd International Conference on Software Engineering, Limerick, Ireland, ACM Press.

Shi, N. and D. Bennett (1998). "Requisite IS Management Knowledge and Skills Construct: A Survey." *ACM SIGCPR Computer Personnel* **19**(1): 3-19.

Speed, J. R. (1999). "What Do You Mean I Can't Call Myself a Software Engineer?" *IEEE Software* **16**(6): 45-50.

Steinfield, C. (2002). "Realizing the Benefits of Virtual Teams." *IEEE Computer* **35**(3): 104-106.

Sterne, J. (2004). *Adventures in Code*. Dublin, The Liffey Press.

Strauss, A. and J. Corbin (1998). *Basics of Qualitative Research*. Thousand Oaks, California, Sage Publications, Inc.

Sumner, M. (2001). *A Report on Industry-University Roundtable Discussions on Recruitment and Retention of High-Tech Professionals*. ACM SIGCPR Conference on Computer Personnel Research.

Surendran, K., H. Hays and A. Macfarlane (2002). "Simulating a Software Engineering Apprenticeship." *IEEE Software* **19**(5): 49-55.

Swanson, E. B. (1976). *The Dimensioning of Maintenance*. IEEE/ACM Second International Conference on Software Engineering, San Francisco, IEEE Computer Society Press.

Tan, M. and M. Igbaria (1993). *Exploring the Status of Turnover and Salary of Information Technology Professionals in Singapore*. ACM SIGCPR, St. Louis, Missouri, ACM Press.

Tomayko, J. E. (1998). "Forging a discipline: An outline history of software engineering education." *Annals of Software Engineering* **6**(1-4): 3-18.

Trauth, E. M. (1999). *Who Owns my Soul? The Paradox of Pursuing Organizational Knowledge in a Work Culture of Individualism*. ACM SIGCPR Conference on Computer Personnel Research.

—. (2000). *The Culture of an Information Economy*. Dordrecht, The Netherlands, Kluwer Academic Publishers.

Trauth, E. M., D. W. Farwell and D. Lee (1993). "The IS Expectation Gap: Industry Expectations Versus Academic Preparation." *MIS Quarterly* **17**(3): 293-307.

Turley, R. T. and J. M. Beiman (1995). "Competencies of Exceptional and Nonexceptional Software Engineers." *Journal of Systems Software* **28**(1): 19-38.

Turner, J. R. and R. Muller (2003). "On the nature of the project as a temporary organization." *International Journal of Project Management* **21**(1): 1-8.

Turski, W. M. (1986). *And No Philosophers' Stone Either*. Information Processing 86, Elsevier Science Publishers B.V.

Vitalari, N. P. and G. W. Dickson (1983). "Problem Solving for Effective Systems Analysis: An Experimental Exploration." *Communications of the ACM* **26**(11): 948-956.

Vroom, V. H. (1964). *Work and Motivation*. New York, John Wiley and Sons Inc.

Walsham, G. (2002). "Cross-Cultural Software Production and Use: A Structurational Analysis." *MIS Quarterly* **26**(4): 359-380.

Walton, J. (1985). *Escort MkI 1, 2, & 3: The Development and Competition History*. Yeovil, Somorset, Haynes.

Weinberg, G. M. (1971). *The Psychology of Computer Programming*. New York, Van Nostrand Reinhold Company.

Wernick, P. (1996). A Belief Model for Software Development. A Framework By Analogy. London, University College London.

Weyuker, E. J. (1998). "Testing Component-Based Software: A Cautionary Tale." *IEEE Software* **15**(5): 54-59.

Williams, L. and A. Cockburn (2003). "Agile Software Development: It's About Feedback and Change." *IEEE Computer* **36**(6): 39-43.

Wing, M. (2005). "Toward a Great and Enduring Profession." *ACM SIGSOFT Software Engineering Notes* **30**(3): 9-11.

Winston, A. W. (2004). "Engineering Management - A personal Perspective." *IEEE Transactions on Engineering Management* **51**(4): 412-413.

Womack, J. P., D. T. Jones and D. Roos (1990). *The Machine That Changed The World*. New York, Simon & Schuster.

Wynekoop, J. L. and D. B. Walz (2000). "Investigating traits of top performing software developers." *Information Technology and People* **13**(3): 186-195.

Yin, R. K. (1994). *Case Study Research: Design and Methods*. Thousand Oaks, California, Sage Publications, Inc.

Yourdon, E. (1975). *Techniques of Program Structure and Design*. Englewood Cliffs, New Jersey, Prentice-Hall Inc.

APPENDIX A

EVOLUTION OF THE INTERVIEW CHECKLISTS

A1. Initial Checklist

The initial interview checklist contained two fundamental weaknesses:

1. The phases of the software development lifecycle given under the "Role" heading were informed by personal experience rather than the literature. The items listed were also too closely packed, allowing little space to write notes.

2. The discussion of skills gathered from other disciplines did not work well in the "Skills" section. Moving it to the "Acquiring Skills" area proved much better as it logically followed questions about the informant's career path.

Interviewee	
Date	

Role

Job Title	
Sales Support	
- RFQ Responses	
Requirements	
- Customer Interaction	
- Modelling/Prototyping	
- Management/tracking	
Analysis	
- Formal methods	
- Scenarios/Use Cases	
Architecture	

- Top Down Hierarchical	
- Object Oriented	
- COTS Software	
Design	
- Structured Design	
- Object Oriented	
- Ad Hoc	
Coding	
- Languages	
- Scripting Languages	
- Code Inspections	
- Coding Standards	
- Version Control	
Test	
- Unit testing	
- Integration	
- System	
Documentation	
- Internal	
- Customer	
Project Management	
- Team Leading	
- Scheduling	
Product Management	
Field Support	
- Installations	
- Fault Management	
Quality	

Skills

Technical	
- Analysis	
- Design	
- Code	
- Test	
- Technical Writing	
Business	
- Costing	
- Planning	
- Recruitment	
- Contract Negotiation	
- Budgeting	
Inter-personal	
- Corporate Politics/Culture	
- Teamwork	
- Team Leading/Managing	
- Motivation	
- Planning	
- Co-ordination	
- Interviewing	
- Customer Interaction	
- Negotiation	
- Understanding	
- Conflict Resolution	
- Supplier Interaction	
- Negotiation	
- Understanding	
- Conflict Resolution	
From Other Disciplines	
- Media	
- Medicine	
- Hardware	
- Government	
- ?	

Acquiring Skills

School	
- Career Guidance	
- Business Studies	
- Civics	
- Oral Exams	
Sports	
- Teamwork	
- Motivation	
- Leadership	
University/Third Level	
- Computer Science	
- Engineering	
- Other (with computing content)	
- Other (without computing content)	
Experience	
- Mentoring	
- Professional Training	
- Book Reading	
- Trial & Error	
- Night Classes	
Hobbies	
- Presentation Skills	
- Committees	
- Teamwork	
- Negotiation	
- Fundraising	
- Budgeting	

A2. Final Checklist

The final checklist draws more formally from the literature. The "Role" question is explored using input from the various IEEE guides. The main source for the revised layout is the Guide to the Software Engineering Body of Knowledge (IEEE Computer Society 2004). However, it also benefits from insights in the Project Management Body of Knowledge (IEEE Computer Society 2003) and the guides to user documentation (IEEE Computer Society 2001) and purchasing third-party software (IEEE Computer Society 1998).

Both the "Skills" and "Acquiring Skills" questions benefit from the skills surveys carried out in the information systems literature (Trauth et al. 1993; Lee et al. 1995; Misic 1996; Sawyer et al. 1998; Shi and Bennett 1998; Bailey and Stefaniak 1999; Noll and Wilkins 2002). The "Skills" question was approached in the early interviews by stating each skill in turn and letting the interviewee answer in any way s/he saw fit. Early analysis showed that the interviewees were taking three different approaches to answering the questions so a prompt was added to the checklist to ensure that the interviewees discussed their understanding of the subject, that they specified the methodology they used (if any) and, finally, that they mentioned any training they received in the area.

Another evolution of the checklist is the increase in the amount of white space provided. As well as giving more room to take notes, it also makes it easier to reference the checklist during the interview.

Interviewee	
Date	

Role

Job Title	
Product Management	
- Sales	
- Pre-Sales Support	
- RFQ Responses	
- Product Roadmap	

Project Management	
- Project Plan	
- Scope Definition	
- Scheduling	
- Costing / Estimation	
- Recruitment Planning	
Requirements	
- Requirements Elicitation	
- Modelling/Prototyping	
- Management/Tracking	
Analysis	
- Formal methods	
- Scenarios/Use Cases	
Architecture	
- Strategies and Methods	
- Attribute Driven Design	
- COTS Software Components	
Purchasing	
- Choosing Vendors	
- Joint Developments	
- Negotiation	
- Acceptance Criteria	
- Long-term Follow Up	

Design	
- Structured Design	
- Object Oriented	
- Ad Hoc	
Coding	
- 3 / 4 Generation Languages	
- Scripting Languages	
- Visual Languages	
- Integration	
Test	
- Unit testing	
- Integration	
- System	
- Performance	
- Customer Acceptance	
Configuration Management	
- Version Control	
-Release Management	
Documentation	
- Internal	
- Customer	
Maintenance/Customer Support	
- Installations	

- Fault Management	
Quality	
- Root Cause Analysis	
- Requirements Validation	
- Design Validation	
- Code Inspections	
- Coding Standards	

Skills (Understanding, Methodology, Training)

Technical	
- Analysis	
- Design	
- Code	
- Test	
- Technical Writing	
Business	
- Feasibility Studies	
- Costing	
- Planning/Risk Management	
- Contract Negotiation	
- Budgeting	
Inter-personal	
- Corporate Politics/Culture	
- Coping with Ambiguity	
- Teamwork	
- Team Leading/Managing	
- Motivation	

- Planning	
- Co-ordination	
- Interviewing	
- Presentation Skills	
- Customer Interaction	
- Negotiation	
- Understanding	
- Conflict Resolution	
- Giving Training	
- Supplier Interaction	
- Negotiation	
- Understanding	
- Conflict Resolution	

Acquiring Skills

School	
- Career Guidance	
- Business Studies	
- Civics	
- Oral Exams	
University/Third Level	
- Computer Science	
- Engineering	
- Other (with computing content)	
- Other (without computing content)	
Experience	
- Mentoring	
- Opportunities for Promotion	
- Personal Development	
- Professional Training	
- Book Reading	

- Trial & Error	
- Night Classes	
From Other Disciplines	
- Media	
- Medicine	
- Hardware	
- Government	
- ?	
Sports	
- Teamwork	
- Motivation	
- Leadership	
Hobbies	
- Presentation Skills	
- Committees	
- Teamwork	
- Negotiation	
- Fundraising	
- Budgeting	

APPENDIX B

SOFTWARE DEVELOPMENT LIFECYCLE DESCRIPTION

This appendix contains a brief description of the software development process as recounted in the interviews. It is divided into four sections, describing the requirements elicitation process, the feasibility study, how the project is managed and, finally, how the software product is constructed.

B1. Defining Requirements

Figure 40. The Artefacts Involved in Requirements Definition

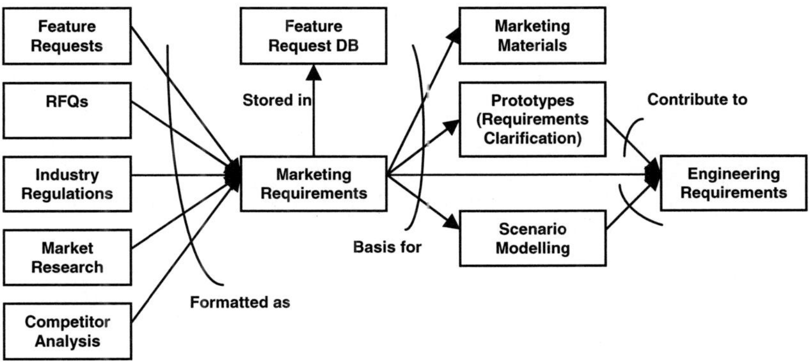

Before any product can be developed, what it should do must be determined. The person responsible for gathering this information is the product manager. The motivation to develop new products or to enhance existing ones comes from a variety of sources. These include:

1. Market research (also called business intelligence). The product managers study the market, assessing the emergence of new technologies and communications protocols. They watch what competing companies are doing (competitor analysis) and may create requirements that allow the product match, or better, the competition.

"So you gather your requirements, either from the market analysis, from your competitor analysis – you're looking at what your competition is doing, you're looking into technology trends. So you're analysing the market and you're talking very closely with your sales and customers, to understand where the market is going."

The product manager may be responsible for carrying this out, but it is often done by a separate marketing function. Indeed, one company in this study used its technical writing group to gather business intelligence. To analyse market information, the product manager must develop a holistic perspective. S/he must understand what market niche the product fits into and how that market is developing. In terms of customer demographics, sales trends and competitor activity, this niche may or may not be viable long-term. The goal is to make the product more attractive to customers, so it is important to be able to identify trends in the marketplace.

2. Existing customers. Having worked with the product, existing customers are in a good position to identify enhancements. The customers quickly realise that the product manager needs to be convinced before a project goes ahead, so they are keen to provide any clarification that is necessary. Development driven by the requirements of individual customers is dangerous as it can pull the product in conflicting directions. A better approach is to choose features that many customers express interest in.

"If you're just being led by customer requirements, what you'll end up with is: All sorts of one-off features which are unusable. So what you really need to do is: When you see something coming up a number of times, or if it's being stressed enough by a small number of customers, you might say: 'This is worthwhile doing'."

These ideas come to the product manager in the form of feature requests (also called change requests). They vary radically in the level of detail provided – sometimes being explained in terms of use-cases. The product manager will often have to arrange meetings with the originator of the request to clarify understanding. In many cases, this will require good listening and comprehension skills, as the customers may not have English as a first language. It also draws on the product manager's analysis skills as s/he needs to elicit enough detail to form an understanding.

"The different sites send in their lists of requirements which are normally pretty rough. They might not be in great English and you have to try and solve for what they really require and send back a list of questions that occurred to you about what they want."

3. Potential customers. These requirements come to the product managers in the form of Requests for Quotation (RFQs). They are also known as Requests for Information (RFIs) or Requests for Proposal (RFPs). These can arrive unsolicited or be the result of successful presentations by the company's sales team. One company estimates that RFQ responses have a one in ten success rate. The product manager has to assure the potential customer that the product satisfies all their requirements either now or in the future. Requesting clarification is a good way of opening dialogue with the tendering company.

"We got the RFI [request for information] from the customer that specifies what they want … Because customers want everything and they will say that they need everything yesterday, in order for you to be able to understand what comes first and how their roadmap looks, you need interaction with customers."

The product manager is tasked with responding to these requests. This requires a certain amount of linguistic legerdemain as the impression must be given that the product satisfies all the customer's needs, even if it does not. Product managers can make good use of the product 'roadmap' here, stating that, while the feature requested is not currently available, it is under development. The features requested in the RFQ often influence the development of the product, as good suggestions may come out of it. Also, if the order is large enough, the product's direction may be changed entirely to accommodate it. The product manager may draw on the systems architect's expertise in responding to these. In return, the exercise exposes the architect to what the market is looking for.

4. Development teams. Just like existing customers, developers regularly produce feature requests for consideration. Often these relate to non-functional requirements like improved performance, reliability and maintainability. These requirements tend to be technical in nature, demanding a good understanding of the product's architecture from the product manager. If a functional improvement is suggested, the product manager will often ask for a prototype that can be used to assess customer demand. Many of the developers' suggestions, while improving the product, do not offer immediate commercial return.

"At the time the releases are being put together we often send a list of things we think should be in the list and sometimes they do get included in the official requirements – some of them might be. They usually have a low priority, but they get in anyway."

5. Industry regulators. In order for telecommunications traffic to pass between operators and between countries, standard communications protocols must be used. As data-based services, such as text messaging (the Short Message Service) and SIP (the Session Initiation Protocol) evolve, new versions of the supporting protocols must be implemented.

   These often take the form of 'recommendations' rather than 'standards' and can be difficult to interpret exactly. Because the company must be able to inter-work with other equipment using these standard protocols, there is often very little up-front work carried out at this stage or during the feasibility studies. There is a tacit assumption that the text of the standard or recommendation will be adequate as a set of requirements. Industry regulations, such as the International Telecommunications Union's (ITU's) standards and recommendations, are often difficult to read and quite legalistic in nature.

6. Product manager's own ideas. Being an expert on the product, the product manager will have an opinion of how the product should progress. These ideas, produced as feature requests, can be validated by presenting them to existing customers or the development teams.

Before the product manager can prioritise these ideas and suggestions, s/he must carefully define what exactly is being asked for. If customers or developers make requests for new features, the product manager will have to ensure that s/he understands precisely what that party is looking for.

Because the ideas for future developments come from such a variety of sources, the product managers may create a set of marketing requirements that present the suggestions in a consistent fashion. Product managers either have a business or technical background.

> "As a product manager coming into a product management role you essentially don't have all the skills. If you come in via technical, there are an awful lot of business – negotiation, marketing – skills required; if you come in via business or marketing you have to acquire quite a lot of technical. Probably more than a lot of jobs out there, a product manager needs further training once they become a product manager because you don't graduate as a product manager!"

Those with technical backgrounds tend to produce very detailed marketing requirements that can be used as the basis for implementation. However, in many cases, a systems architect will get involved to produce what will be termed here engineering requirements.

Engineering requirements represent a formal description of the functionality that has been requested. Such requirements need to be both testable and measurable. For instance, a marketing requirement, such as: "The system will have the capacity to process all traffic during the busy hour" would have to be replaced with: "The system will be able to process X MAP transactions per second. If further transactions are initiated beyond this figure, they will be rejected by sending a MAP-P-ABORT protocol data unit".

Arriving at this level of detail is difficult and several techniques are used to elicit further insight. These usually involve input from both the product manager and the systems architect:

1. Arrange a review of the marketing requirements document. By presenting the product manager's perception to the originator of the request, s/he will be able to correct any misconceptions. Obviously, this technique is only useful if a specific party generated the idea.
2. Examine how the feature is to be employed. This can be done by means of scenario analysis, using representations such as the Unified Modelling Language's (UML's) use cases. This

technique can be practiced by the product manager on ideas that arise from market research or competitor analysis.

3. Prototypes are an ideal way to demonstrate understanding. Some aspects of a product, such as the user interface, benefit from rapid prototyping tools that can be demonstrated without significant up-front costs.

The engineering requirements document is the responsibility of the systems architect who works with the programmers in the relevant functional areas to build up requirements that are possible to implement. This document, sometimes called a requirements functional specification, may also contain high-level descriptions of proposed solutions. If this is the case, it is useful to include a section describing rejected alternatives. This can be helpful if the feature is expanded some time in the future.

Some companies take a very legalistic approach to requirements, stating every possible action the product may perform. This approach can lead to extremely complex solutions and might make the work too expensive to justify.

> "Rather than saying: 'When the switch receives message X, it shall do Y', you'll write: 'When AND ONLY when it receives message X, it shall do Y, AND ONLY Y' and you start writing like a lawyer which will mean that you'll win the argument in court as to whether you were wrong or right when it screws up, but it will actually increase the possibility of screwing up because it will lower the comprehension of the next person down. … People have doubled and tripled the cost of a feature with things that are totally useless."

Requirements definition requires the skills of both a product manager, who provides the customer-facing functions and the systems architect, who handles the interface with the programming team. While the product manager and the systems architect are the main people responsible for this work, interviewed programmers have had to resolve vague requirements – ones that have not been refined by a systems architect. As the programmer begins work on implementation, other, more detailed requirements may be identified. It this situation, the programmer is effectively acting as a systems architect. This appears to be the experience of the senior programmers interviewed for this project. Thus, senior programmers need to possess the product knowledge, domain knowledge and analysis skills of the systems architect.

> "You can go from getting a one-page, or one-line requirement for something, that comes straight from the customer's mouth, or you get something that's been well processed through product development or product management … I would be involved in reviews of requirements. Generally, once the requirements spec. has been issued, or reviewed, it is usually up to one of the developers then to see how we can implement those requirements."

Similarly, once the project is approved and planning begins the project manager may have to carry out requirements definition work. An example of this situation is where the company decides to implement a new version of a communications protocol. The project manager may receive a single line requirement to implement the latest version. S/he will then have to define exactly what new messages have been added and how the existing messages have changed. In this case, the project manager will need to display the analysis skills of the product manager. The systems architect will create the engineering requirements as before.

Considering each of the artefacts in Figure 40 gives:

B.1.1 Related Artefacts

Feature Requests

A feature request relates to an existing product. It is used by existing customers to indicate new functionality that they would like to see in the product. It is also the mechanism used both by the product manager and the programming team to convey their own suggestions.

Feature requests are sometimes called change requests and facilities are often added to companies' bug-tracking software to allow both customers and internal staff to raise such requests.

Requests for Quotation (RFQs) and their Responses

A Request for Quotation is a detailed document listing a customer's requirements for a certain type of network entity. The product manager must respond to this by indicating how the current product line will satisfy all the requirements, either now or in the future.

> "The issue with the RFP is that you have to describe the product, whether it exists or not. We'll step back: You have to decide whether you're going to bid. You have to decide what you're going to bid and then you have to

> describe the product, usually in quite a lot of detail. Aside from the administration and the paperwork and just filling in the boxes, there's an awful lot of design work to be done there at a high level."

Industry Regulations

The telecommunications sector is strongly regulated. An obvious example is the way the radio frequency (rf) spectrum is divided up between radio and television broadcast media, mobile telephony, satellite communications, etc. If the telecommunications standardisation bodies, such as the International Telecommunications Union (ITU), the Institute of Electrical and Electronic Engineers (IEEE), the International Standards Organisation (ISO), the Third Generation Partnership Project (3GPP) or the European Telecommunications Standards Institute (ETSI), create a new communications protocol, for instance, equipment providers have to consider the consequences of not supporting the new protocol.

Market Research/Competitor Analysis

Market research and competitor analysis are activities that may or may not lead to formal artefacts. Some of the larger companies subscribe to commercial research organisations, such as the Gartner Group (Gartner 2008) and Ovum (Ovum 2008), which produce reports on different market segments. Alternatively, they may employ their own marketing divisions to generate more tailored reports. The smaller companies rely on what information is freely available on the web and on what their customers feed back to them.

> "Here we tend to research technologies as opposed to researching the market. We don't really research the market – we get the market from our customers directly … In terms of going out and trying to measure the market, or predict the market, we listen to what the customer tells us or what our partners tell us. We don't have a big enough company to go out and do market research."

Marketing Requirements/Materials

Marketing requirements are also called feature descriptions. These contain the product manager's descriptions of the features requested. Strong technical writing skills are needed here, especially if the marketing requirements are reviewed externally. The goal is to ensure that the product manager's understanding of the feature matches that of the customer. These requirements will evolve into marketing documentation (such as press releases) if it is decided to implement the feature. They also are helpful in eliciting feedback from other customers.

> "We're responsible for the marketing materials. So we would actually generate the presentations, review all documentation and then we would be responsible for presenting what has been delivered or developed back to the customer."

Feature Request Database

This is the repository for all the marketing requirements. Ideas for new features come from a myriad of sources. The product manager has to ensure that each one is recorded – often placed in a feature request database – and that each gets due consideration. Whatever course of action is decided upon will have to be communicated back to the feature's originator. These requests, along with the artefacts generated, are archived for future use. The same feature may be suggested at a later date by a different source.

> "We have a method for formally capturing that need and recording it, which is called the FR Database – the Feature Request Database. And then we have what's called a FERB, which is a Front End Review Board. So we have all these processes, but this is the part of the process that I am actively involved in. First of all, I open a large number of feature requests myself and secondly, any feature request that comes in for my product, I assess."

Prototypes (to Clarify Requirements)

One of the ways of initiating a discussion with the customer is for the systems architect to prepare a prototype that illustrates how the feature will work. This is often useful in demonstrating the user interface, as tools are available to prototype the area rapidly. Prototypes developed in this sub-process are used to gain understanding; they are not used to prove concepts. Sometimes companies will have demonstration systems that they can use to explain existing functionality. These demonstrations can provide a basis for meaningful requirements discussions.

Scenario Modelling

Another effective way to elicit requirements is to work through some usage scenarios with the customer. In the telecommunications sector, this often involves message sequence charts showing the message exchange between various network entities. While standard transactions tend to be straightforward, error cases can be quite convoluted. Just like the marketing requirements review and the prototype demonstration, the scenarios are used to determine what needs to be done, not how to do it. Scenario modelling will be carried out by the systems architect, who must be adept at asking 'what if?' questions.

> "You normally paraphrase, or give examples – make up a number of different subscribers and different sample data and go through a scenario then of what would happen. That's normally the best way because they can see it. The most frustrating part of requirements is trying to tease out the actual requirement."

Engineering Requirements

These must contain enough detail to allow the building of a computer-based software system that can be demonstrated to satisfy the requirements. This is important because the engineering requirements often form the basis for the contract between the customer and the developing company. Traditionally, requirements take the form of numbered lists. One of the architects interviewed for this study recommends that some explanatory text be added to place the requirements in context. He feels that this makes the documents more legible.

> "I might draw [the screen layout] and I might write a whole load of requirements around it and a discussion and things like that and I might have one sentence like: 'The screens might not look exactly like they do here, but these are for the purposes of illustration and discussion'."

B2. The Feasibility Study

Figure 41. The Artefacts Involved in Feasibility Assessment

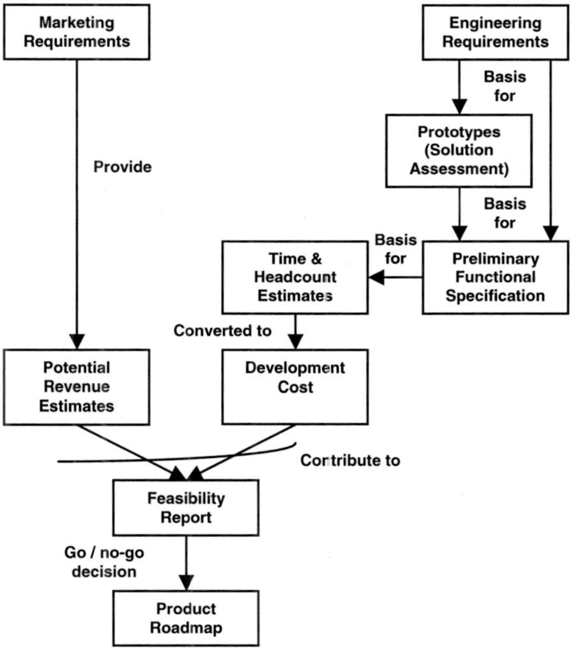

To select features to include in the future evolution of the product, the systems architect has to decide on solutions that satisfy the requirements. Ideally, the architect should be in a position to consider several, competing solutions. However, one of the companies in this study wants estimates to be provided within two weeks of assessing the requirements. Unless the new feature is very similar to a previous one, it is unlikely that these estimates will be very accurate.

Assessing the feasibility of a development seems to be a straightforward task. Decide on how the requirements are to be met, estimate the likely development costs, assess the potential revenue from such an undertaking and make the decision based on which figure is larger.

Unfortunately, accurate development estimates are difficult to produce. This is particularly true if the new feature differs radically from what was done before. On the other side of the equation, the proposed development may not yield any revenue, but may be essential for survival in this marketplace. For instance, changes mandated by industry regulators have to be made just to remain viable. Also, features already available on competing products may be approved, despite not having an identified customer.

> "With O&M [Operations and Maintenance] features especially, sometimes it's: 'We've got to do this because our competitors do it and we may be out of a market because of that'. Then they put pounds, shillings and pence against the cost of being kicked out of the market because we haven't done something. So, sometimes, we could lose a potential twenty million in future sales over the next five years, for the sake of investing three hundred thousand and something."

According to Boehm (1981), estimates should be based on historical data. This view is endorsed by the interviewees who acknowledge that, if the new feature resembles a previous one, the estimates tend to be accurate; if it is something radically different, the estimates can be completely wrong. Some of the companies studied use methods such as Wide-band Delphi and Function Point analysis to improve accuracy.

The more the architect understands how the feature will be implemented, the more accurate the estimate is. Some companies commission quite detailed prototypes as part of the feasibility study. This is appropriate when evaluating alternative implementations. If a radical proposal is made, the better the technology involved is understood, the less risk will be associated with choosing that proposal. In these situations, it is better to determine if the solution is possible as part of a feasibility study than to commit to a full-blown development effort and discover that the proposed solution cannot work.

> "When you look through the architecture, you might identify certain areas where the requirements are kind of thin, or where there are certain risks associated and, as a way of mitigating the risks, you tend to do early prototyping to make sure it's feasible. It's a way of finding the problems up front rather than six months down the road when you go and implement it and realise we have to change it all."

Any solution must be considered in terms of the existing product line and how it will affect existing customers. Of course, there is always the possibility that the feature is impossible to implement. Then the architect will have to explain that the requirements are technically infeasible. Another way they could be deemed infeasible is if the solution would take the architecture in an undesirable direction – away from the product strategy.

If a solution is found, the systems architects determine what functional areas are impacted by the new feature and derive estimates for each area with help from individual programmers. This is done by commencing work on the functional specification (also called the architecture specification).

It is possible that several competing solutions are possible. At this stage of development, it is appropriate that the systems architect considers every possible option. As Uwe Bahnsen, Ford's erstwhile Vice President of Design recommends: "Never ask a designer to design a bridge, but ask him to make a way of crossing a river. That way there is no limit placed on creativity." (Walton 1985, p.220) If more than one implementation is valid, the architects will describe each of the alternatives and produce estimates for each. They will also list the advantages and disadvantages of each option.

The result of this work is a preliminary time schedule and headcount estimate. In one company, for instance, the development estimates are based on the architects' own experience, but the test and support estimates are calculated from the development estimates using standard formulae. These estimates must be translated into monetary amounts, a task carried out by the finance department.

The potential revenue side of the equation is based on market research. The product manager may be assisted by sales and marketing people in determining how much this feature will be worth. One company bases their business case on the anticipated return on investment over five years. In another company, licensing is used in order to make up revenue while still having an attractive base cost.

> "If it's something that looks like it's once off, we try to make all our money back on it in one go and you price it accordingly. But if you think you might resell it because it's a nice feature and will help to sell the product in the future, you mightn't be looking to get the money back off the first customer that asked for it. It would be nice if you did! … You have a cost for having the product and then you have a licence based on the amount of throughput it handles. So if you sell the same product to two

> different customers, you'll work out two different prices based on the amount of traffic they expect to handle. Both of them could be scaled so they have the same hardware. Their hardware costs may be the same and their basic licensing costs may be the same, but they'll have a certain throughput licence on top of that, so the guy who uses it the most, will pay more."

As well as raw figures, the systems architect will have identified risks that may occur in development – untried technology or new programming staff, for instance. All this information is compiled into a feasibility document by the product manager. This is then reviewed by senior management. While the go / no-go decision lies with them, the architects and product managers can influence these decisions. One interviewee made the cynical observation that if the development group did not want to work on a particular feature, they could reduce its chances by exaggerating the estimates.

> "You can always alter priorities by how long you estimate something will take. That's a great way of altering priorities. If there's something we think is essential for the product, you can always give a good, optimistic estimate for it to make sure it stays in and vice versa."

If it is decided not to implement the feature, the originator must be informed. This might not involve a blank refusal. Instead, alternative ideas may be presented that might satisfy the underlying need. It is important for the product manager to maintain a good relationship with the customer in these circumstances.

If the decision is to proceed with the development, the feature must be added to the product roadmap and this update distributed to the customers. If an existing product does not have the feature set required by potential customers, the product's roadmap can be used to reassure them that the product will satisfy their needs eventually. The roadmap details the contents of the next several releases of the product. It is very much a moving target, changing to reflect market dynamics. While changes to distant releases are not a problem, requests to change things in the release under development cause friction with the programmers. The product manager must ensure that all existing customers are reasonably happy with the state of the roadmap.

B.2.1 Related Artefacts

Potential Revenue Estimates

This information will be gathered by the product manager, but is likely to originate with the sales and marketing teams. Extra analysis may be provided by the finance department. As shown earlier, revenue estimates can also have a negative consideration – the cost to the company of NOT developing a particular product. Also, many programming team suggestions relate to non-functional aspects that do not generate obvious revenue, but will improve the reliability or maintainability of the product.

Prototypes (for Solution Assessment)

Unlike the prototypes produced when defining requirements, these ones explore possible solutions. The architect must consider various implementation strategies and decide which approach is best. Prototypes can, in themselves, provide useful data; they can be used to model the performance of the proposed system. For instance, one company has to provide certain performance characteristics and the architect uses prototype modelling to ensure that such figures are possible to achieve. Their most usual application is to assist in creating a preliminary work breakdown structure that contributes to the estimation effort. However, they can also allow the technical feasibility to be assessed.

Preliminary Functional Specification

Before a development can be estimated, it must be decided how to satisfy the requirements. This document provides a high-level description of the software involved. In particular, it details which functional areas have to be changed. Based on this breakdown the architect can, with the help of functional area experts (i.e. programmers), build up reasonably accurate estimates.

Often companies will begin a tendering process by sending out RFQs to vendors. In response, they will want black-box level descriptions of how the vendors plan to address the various requirements. The material for the functional specification is often found distributed throughout the RFQ response.

> "If it's a product you don't have and you still bid, you end up with a functional spec. – the bones of a functional spec. – the information would

be dispersed throughout the response to the RFP [Request for Proposal], so it would be a set of fragments. It wouldn't be a document. So you would have all the decisions made, all the high-level sketches made. But you would then have the task of putting it all into a document, which would be the functional spec."

Time & Headcount Estimates

Although all the interviewed systems architects agreed that estimation draws heavily on personal experience, some companies maintain records of previous project schedules and use formal techniques, such as Function Point and Wide-band Delphi analysis. The attraction of the Function Point approach is that the components map onto the customers' views of the world. Product managers can then use the estimates to discourage customers from functionality that takes too long or is too expensive.

> "For estimating, I think function points and evolutions of those ideas, are the best thing because if you're talking to a product manager and he's familiar with it, then you can come back and say: 'Here's how I estimate it, there are the five function points, blah, blah, blah' and he can look at your detailed analysis and say: 'Oh yeah, I know what all those things mean'. Whereas if you tell him: 'We thought we were going to have to do a detailed design document and this and that', he's not going to be able to come back and say: 'Well no, I think you shouldn't. I want to skip that part'. So you need to be talking in the language of the person asking for the feature because they need to be able to then say: 'Well I don't really need that part, can you take that off the shopping list?'"

Headcount estimates can also include other overheads, such as equipment or consultancy services needed.

Development Cost

Although the architects produce estimates in terms of time and headcount, those figures are translated into monetary amounts by the finance people. The way developers are isolated from financial aspects surprises one development manager. In his previous company, that interviewee had to track costs in terms of time, materials, depreciation, etc. He feels that this isolation gives little incentive to economise on day-to-day overheads.

> "When I came here, I asked people how much an engineering hour cost or what was the cost of a phone call? Nobody knew. I remember saying: 'You can't run a business like this. Everyone is just wasting money all over the place' and I was basically told: 'That's not your business' … I

could have saved a fortune of money. … But nobody was interested, because there was no incentive to save the money."

Feasibility Report

Depending on the size and complexity of the feature, the result of the feasibility study may not be an actual document. Features may be rejected out of hand if they have no bearing on the current development strategy for the product. These decisions will be noted in the feature request database and fed back to the feature originators. Another possibility is that the feature list is reviewed regularly and the results of the feasibility studies are presented at these review meetings. The analysis in the feasibility study relating to the development cost and the resources required will find use in the project plan if it is decided to develop the feature.

Product Roadmap

If it is decided to proceed, the feature must be scheduled into a future release. Here again, politics comes into play; important, or 'high yield', customers will get priority for their requests. The roadmap is very much a moving target, changing to reflect current priorities. It is an important part of the product manager's role to keep customers apprised of changes to the roadmap.

> "There's a lot of lobbying that goes on from local offices and you have to balance that kind of lobbying and that kind of individual customer demand or requirement – you have to balance that against your product strategy and the other thing is, you don't put features in there that are going to confuse your product strategy."

B3. Managing the Project

The management of a project covers two principal activities:

1. Project planning and definition.
2. Project tracking.

The following sections describe these activities in depth. Note that some management related artefacts – the bug tracking mechanism and the final test and installation reports will be detailed in section B.4.

B.3.1 Defining a Project

Figure 42. The Artefacts Involved in Project Definition

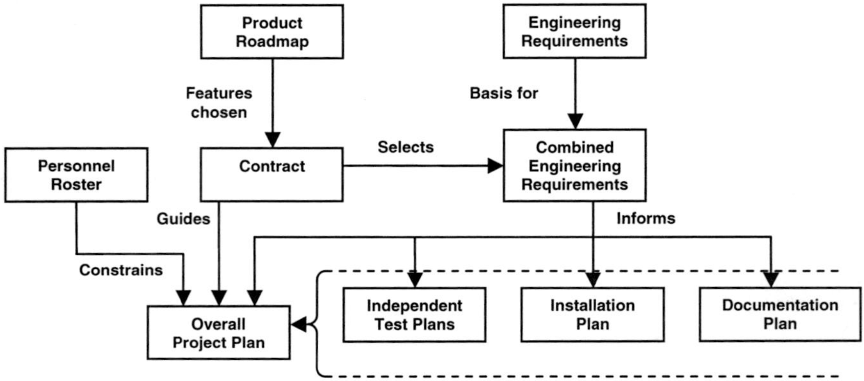

According to the Project Management Institute, a project "is a temporary endeavor undertaken to create a unique product or service" (IEEE Computer Society 2003: p4). In this sector, a project is set up to develop those features that have been assigned to the next release in the product roadmap. Therefore its goal is to implement a system that will satisfy the engineering requirements for all the features in the release.

The project manager now has to combine the requirements for all these features and produce a project plan. The plan contains headcount and resource requirements, the work breakdown structure, the preliminary schedule and the risk analysis. Very often, the project manager will have to commence work on the next release of the product before the requirements are fully defined and all the feasibility work complete. Indeed, some features will be added to a release with little or no technical consideration.

All the aspects of the project plan should have been considered previously, for the individual features. Now the project manager must regard them as a unit and produce an overall work breakdown structure. In doing so, shortcuts taken during the feasibility studies must be addressed and a full set of activities must be included. The project manager may have to refine certain requirements and commission prototyping work in order to complete the plan. The project manager also has to be more pragmatic over personnel assignment – while the architect can consider roles, the project manager must find actual people to fill those roles. There is a real possibility that there are not enough people available to do the work. This is a particular problem for smaller companies.

In such a case, the project manager might make out schedules for different numbers of people and see which works best.

> "If there are two or more people working on a release, then you would do a project plan – Gantt charts, that sort of stuff, using Microsoft Project – and you move things around and see whether or not you can make this date. I would have done outline ones of these already before this – assuming there's one engineer, assuming there's two engineers, assuming there's three engineers. Some of them you don't need tools like Microsoft Project to work out but sometimes you do."

Several factors need to be considered when assigning work to a person:

- No one person is available 100% of the time to work on a project. Boehm (1981) estimates that 30% of a person's time can be taken up with training and non-project activities. He also points out that 40% of the total project time can be spent fixing problems, reading and attending meetings.
- Echoing DeMarco's (2001) point that people are not 'fungible', one of the interviewed project managers finds that swapping people between tasks can be both de-motivating and inefficient.
- It is a good idea to add some spurious activities to a schedule for contingency purposes.

Another problem for the project manager is the delivery date committed to by the sales people. They usually promise delivery within so many months of receipt of order. This delivery date may have to be renegotiated. One way of doing this is to suggest a phased delivery. Thus a generic product can be installed straight away with new features given more generous deadlines. One company notes that deadlines tend to be 'soft' in this industry. For instance, key customer personnel may not be available, or the deadline coincides with a critical period (such as a bank holiday) where service cannot be interrupted.

Risks will have been considered by the architect in terms of a go/no-go decision. At this juncture, the risks must be assessed in terms of likelihood of occurrence and impact if they do occur. Contingency or mitigation plans need to be put in place to deal with risks should they arise. As the project progresses, some risks will become irrelevant while others are noticed for the first time. Risk management is an ongoing part of project tracking.

The person managing the software development project can be a professional project manager. Such a person may have a background in a totally different industry, such as building construction. This situation can arise in companies where a matrix or fully project-based structure is in place. Here, the people available to develop the software are considered to be a pool of resources. A team is assembled from that pool to complete the project.

More typically, the project manager is either a senior programmer or team leader. Sometimes, the systems architect will carry on and provide administrative as well as technical leadership. For senior programmers in this role, there is the danger that they are responsible for the release, but have no control over the people who have been assigned to carry it out.

> "That can be very difficult and sometimes, when you don't own the resources – either physical resources or people resources – it's very frustrating. We're given all the responsibility of delivering something without being given the full authority to do it."

One of the problems faced by project managers is dealing with a hard deadline. This may have been decided based on the feasibility study. When the project manager explores the schedule in more depth and considers all factors, such as vacation times and administrative overheads (training courses and project meetings, for instance), s/he may find that the schedule stretches out beyond the deadline. Project leaders have been known to commit to the deadline, despite their analysis showing that it is impossible to meet.

> "Essentially you would think of everything you had to do and think about how long you had to do them all in and you add it all up. Now 'Estimate 101' is that, if you're going to do your project plan at that stage, you're going to fail – you're not going to think of half the things you really need to do. You're going to put down how long it SHOULD take rather than how long it usually does take because you're trying to please people. So you'll generally markedly under-estimate it if you do that."

If the deadline has to be met, the project manager can either request more resources or drop features from the release.

B.3.1.1 Related Artefacts

Personnel Roster

In some companies, the project manager is also a team leader and the team will have enough expertise to carry out the work of the release. In other organisations, a matrix structure is used (Galbraith 1973); this involves sharing the developers among projects. Conflicts tend to arise between project managers over good personnel.

Contract (Release Definition)

The definition of a new product release may or may not involve a legal contract with an individual customer. In most of these organisations, new features are being added to existing products, so the delivered software comes under the heading of a support agreement.

Although the product roadmap is a very fluid document, when the time comes to define the next project, decisions must be taken to 'lock down' the project and define the requirements that the release will satisfy. As well as prioritising the marketing requirements, the release definition should have a cohesive theme to it. In this way several related developments may occur together.

The release definition can be the basis of a "Statement of Work" that defines what the customer is getting. Contract negotiations with new customers also involve the arrangement of a support agreement that includes the supply of future releases.

Combined Engineering Requirements

While the requirements for each feature may be well-defined at this juncture, the project manager will have to consider the requirements for the release en-masse. Certain synergies may be achieved by implementing these together, although conflicts may arise also. A set of requirements for the overall release may appear in the project plan.

Overall Project Plan

This is the key document for the entire project. In larger companies, where several different products are produced, there may be many levels of project plans. For instance, there could be one overall plan for the entire product range. This refers to project plans for each product and these in turn reference plans for each group.

> "There would be a project manager for an overall project, which involves work from the different groups. But within each group then, the group manager would schedule the work."

This study only considers plans at the group level. But even with this restriction, the ancillary groups (test, documentation, training, customer support) may all produce plans to manage their own areas. The project plan should contain a statement of work (most likely references to the engineering requirements), a work breakdown structure, a schedule (or a reference to a software package where the schedule is managed) and an assessment of the identified risks.

If the requirement definition and feasibility studies are carried out with due diligence, the project plan should be a straightforward document to prepare. However, in many companies, requirements definition and estimation work has to be done as part of the project definition sub-process. One leader described the steps needed to 'lock down' a feature as:

1. Validate the requirements with the systems architect and get the customer to sign off on them.
2. Create a work breakdown structure.
3. Gather estimates from all parties. Note that some parts of the feature may be developed in remote sites.
4. Generate a project plan document based on a template.
5. Ensure that the feature schedule fits in with the overall release schedule.
6. Identify and document potential risks.

B.3.2 Tracking a Project

Figure 43. The Artefacts Involved in Project Tracking

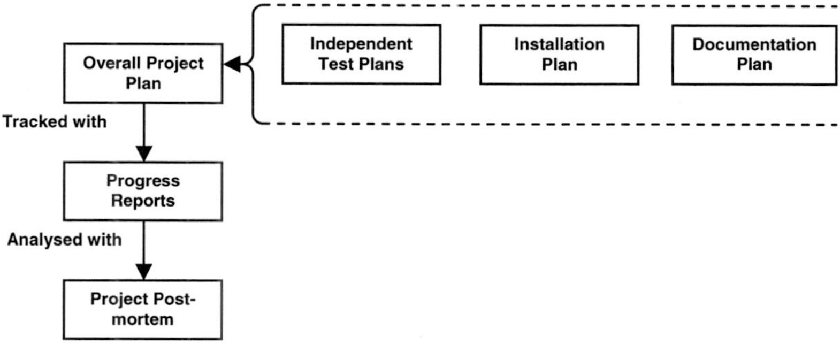

The guide to the Project Management Body of Knowledge (IEEE Computer Society 2003) states that there are five types of processes involved in project management:

Figure 44. Project Management Processes

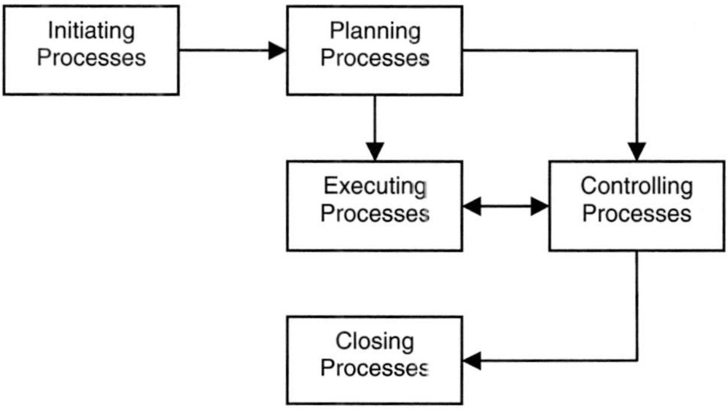

The market research and feasibility activities are the initiating processes; the project definition activities are the planning processes and the construction, installation and maintenance activities are the executing processes. This section concentrates on the controlling processes.

It has been mentioned already that there can be a hierarchy of project plans, placing each sub-project in the context of the bigger project. This will put external constraints on each sub-project that has to be managed. Even at the overall project level, it is likely that other projects are being carried out contemporaneously. These create competition for resources such as personnel and test equipment. Another factor to consider when managing a project in its executing phase is that other projects are now being initiated and planned. Thus, if this particular project is delayed, subsequent ones will also be held up.

> "If one project gets delayed for some reason, or has to get re-planned, because of either inbound dependencies or technology constraint, well the resources have to be held on that project for longer. Which means they're not freed up to feed into the project that follows. … You just have to limit the knock-on effect as much as possible … You may go for sub-contracts as resources; you may go to other resource pools that have similar skills."

One of the interviewees described project management as continuous fire-fighting with issues arising all the time. The main goal of project tracking is to ensure that the project plan is implemented. Regular meetings are held (generally on a weekly basis) to record progress and to address issues raised, such as:

- Delayed external deliverables
- Changes to requirements
- Higher-priority tasks (such as bug-fixing on a previous project) drawing people from project work

Several of the companies in this study used earned-value analysis to track progress (Boehm 1981). This has the benefit of highlighting the amount of effort that goes into completing a task. For instance, a project can appear to be running perfectly according to schedule but, thanks to earned value analysis, it can be seen that everyone in the project team is working seven days a week to achieve this. Other measures are also taken into account, such as: risks, defects, test execution status and requirements changes.

The project manager is also responsible for ensuring that the company's quality standards are maintained. Thus, s/he must ensure that documents are reviewed and code is inspected. Some companies use a gating process, whereby all validation and verification steps must be completed before the project can proceed to the next step. Tracking requirements down to code level does not seem to be widely practiced, although bug fixes will have the bug report number documented in the code comments.

> "We wouldn't go to the stage where we would put comments into the code that would reflect that a particular piece of code is to meet certain requirements in a certain document. The only place where that would specifically happen, maybe, would be for bug tracking, where you would have a bug reference and, when you fix it, ideally you'd make a comment in the code saying: 'This was to fix such and such a problem'."

As noted in section B.3.10, the person responsible for the tracking and control of a project may be:

- A professional project manager (as might be found in a matrix or project-based organisation).
- A group leader, who is also responsible for the welfare and career development of the group members.
- A systems architect, who continues working on the project after the feasibility study is complete.
- A senior programmer, who also has to contribute to the construction of the product.

A major concern with the group leaders and project managers is that they do not really know what is going on in the project. The interviews highlighted three solutions to this problem:

1. If the company has a comprehensive development process, the figures needed to control the project are well-defined and the project team is familiar with what needs to be reported. In this situation, the project manager does not need any hands-on, technical knowledge.

2. One of the group leaders takes responsibility for the version control of the software and finds that this gives him a good feel for progress. He also runs the sanity tests to make sure that the code is fit for independent test.

> "I think that's nearly essential to keep an eye on what's going on. I use that as a way of keeping track of what's been changed. Rather than going through all the code and attending all the code reviews I do a bit of the configuration management and that means I know what's going on."

3. Another leader, who works in a matrix structure, has to manage a number of programmers as well as tracking projects. He finds that, being exposed to such a range of problems, gives him more experience than if he was a programmer confined to one area.

> "When you're actually an engineering manager you actually can learn quicker than people who are actually doing technical work. A lot of people don't know that: That you can develop such a wealth of experience because you can actually work on every tough problem."

B.3.2.1 Related Artefacts

Progress Reports

These are very important documents politically. In some situations, they are made available to customers, but they will always be of interest to senior management. The reports should highlight how actual progress compares to planned and explain the discrepancies between the two. To gather information for these reports, regular meetings are arranged, where issues can be raised and addressed. In companies with deep management hierarchies, reports at one level are based on reports from the lower level. If there are enough levels, an absurd situation can arise where the reports at the bottom levels have to be prepared before the reporting period begins, in order for the top-level reports to be ready in time (Weinberg 1971).

Project Post-mortem

At the end of each project, it is a good idea to review the project and identify the successes and failures. Lessons can be learned and applied to future projects. Often, the project team will gather for a post-mortem (or post-partum, as it is called in one company) meeting. This allows everyone the opportunity to highlight aspects of the projects they felt worked or those that could be improved. The actual durations for each activity in the work breakdown structure should be archived to build up a basis for future estimations.

> "Well hopefully not post-mortem, post-partum. Post-mortem means something died. But here we do those too. We try to document what went well, what went badly, lessons learned, what can we do better the next time?"

B4. Construction

The main goal of any software development project is to produce a validated and verified software product that includes tested code, documentation and training materials. This section will detail the activities required to reach this goal. They will be presented under the following headings:

1. Designing and creating the raw artefacts.
2. Testing the product.
3. Preparing for the installation.
4. Installing the product on site and demonstrating that it passes the customer acceptance test plan.
5. Maintaining the product.

B.4.1 Creating the Raw Artefacts

Figure 45. The Artefacts Involved in Product Creation

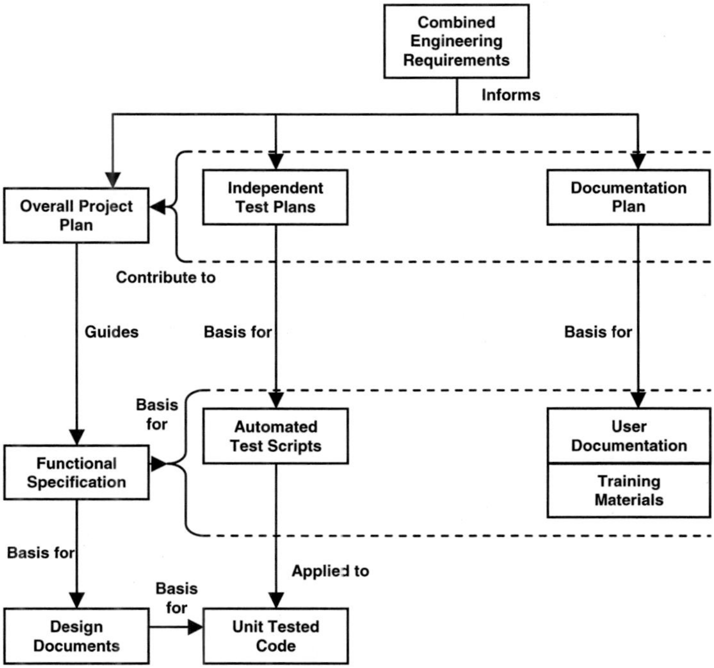

Creating a software product involves those activities most closely associated with software development. It begins with the creation of the functional specification. Some specification work will have been carried out during the feasibility study in order to decide on solutions for each feature and formulate enough of a work breakdown structure to generate estimates. Now that the go-ahead has been given to proceed with development, an overall specification can be properly written.

This specification will describe all the features being implemented in this release. It will highlight common areas affected and should identify opportunities for code reuse between features. This document will present the architectural and interface changes caused by the new features and explain how they fit into the existing product. A useful section to include in this document is a list of rejected alternatives with reasons why they were unacceptable. As Jackson and Carter (2000) point out: "Perfect rational behaviour would imply that, when making a decision of any kind, the decision-maker is able to gather all the information relevant to that decision, rank it in significance and make a reasoned choice between alternatives" (p.98). Since all the facts are often not available, it is common to act using what information is at hand; this is called bounded rationality. If the feature is to be enhanced in future, more experienced reviewers might be in a better position to assess the alternatives.

The review of the functional specification can be considered the launch point for much of the project activity. Several of the interviewees who work in the ancillary functions, such as test, documentation and customer support, cite the specification as the indication that this development is actually going to happen. Although they do take part in the requirements review and contribute to parts of the project plan, the functional specification contains those features that definitely will be developed in this release.

Once the functional specification has been reviewed and approved, the various parties can commence work. Steve McConnell (1993) defines construction as covering design, code and unit test activities. This section will consider the construction of all the deliverables associated with the product, including independent test plans, user documentation and training materials. Thus, various roles are involved:

- Programmers. The project manager will assign development tasks among the programmers based on either a feature or functional area basis. Functional area breakdowns are popular because the programmers can then build up useful expertise in a given area. Recently, the adoption of agile methods has meant that the work has to be divided into smaller portions, with programmers (or programming-pairs) selecting their own assignments.

- Testers. The test group leader may have already contributed to the feasibility and project plan estimates. Now a proper test plan is created and the testing work will be divided among the group. In situations where the programming work is delayed, project managers tend to compensate by shrinking the testing interval. This proves to be a constant irritation for one test group leader in this study.

"Some of my schedules reflect zero days for both these tasks [setting test objectives and designing test cases] just to indicate that we haven't forgotten about it, but we're just not going to do it, because we haven't the time – they've only given us X weeks."

- Technical writers. Customer documentation has to describe how the product works, from an end-user perspective. This suggests that the documentation can only be written when the software is physically available to work with. Although the details in the manuals have to wait until this point, much work can be done beforehand. As well as drawing from the functional specification, the writers develop informal relations with the programming teams and manage to get access to early versions of the software. Some writers have been able to return the favour by proving to be effective testers. Indeed this informal relationship is so important that one interviewee suggested that the documentation function cannot be separated from the programming one.

"I don't see how people can do technical writing off-site, at home. You can do certain aspects of it but really, to do an entire project from the comfort of your own home, would be, to me, next or near impossible."

B.4.1.1 Related Artefacts

Independent Test Plans

The test group bases its test plans on the engineering requirements. The goal is to find deviations from the requirements. The testers often determine the relative importance of each feature and target the main testing effort to the most important ones. The test plans are reviewed by the programmers and architects. Some companies present a very basic test plan for review, with each test comprising a single, one-line description. Once the suite of tests is agreed, the test plan is developed further, detailing the steps needed to carry out each test. Test plan documents are often template driven. A subset of the system test plan is used for customer acceptance testing.

Documentation Plan

The suite of user manuals accompanying any new release of software needs to be written by the technical writing team in time for shipping with the product. The writers need to plan their work in the context of the company's other products and in terms of available personnel.

Functional Specification

This is based on the preliminary specifications that were created as part of the feasibility studies. An important aspect of this work is identifying features that impinge on the same functional areas. Here, conflicts will have to be resolved but, on the other hand, opportunities for code reuse may be identified. Because this document represents the basis for so many project activities, it will be carefully reviewed.

Automated Test Scripts

If automated test scripts are used, much of the documentation that goes into the test plan will instead be included in the script body. In the companies studied, C, PERL and TCL are used to write the scripts. To make test calls as realistic as possible, some companies try to capture actual call traces at customer sites. These messages are then injected into the system under test by the automated scripts. The scripts are validated by running the call scenarios manually and comparing the results with the script output.

User Documentation

The technical writers base their work on the functional specification as they have to describe how the product works. Each company has its own documentation formatting standards (called style guides) and the technical writers have to ensure that their products conform to these. The user documentation cannot be completed until the software is available to work with. This is particularly true when there is a user interface component – the technical writers need to capture actual screens to illustrate their manuals. In one company, a suite of four documents is produced for each new development:

1. Service Description. This is a high-level product description that should be understood by non-technical readers.
2. Administration Guide. This gives details of the configuration of the product and assumes a certain level of knowledge by the reader – such as how to use the operating system, for instance.
3. Operation Guide. This describes the graphical user interface and generally does not require technical expertise on the part of the reader.
4. Installation Guide. This is used by both internal customer support and by customers themselves.

It is important for the technical writers to establish good, informal relations with the programmers, in order to gain access to early versions of the code.

> "You need to have good interpersonal skills. You need to be able to communicate. You need to be able to ask the right questions. You also need to be able to stand back and not annoy the hell out of people. People will always be forthcoming with information if you can do it in a nice way. If you do it through formal channels and complain, people will switch you off. You need people to help you."

Training Materials

Training is an area that differs radically among the companies in this study. Sometimes the customer support people provide the training, but the product managers, architects and individual programmers can also get the job. Only one company has a dedicated customer trainer on site – most of the others having training departments in head office. The course materials are provided by the architects and programmers and they may be formatted to company standards by the technical writers.

Design Documents

The number of design phases between the specification and the code varies depending on the complexity of the feature and the experience of the assigned programmer. Object-oriented design and the Unified Modelling Language (UML) are used by most of the programmers interviewed. In one company, UML is used for modelling purposes, but the International Telecommunications Union's (ITU's) Z.100 Specification and Description Language (SDL) and message sequence charts are used for the actual designs – most of the programming revolving around finite state machines.

An interesting development in the programming world is the use of agile methods, where the unit tests are written before the code and the work is divided up into much smaller units. None of the interviewees mentioned writing a separate unit-test plan document.

> "Unit testing isn't after coding, it's more like while we're coding. We're kind of extreme programming-type testers and developers. I'm a big fan of that, where you, in a lot of cases, write your tests first – especially in OO [object orientation] where you have classes, you can test at the class level. You write your test first and then you define your interface and then you write the guts behind it and suddenly you find that it all works and you're happy."

Unit Tested Code

This is the deliverable from an individual programmer. If the design phase is comprehensive, coding should be mechanical. The languages used in these companies include: assembler, C, C++ and Java. Although agile methods insist that unit test code is written before the production code, traditional development has not been very diligent in this respect. Indeed, many of the practitioners interviewed have little or no understanding of testing theory (Roper 1994; Myers 2004). Before the individual units of code are presented to the independent test group, some rudimentary integration, or sanity tests are carried out to ensure that the system as a whole will run in the test lab.

B.4.2 Testing the Product

Figure 46. The Artefacts Involved in Independent Testing

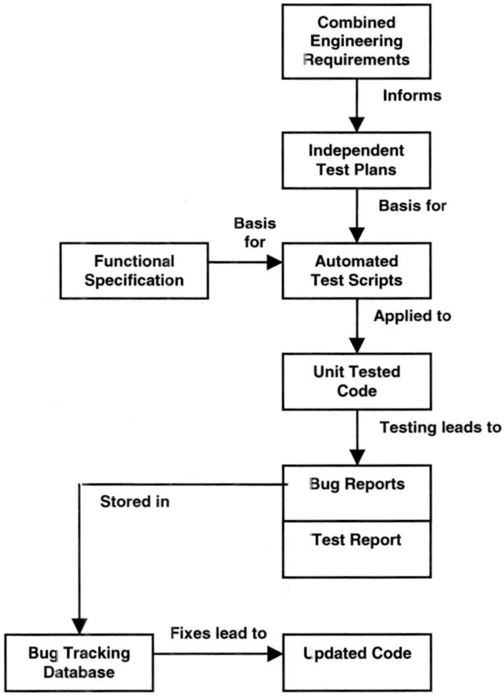

Telecommunications network products basically receive data from external sources; carry out some processing and send data to external destinations. This makes it difficult to test them satisfactorily without access to the other entities in the network. The independent test group is in a position to test the product in the context of a network. Ideally this is done using actual network entities, but these are often simulated. Another useful piece of test equipment is a traffic-generator that can produce heavy loads of mixed traffic. For best results, this traffic should be based on actual call-traces captured from customer sites.

Figure 47. The 'V' Development Model

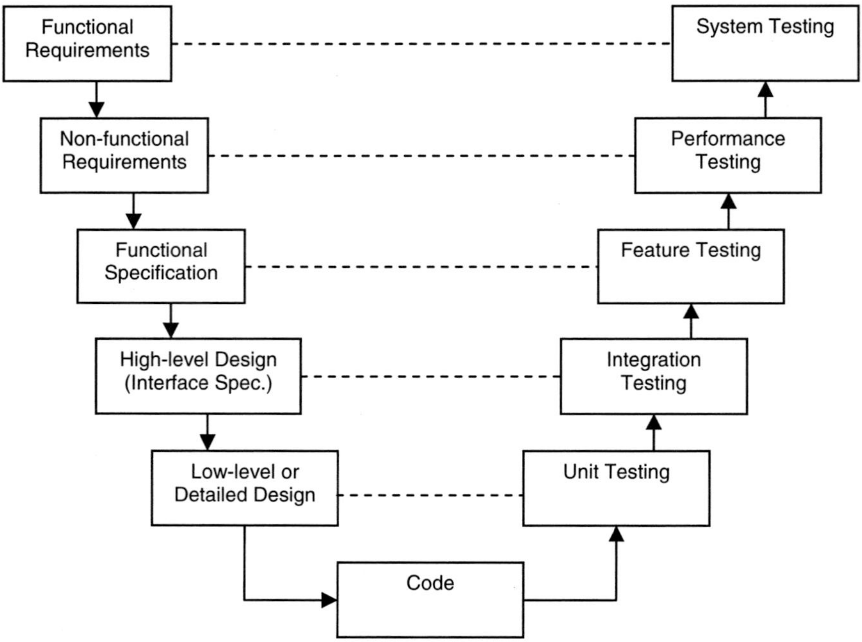

The independent test group is responsible for feature, performance and system testing. If a feature is implemented across several network entities, it may also carry out some integration testing. Each level of testing corresponds to a stage of development as shown in Figure 47.

Two levels of testing can be carried out based on the amount of simulation used:

1. Feature integration testing. This is where the new feature is loaded on a real network entity and the remainder of the network is simulated.
2. Product integration testing. Now, all the changed network entities are available and only the unaffected entities are simulated.

Before the programmers hand over the code officially, they often visit the lab and attempt to get their software running on the test system. This exercise benefits not only the programmers (who get access to better test equipment) and the testers (who get help setting up their test system), but also the customer support people who can see how the equipment is installed.

Once installed, the test group will run a set of sanity tests to see if the product is worth testing. If it is, the system test will begin. Sometimes a lot of time is taken up debugging test scripts at this stage. Besides finding defects, one of the main deliverables from the test group is an indication of load capability. This is a major selling point for a telecommunications product. To get these figures, the group must carry out performance tests. These break down into two types:

1. Load testing, where the product is put under load and the system is observed. Then the load is progressively increased until such time as the system cannot cope. If the test equipment is incapable of generating such a load, then the observations taken will be reviewed to estimate at what load problems will occur.
2. Soak testing, where the product is left run over time to see if there are cumulative problems like memory leaks.

Another type of performance testing involves loading a protocol stack one layer at a time. This is a useful exercise when evaluating competing third-party stack products. It involves detailed knowledge of the interfaces to the stack layer and may require that code is written to interface with the traffic generators.

Independent testing suffers from two scheduling problems. The lab resources may be temporarily reassigned to the customer support group in order to investigate an urgent field problem and test the solution. Reconfiguring a lab to emulate a given customer configuration is a non-trivial task, often taking several days. The other scheduling problem relates to the programming team.

> "It's a case of whoever shouts loudest, whoever's most important. So if you've a problem on site that needs to be fixed, that gets higher priority. … You're supposed to have two weeks for testing and that would give you enough time to do it, but normally you get pushed out and test time becomes development time."

If the delivery deadline is contractually fixed and construction work slips, the test interval has to be reduced somehow. There are two resolutions to this: either reduce the amount of testing done or get the tests completed by "working savage hours".

Figure 48. Obstacles to Independent Testing

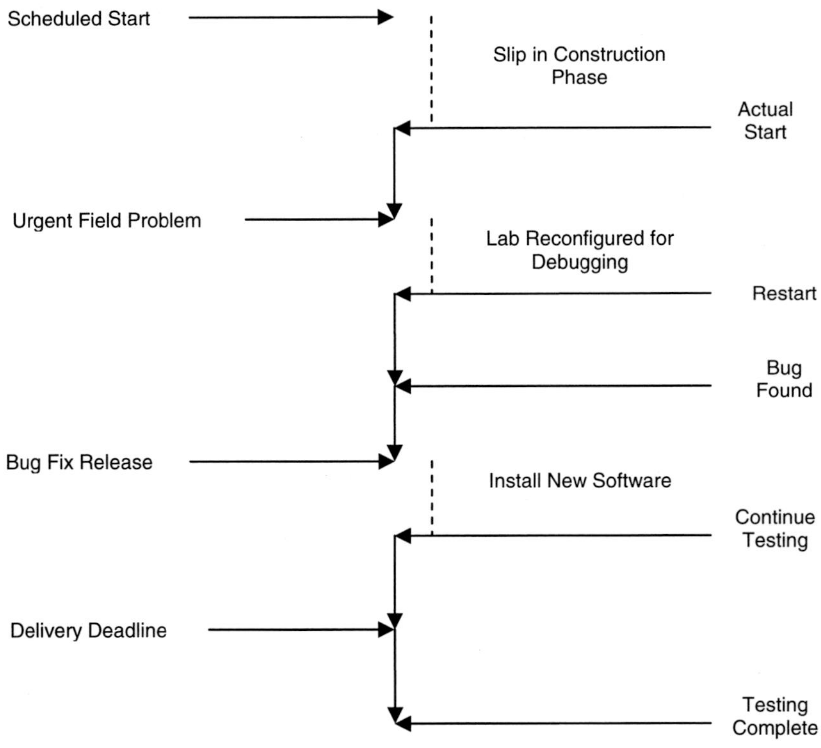

B.4.2.1 Related Artefacts

Bug Reports

Once the software is released into test, communication becomes more formal. Although there may be unofficial cooperation between the programming and test teams in deciding whether a failed test is due to a genuine defect or a problem with the test script or test equipment, all bugs are recorded in a bug-tracking database. For each defect, the tester will record the build version of the software, a description of the problem and instructions showing how to reproduce it. When a programmer develops a fix, s/he will describe the solution and indicate which release the fix will appear on. Companies also are keen on determining why the problem occurred – in particular, which development process introduced the defect.

Bug Tracking Database

Once the product is released to the independent test group, a formal mechanism is needed to report any faults. This is particularly true when the test group is physically remote from the programmers. All detected faults are recorded and stored in a bug tracking database.

This database will also be used by the customer support people to track faults found during the installation of the product or during its commercial operation. Customers often have access to this database in order to report their concerns and to keep up to date with how they are being addressed. This access is part of their support contract.

The bug tracking database may also be used to allow the customer suggest possible new enhancements – these are elaborated by the product manager and entered into the feature request database as marketing requirements.

Updated Code

Ideally, the programmer will be able to see the incorrect behaviour on the lab system and be allowed time to debug the problem. If the behaviour is due to a coding error, this must be corrected and a new version of software prepared for testing. For many network entities, loading a new software release is very time consuming, so new releases often contain several fixes.

Final Test Report

Once the test team has run all its tests, it needs to communicate its opinion of the release to the management team. Essentially, they need to recommend whether the product should be shipped or not.

Telecommunications products are rated on their throughput, so an important part of the test report is an indication of the product's load capability. This information feeds back to the product management and sales teams.

B.4.3 Pre-installation Planning

Figure 49. The Artefacts Involved in Pre-installation

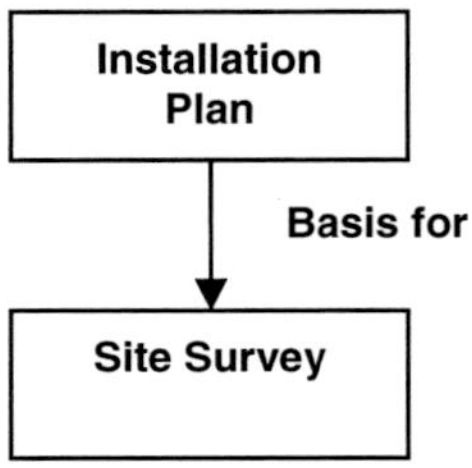

Site installations can have two flavours:

1. New sites that need to be prepared for a first installation. In this case, the new release will represent the first time this product is included into the customer's network.
2. An upgrade to an existing site.

For a new site installation, the customer support group will carry out a site-survey. This details the physical layout of the customer's facility. They need to establish where the equipment will be physically located (will new racks have to be purchased, or can they make use of space in existing ones?), what type of power supply is available and what types of connections are used to interface with the network?

If the task is to upgrade an existing system, customer support personnel are very interested in those aspects of the functional specification that signify changes to the customer site – additional cabling or more equipment for instance. As well as alerting the customer to these changes, the customer support staff must order any new equipment in good time and arrange for it to be shipped to the customer site. They must also develop an installation guide so that the upgrade can be made with minimal downtime.

B.4.3.1 Related Artefacts

Installation Plan

The installation or upgrade of a telecommunications network entity is a very visible operation and, as such, must be carefully planned. The plan will detail the exact set of activities to be carried out on-site. If preparing for new releases was the only responsibility of the customer support group, it would be possible to plan things better. However, the group is exposed to a constant stream of problems from the field.

> "The bottom line is: if there's a crisis with any customer, that is number one. So the reality is: the stuff that I'm doing back up at the start of the project – requirements and design, etc – that goes out the window if I've a crisis."

Another difficulty the group faces is schedule slippage in the construction or test phases. This makes it difficult to arrange a suitable time with the customer.

One of the interviewees stressed the importance of planning an upgrade to an existing system, but felt that it was possible to carry out less planning for new installations. This is because other network entities, some from other vendors, are often being installed at the same time. The integration of all this equipment is overseen by the customer who has the main planning burden.

Site Survey

This is usually only carried out for new customers. The group has to be aware of the physical layout of the customer's site and the facilities available. This will indicate, not only what type of plug-tops and connectors to use, but also what tools to bring with them. An example would be a protocol analyser. This is a very expensive, bulky instrument and it would make journeys simpler if the customer had one on site.

Security arrangements on site also have to be considered. For instance, one product manager recalled that the security guards in one site had to be aware of the passport numbers of each member of the installation team before they would be allowed in.

> "The silly things you had to remember like: you can't get onto a site unless your passport number had been given to the head of security in [the customer's headquarters] and they had faxed the site to say that you were allowed on that site on a particular day. So I needed to know all the people that would be on site and all their passport numbers – that little kind of detail. If you didn't look after that detail, everything was up in the air."

The site survey will also be of benefit when preparing for subsequent visits, especially if new staff members are involved.

B.4.4 Installing the Product

Figure 50. Artefacts Involved in Product Installation

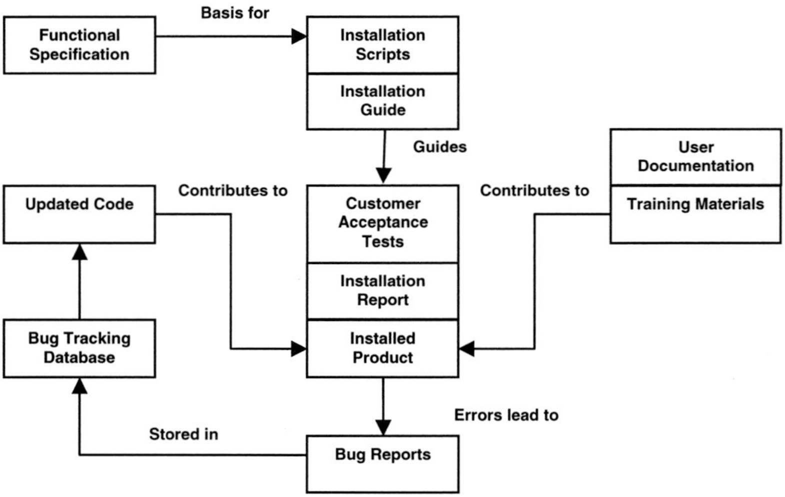

Installation involves either the initial installation of the product in a new site, or the upgrade of an existing product. A new installation involves connecting the product into a live network for the first time and can expose some fundamental errors. If there are no hardware changes to be made, a software upgrade can often be carried out remotely using a modem connection. Customers often prefer to have someone on site, however, in case of problems.

Any sort of installation is very visible. Senior management pay particular attention to 'Tier One' operators, whose endorsement of the product is a very effective form of advertising. In these circumstances, the installation must be well-planned and upgrades carried out with minimum (or ideally no) downtime.

> "There is downtime all right. The core - to go from one major release to the next major release - would be a significant upgrade, with significant downtime. But for the patch – we turnaround fixes in patches – they're pretty well packaged so that there would be minimal downtime, unless it was an unusual fix. We're even at a level now where we actually develop some features in patches."

New installations are often planned by the product manager – particularly if the existing product meets all the customer's needs. The installation of new versions of software is usually the responsibility of the project manager. Both work with the customer support team leader.

Customer support personnel tend to have a system-wide perspective and are very knowledgeable about how the product should be connected into the network – understanding physical-layer protocols for instance. They also know how to configure the product and how to make its statistical information (such as billing and performance figures) available to customers' analysis equipment.

Because of their own expertise in configuring lab systems, test personnel are often assigned to installation work. Because neither group has deep, white-box knowledge of the product, programmers can be asked to take part in the first installations of a new release. This is usually the case when extensive changes have been made, such as support for a new protocol version. The programmer will be expected to solve any coding problems on site. This practice demands discipline on the part of the programmer. If code is changed on site, those changes must be sent back to head-office and included in the software archives. If this does not happen, the on-site system cannot be reproduced in the lab if problems crop up later. However, this has to take place in a fire-fighting atmosphere:

> "When you were on site, they didn't care how you got it working, as long as you got it working. So there was a sort of attitude: 'Just get the bloody thing going. I don't care how'."

To minimise the impact of any downtime, installations are often carried out at night time. If there are any complications, significant amounts of unpaid overtime are involved. However, installations have been cited by several practitioners in this study as being profound learning experiences.

> "Within six months I was out in the field installing software in a major upgrade, which was really good. I really learned a lot that time, I have to say. I learned more in the first year than I did later. It was purely because I had no choice but to learn."

For a first installation or a major upgrade, the customer support team leader or the responsible manager will lead the installation personally. S/he can protect the installation team, often simply by engaging the customer representatives in conversation during the work. For a product manager, this is an opportunity to learn more about the customer's plans and to arrive at ideas for new features. A more difficult aspect of the job is reassuring the customer when problems arise. At all times, the leader must preserve a good public image.

> "You have to protect your own site and your own company when you go to customers. But then when I'm here, I have the other shoe on, because I'm telling everyone here that [the product is] rubbish and then I go out and have to say it's not so bad and that's definitely a conflict."

B.4.4.1 Related Artefacts

Installation Scripts

Because these systems are so highly configurable and work with a great deal of customer data, installations tend to be complex with each site having unique requirements. Customer support personnel often have to write shell scripts to transfer billing and statistics information to customer machines and also to schedule housekeeping tasks using the UNIX cron facility.

Installation Guide

The customer support people need to understand what they will have to do on-site. Their main concern is with the hardware requirements. Obviously, a new customer will need a complete new system, but an existing customer may need to purchase extra processing or interfacing capacity. The product managers and the customer support group work together to ensure that this is available on-site in time for the installation. They will also study the planned software changes to predict how much pre-installation work is required. For instance, database table layouts may be changed in this release and existing customer data will have to be reformatted to work with the new software. Scripts must be written to achieve this.

> "If we were doing a migration, taking over from another [customer] – they were being kicked out and we were replacing them. In that case, I would be directly involved in dealing with the customer. If they had a set of subscribers and you want to move those into our system, I try to work out how they map across – what features they have, what we have."

The step by step guides to the installation will have been trialled in the lab. The idea is to make the actual installation as mechanical a process as possible. With the customer present, important steps can be forgotten by a nervous team member. This can be a very frustrating document to write, as scripts written to aid the installation are often the last things developed. There is a distinction to be made between new, 'green field' installations and upgrades to existing systems:

> "We would receive some kind of guide on upgrade plans from individual [programming] groups. We've three or four elements producing software so they'd say: 'This is how we go from A to B in our software' and then we'd try and take all that and come up with an overall plan. We should be doing the same for new installations, but we haven't got around to it that much. So the installations are more ad-hoc. Because it's a green field site, you can get away with it. But with the upgrade, if it doesn't work, you know what happens… We have enough expertise and rough documentation to get us through [a new installation], fixing as you go along. Make it happen!"

Customer Acceptance Tests

These represent a subset of the system test plan. Surprisingly, most customers do not develop their own test suites, preferring to review the vendor's. No matter how constrained the test interval is, every effort will be made to run the acceptance tests before shipping the product.

Final Installation Report

Much can be learned during an installation and these lessons are detailed in the installation report. The report provides useful feedback to everyone involved in the project and may provide a list of development activities to be included in the next project. It is essentially a post-mortem document for the installation phase.

Installed Product

The goal of the installation is to put in place the new functionality. This is achieved by physically making the updates (or installing the product for the first time) and confirming that it works correctly by demonstrating to the customer that it passes the acceptance tests.

Bug Reports

Although bugs tend to be fixed as rapidly as possible on site, it is important that these bugs are recorded. This allows the programming team at home an opportunity to assess the problem without so much pressure. Even if they arrive at a better solution, the original quick fix must be included in the code archive. At all times, the on-site system needs to be reproducible in the lab. The number of site-generated bug reports is recorded as part of the product's quality assessment.

B.4.5 Maintaining the Installed Product

Figure 51. Artefacts Involved in Product Maintenance

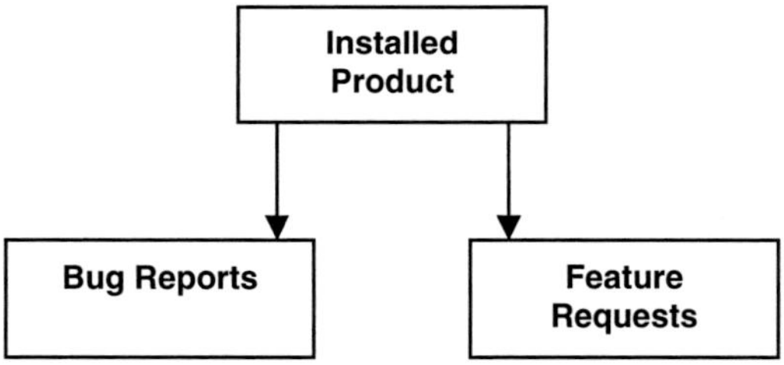

Software maintenance is often overlooked in project schedules. However, it can take up between 50% and 80% of a project's total duration (Boehm 1981; Hatton 1998). Maintenance can be classified into three types (Swanson 1976):

1. Corrective maintenance. Fixing defects in the code.
2. Adaptive maintenance. Coping with changes in processing or data environments. This work can often yield revenue.
3. Perfective maintenance. Improving performance or maintainability.

Once a product is released, the customer support team is responsible for ensuring that customer-reported defects are dealt with. This requires them to establish mechanisms that allow the customers report problems. In some situations, the company will be required to provide around-the-clock support. Globally distributed development departments can provide this level of support by handing over support duties so that the support responsibility falls on a site only during normal working hours. The bigger companies often have organisations in the customer's country and these provide what is called 'First Line' support.

> "It's out there then and the first level of support is CNRC, so there are men around from the [Cellular] Network Resolution Centre. So they're the first line of support I suppose and then we're next. Each of the customers has a local office or a local account team on site with them. So they, depending on their level of technical ability, sometimes they look at the problem; more times they push them over. CNRC looks at every problem that comes in and they get opened on the database system. There could be an enquiry; there could be a product change; everything. So they contain about 80% of the issues and the 20% of the problems come to [our site] and the problems that come to us, at least half of them are ones that require a code change."

Many customer problems relate to configuration issues and are caused by incorrect customer action. Whatever organisation handles First Line support must have the expertise necessary to address these problems. However, in the case of a genuine software error, the code will have to be changed.

In one company, field problems are distributed as follows:

1. ~70% of problems relate to other vendors' equipment. Part of the customer support role is to help the customer to isolate network problems. Tracing and isolating problems is a major part of this work.
2. ~20% are complaints relating to configuration issues.
3. ~10% are genuine coding errors. As the product matures, these are reduced. In these situations, the customer support people must find out as much information as possible about the problem, ideally being able to supply call traces that allow developers to reproduce the troublesome call at home.

Diagnosing a genuine error can cause inconvenience to the test team as their lab may be confiscated with a view to reproducing the problem. If it is not possible to reproduce it at home, a customer support person may have to travel to site to witness the problem there. One of the interviewed customer support people offered the following step by step approach to problem solving:

- Begin by gathering all the available data. This can be quite difficult if trying to communicate across language barriers.
- Get the facts. Do not make assumptions. This lesson is learned from experience.
- Has this problem been seen before?
- If not, try to reproduce the problem. This might involve getting use of the independent test group's lab system.
- If the problem is reproducible, try to get it fixed as soon as possible.
- Otherwise, go on-site and try to reproduce the problem there.
- During all this, keep the customer up to date.

In some companies, the support group will design and implement the fix themselves; otherwise the programmers will have to do it. As Brooks (1972) points out, fixes to problems can introduce further problems. The reasons given for this are:

- Bugs cause localised problems leading solution providers to think locally.
- The solution provider usually has not written the original code so s/he does not have a perfect understanding of the consequences of the fix.

This suggests that bug fixing should be left to the original programmers. Unfortunately, the original programmer may now be assigned to another project or indeed may have left the company.

When the same product is installed on many sites, a problem seen on one site may appear on others. For this reason, it is important that all bugs are recorded in a bug-tracking database. Part of the documentation for an upgraded product is a set of release notes, detailing the defects corrected in this release, as well as the new features.